DEFOE
and the Idea of Fiction

Frontispiece. Daniel Defoe.

DEFOE
and the Idea of Fiction
1713–1719

Geoffrey M. Sill

NEWARK
UNIVERSITY OF DELAWARE PRESS
LONDON AND TORONTO • ASSOCIATED UNIVERSITY PRESSES

Associated University Presses, Inc.
4 Cornwall Drive
East Brunswick, NJ 08816

Associated University Presses Ltd
27 Chancery Lane
London WC2A 1NF, England

Associated University Presses
2133 Royal Windsor Drive
Unit 1
Mississauga, Ontario
Canada L5J 1K5

Library of Congress Cataloging in Publication Data

Sill, Geoffrey M., 1944–
  Defoe and the idea of fiction, 1713–1719.

  Bibliography: p.
  Includes index.
  1. Defoe, Daniel, 1661?–1731—Political and social
views. 2. Fiction. I. Title.
PR3408.P6S5   1983   823'.5   82-60073
ISBN 0-87413-227-4

Printed in the United States of America

Contents

Preface

Though his life was abundantly full of dangers and disasters, prosecutions, bankruptcies, intrigues, secret spy missions, slanders, and plots against him by his enemies, Defoe was perhaps never more truly Daniel in the lions' den than during the years 1713 to 1719. It was in this time that he managed to establish himself as a writer more or less free of political connections while negotiating the extremely treacherous passage from the Stuart to the Hanoverian monarchies, and from Robert Harley's moderate Tory ministry to that of his late adversaries, the Whigs. Unlike his earlier adventures in which he had been imprisoned and pilloried, he had this time neither the approbation of the mob nor the protection of men in high places; one often has the sense, in reading his pamphlets from this period, of a man literally writing for his life. His effort to impose his own versions of the political and ideological history of his times on his readers seems to have been his own best life insurance policy, and the doctrines of liberalism and the pursuit of ease and safety that he offered the world were both the products of his experience and the means of his salvation. But his course through this transitional period has never been clear, nor has its impact on his later, better-known writings. The first acknowledgment of gratitude owed by the writer of this study, therefore, is to the many people who have expressed a desire for sound information—such as there is—about Defoe's activities in the years immediately preceding *Robinson Crusoe*.

A book such as this one is truly the work of many hands. The patient spadework of William Lee, John Robert Moore, Maximillian Novak, and many more scholars has uncovered the foundations of Defoe's career, without which this book could not have been contemplated. Moore's *Checklist*, though much abused on the academic cocktail circuit for its sometimes overly confident attributions of pamphlets to Defoe, remains the best guide through very confusing territory; the greatest difficulty in using the *Checklist,* perhaps, is in trying to determine Moore's grounds for having included a particular work. It is frequently necessary to do Moore's detective work over again in order to confirm his attributions, and in this task the assistance of professional reference and rare book librarians has been invaluable. The writer has benefited in particular from extended periods of study in the British Museum; the Trent Collection of the Boston Public Library; the William Andrews Clark Memorial Library, University of California at Los Angeles; the Henry E. Huntington Library; the Rosenbach Foundation of Philadelphia; and the microfilm collection at Princeton University, as well as from the collections of the University of Pennsylvania, Rutgers University, and the New York Public Library. The Huntington Library has kindly granted permission for the use of quotations from the manuscript letterbook of Jean de Robethon in chapter 2, and the Clark Memorial Library for permission to reproduce engravings from William Stow's *Remarks on London: being an exact survey of the Cities of London and Westminster* (1722).

Among the many individuals who have given me help along the way, I wish particularly to thank Professors John M. Beattie and Peter Linebaugh, who gave the book their support when it was little more than a promise; Maximillian Novak, who assisted me to a very profitable tenure as an Andrew Mellon Fellow at the William Andrews Clark Memorial Library; Jerry Beasley, Alan Downie, Robert Fishman, Leland Peterson, and Manuel Schonhorn, who read early drafts of the manuscript and saved me from many grievous errors; and two very good friends, Susan Chromiak and Richard Gilder Jr., who gave me both criticism and support when I needed it. I wish also to acknowledge the steady support of Rutgers University, which provided me with two research grants and a semester's leave, and of my division, University College, whose faculty and staff made my project their own.

DEFOE
and the Idea of Fiction

1

Ideology and the Idea of Fiction

No intensive study of the career of Daniel Defoe between the succession of the elector of Hanover in 1714 and the appearance of the first of Defoe's famous novels in 1719 has ever been undertaken, despite the frequent acknowledgment that this formative period must contain valuable clues to his development as a maker of fictions. Defoe's biographers have usually skipped over this turbulent period in a single chapter, while lavishing attention on his early activities as the author of *The Shortest Way with the Dissenters* and as the government's agent in Scotland during the negotiation of the Treaty of Union.[1] Important as they were, these activities tell us little about the process through which Defoe came to accept fiction as a legitimate means for regarding human experience (even if he never quite admitted it was), and even less about what he intended his fictions to accomplish. We are left with the false impression that Defoe jumped from his career as a journalist at the end of the *Review* in 1713 to that of novelist with the publication of *Robinson Crusoe* in 1719. Between these dates, it is thought, there is only a broad chasm of infertile years that he spent as a spy and propagandist for a number of contradictory interests to which his attachment was hypocritical at best.

The reasons for this lack of critical attention are not hard to find. Defoe's letters to Robert Harley and others, which have been a rich source of insights for interpreting his career under Queen Anne, come to a sudden stop after Harley's fall from power in 1714, and except for a few somewhat ambiguous letters to Charles De la Faye in 1718, virtually no record other than Defoe's literary productions is available. The literary productions—newspapers, pamphlets, satires, short biographies and secret histories of political events—are extremely difficult to interpret. There is, first, the problem of attribution—how does one determine the true thread of meaning that runs through an author's works without knowing absolutely what he wrote? And how can the canon of an author famous for disguising his style be established without knowing the thread of ideological continuity that can lead us through the maze? Second, there is the bewildering complexity of English politics in this period, which until recently has defied the best efforts of historians to describe its structure and operation. The interpretation of a particular Defoe pamphlet as pro- or anti-Whig, for example, presumes some consensus on the nature of the Whig ideology, as well as on the simple existence of such an ideology, and even on the existence of the party itself.

Unfortunately, there have been no major discoveries of new sources of information on Defoe's activities in this period, nor are there likely to be. Instead, there has been a painstaking sifting of the available evidence, both on the question of Defoe's canon and on the structure of politics, and it is this sifting that makes this study feasible. John Robert Moore's *Checklist of the Writings of Daniel Defoe,* which in 1960 had brought to light dozens of pamphlets that plausibly were Defoe's and had omitted others once thought to be his, appeared in a corrected second edition in 1971; in the same year, Maximillian Novak's checklist of Defoe's writings was published in the *New Cambridge Bibliography of English Literature,* providing the Defoe scholar with a second opinion where Moore's attributions seemed doubtful. Work on the Defoe canon by such scholars as William L. Payne, Henry Snyder, Alan Downie, and Pat Rogers has clarified some of the many remaining obscurities. Though individual titles are still occasionally disputed, a consensus does exist on the most important works attributed to Defoe in the period under study; in any case, there is sufficient redundancy in the nearly 200 titles attributed to Defoe between the years 1713 and 1719 so that no conclusion about Defoe's stance on a given ideological issue rests on a single disputed title. While the student of Defoe must remain mindful of the snares and pitfalls that abound in the interpretation of anonymous pamphlets, a point comes when further knowledge of the canon of an author's work depends not on newspaper advertisements or quirks of style, but on the consistency of the ideas in a pamphlet with what is known about the activities and ideas of that author at that time. One of the purposes of this study, then, has been to sketch in the web of ideological connections that helps explain the existence and intention of one title in terms of the others that Defoe is known to have written.

1. Ideology and the Eighteenth Century

The sifting that has produced a consensus on the structure and operation of politics requires a more elaborate explanation. Previous efforts to describe Defoe in ideological terms have resulted in gross oversimplifications that take Robinson Crusoe as the author's persona and project Crusoe's "emerging individualist and liberal ideology" onto Defoe's own life and writings.[2] More serious efforts have been baffled by the influence of Sir Lewis Namier and historians of his school, notably Robert Walcott's *English Politics in the Early Eighteenth Century*, which discredited the notion that political behavior had been guided by ideological ends, and even that the distinction between *Whig* and *Tory* had any ideological significance.[3] The biographies of Defoe by James Sutherland and John Robert Moore were written during a time when politics in the early eighteenth century was believed to have derived its content chiefly from personal relations between individuals based on ties of kinship, friendship, or patronage, with a consequent diminution of emphasis on the role of ideas. In the words of one recent critic of Namierism, the ideas and principles of the period were reduced to mere "rationalizations of selfish ambition and base motives."[4] Ideology was seen as a superstructure imposed on consciousness, rather than inherent in it; the basis of political behavior was believed to be the desire for power, or at least for place, and what counted for the historian were verifiable patterns of influence by which places and power were distributed. For this reason, historical and literary research in the period tended to focus on the formal structure of political and cultural phenomena and to discount their ideological content as either "feigning" or as false consciousness.

The way toward restoring considerations of ideology to the study of this period was opened by Geoffrey Holmes in the late 1960s in his *British Politics in the Age of Anne*. Holmes disputed the Namierite view of early eighteenth-century politics as dominated by a small number of men, each or several of whom headed a faction or "connection" that acted sometimes in concert with other factions and sometimes independently. Holmes did not reassert the preeminence of ideas in history, nor did he attempt to assign fixed ideological meanings to the terms *Whig* and *Tory* that had been used so freely in the reigns of Anne and George I. But he did argue that a "clash of interests" between moneyed and landed men surfaced after the Revolution of 1688 and made its way into the political rhetoric. With two "quite essential" reservations—that neither the Whig nor Tory party was ideologically homogeneous, and that the Tories had sufficient interests in overseas trade not to be hostile to merchants (as, indeed, the Whigs had sufficient interests in land not to be hostile to property)—Holmes showed that connections could be made between interest and party ideology. The Tories, for example, came to be "identified with the defence of the special interests of the landed men,"[5] which included not merely the land itself, but all those institutions and ideas that tended to preserve the value of land. As a subsequent historian has shown, the divine right of the monarch to his crown, the duty of the subject to obey, the episcopal structure of the church, the religious and property tests for political office, and the acceptability of a standing army in peacetime were ideas that were strongly attractive to landed men generally, and less attractive to men for whom social mobility and new investment opportunities were important.[6] Rejecting the effors of Marxist historians to find rigid and deterministic connections between interest and party loyalty equally with Namierite efforts to eliminate ideology altogether as a basis for political behavior, Holmes concluded that "this conflict of Tory and Whig was one in which considerations of ideology, policy, power, self-interest and class-interest were all involved," thus opening the way for a continuing debate about the delicate and complicated links between the sources of a man's wealth and his ideological beliefs.[7]

Among the more important moments of this debate have been books by J. G. A. Pocock and H. T. Dickinson that trace the connections between ideology, political rhetoric, and party allegiance in the early eighteenth century. In *The Machiavellian Moment*, Pocock is as skeptical as Holmes of what he calls "old fashioned Marxism," with its reliance on historic inevitability and its readiness to interpret the conflict of interests as a struggle between the classes. Instead, Pocock offers a new framework in which to understand such writers as Defoe, Jonathan Swift, Andrew Fletcher, and Charles Davenant, the major "neo-Machiavellians" of their time.[8] These men "belong in the civic humanist tradition" of Machiavelli and his contemporaries "by reason of their concern with virtue as the moral as well as material foundation of social and personal life."[9] They were "not constant in their political allegiances"—a gentle way of acknowledging the charge of opportunism that is frequently leveled at Defoe in particular—but that inconstancy does not displace them from the tradition; in fact, it is *part* of the way the citizen of the Machiavellian state met his responsibilities.[10] The inconstancy of their political allegiances does not disqualify them from consideration as ideologists, but rather suggests that civic humanism *was* their ideology, which transcended Whig and Tory party questions. In the pursuit of this end, they employed "a highly ambivalent rhetoric, replete with alternatives, conflicts, and confusions, of which they were well aware and in which they were to some extent trapped."[11]

According to Pocock, the ambivalent rhetoric originated, at least in part, in the discovery that credit, rather than land, was becoming the basis of the political value system.[12] The stable and traditional notion of civic virtue grounded in the ownership of land was being challenged by the illusory and subjective values of the exchange. Where the ownership of land had encouraged a definition of virtue as the capacity of an individual to know and rule himself and to know the part he might play in a social structure, the new value system based on credit substituted a definition of virtue as the possession of passion, opinion, and imagination by the citizen. The problem of government became not the defense of the "order of nature" (i.e., traditional patterns of ownership and influence), but rather the proper management of the passions. What was particularly Machiavellian in Defoe's thought was his continuous effort to find a middle way between these "two directions in which the Augustan mind might go," a way to define virtue so that it might include both passion and order. For example, Pocock suggests that Defoe's special study was to show "how opinion and passion might be grounded upon experience rather than imagination," thus legitimating passion as a source of virtue while, at the same time, restricting it to men who already possessed some wealth and social standing. Though Pocock's remarks apply to Defoe's polemics with Swift in 1710–11, this study will show that Defoe continued his efforts to mediate these conflicting definitions of virtue throughout the decade and that the struggle to arrive at a station of virtue that combines passion and order is a major theme of *Robinson Crusoe.*

Shortly after the publication of Pocock's *Machiavellian Moment,* H. T. Dickinson's *Liberty and Property* described the contradiction between land and credit not in terms of its effect on political rhetoric, but through its impact on ideological formation. Rejecting the Namierite prejudice against attaching any ideological significance to the Whig and Tory parties, Dickinson argued that while both parties intended to restrict power to the owners of property, the Whigs could be distinguished by their recognition that financial and commercial revolutions at the end of the seventeenth century had created new forms of property. The Whig ideology was shaped by the efforts of these men to extend and legitimize their power at the same time that they protected the idea of property as the basis for enjoying the liberties of the political state. Thus, such important matters of state as the settlement of the succession in the Protestant line, the resolution of the war with France, and the question of reopening the French trade in 1713 were decided not primarily on their merits, but on the effect the outcome would have on the political emergence of these new forms of property. This new means of ideological formation, according to Dickinson, was grafted onto the older distinction between Court and Country politicians, in which the Court—by which Dickinson means those "professional politicians who wanted power and were anxious for office"—was traditionally opposed by the Country element, which defended the interest of the private (usually landed) citizen against the threats posed by the Court politicians and the financial interests of the City.[13] The resulting confusion, in which two essentially Country politicians such as Robert Harley and Henry St. John could wind up struggling for control of the ministry because of their ideological differences over the legitimacy of money and credit as sources of civic virtue, helps to explain the ambivalent rhetoric and the embrace of civic humanism encountered by Pocock.

The conflict over the reopening of the French trade in 1713 is an important case in point for examining the formation and use of political ideology and rhetoric. The treaty that would have reopened the trade was negotiated by St. John, by that time Viscount Bolingbroke, in what was apparently an attempt to diminish the power of city merchants and of the moneyed interest generally by opening up a relatively free trade directly between English manufacturers and French buyers.[14] The history of the struggle over the Treaty of Commerce reveals another form of the contradiction between land and money, which was recently explored by Joyce Oldham Appleby. Appleby describes what is apparently the same clash of interests identified by Holmes, Pocock, and Dickinson taking place between the manufacturers and the merchants.[15] The manufacturers, who shared with landowners a common interest in the production and working-up of English wool, found their path to the market blocked by the urban merchants, who, in order to make English wool competitive on the Continent, were not above manipulating the flow of exports and the extension of credit in order to control the supply. The manufacturers, which included not only the country woolen clothiers but also their urban counterparts in the silk trade, saw the reduction of duties on French cloth to the same levels as the duties imposed on imports from other nations as the end of their competitive edge in the home market, while the merchants saw the treaty as an opportunity to displace the Continental middlemen through whom the trade was presently routed. The debate between these two groups, neither of which was dominant, gives Appleby an opportunity to refute "Marx's theory of the class-based formation of ideology," which rests on "Marx's insistence that people holding similar ideas must have formed alliances prior to the acceptance of the ideas rather than subsequently."[16] Rejecting the notion that ideology is either "feigning" or false consciousness, Appleby argues that an ideology is a system of ideas, or a "plan," by which consciousness orders its world. Rather than a means of concealing or advancing special interests, ideology is an "intellectual response" to changing circumstances by writers and economic thinkers, who "created interpretive models that shaped the consciousness of their contemporaries."[17] One ideology becomes dominant, in Appleby's view, because it is "selected" on the basis of the appeal of its values to people of differing backgrounds, who join together around that ideology to form a "modern class" with which to resolve their shared economic problems.[18] This strongly idealistic theory makes ideology the basis of social behavior, rather than the product of it; instead of the Marxist class-based theory of ideology, Appleby offers us an ideology-based theory of classes.

Appleby's opposition to Marxism poses some important, yet ultimately refutable, challenges to a Marxist approach to the politics of this period. As the succeeding chapter will show, the ideological arguments that developed as a result of the conflict over the Treaty of Commerce were not selected in a free marketplace of ideas on the basis of their intellectual or economic merit. They did not result in the formation of a "modern class" that had not existed before, although the defeat of the treaty was an important part of the process of demoralization of the Tory party that opened the door to the hegemony of the Whigs.[19] Though it cannot be shown that the ideological arguments were based on class differences, as Appleby believes it necessary for Marxists to maintain, yet neither can it be shown that they originated in a clear and correct apprehension (or rejection) of the ideas that the treaty represented. In fact, it was the aim of propagandists on both sides to obscure, rather than to clarify, the true intentions and probable consequences of the treaty. Defoe's antagonists among the Whig writers were not interested in proposing an articulated vision of a "new social reality" known as Whiggism, but only in blowing holes in the treaty by evoking fears of the loss of the Portugal trade or fears that the treaty would let in a flood of cheap French manufactured goods. Defoe, for his part, showed very little interest in defending the free-trade theories of Nicholas Barbon and Sir Dudley North, which Appleby believes were at stake in the debate over the treaty, but instead chose to defend it on the same grounds as his antagonists—how the treaty would affect the balance of trade. His reason for this choice may have been that he was not a believer in free-trade theory, but a more obvious explanation is the fact that he, having unique access to the Customs House records, could disprove the assertions of his antagonists without requiring his audience to accept a new and untried economic ideology.

The problem, then, is not whether there was a clash of interests in the early eighteenth century, but whether Appleby is correct in describing this clash as an intellectual competition between two divergent ideological systems or whether Marxism is correct in regarding ideology as the product of a struggle for dominance by a particular class. This problem calls for a brief reexamination of the concept of ideology, especially as it is used by Marxist writers. According to Destutt de Tracy, a member of the Institut de France at the end of the eighteenth century and the man who first described the concept, ideology was a "science of ideas," or a means of discovering the empirical origins of ideas in the mind on Lockean principles; his assumption was that if the human mind could be freed from the religious and metaphysical prejudices that interfered with the derivation of ideas from sensations, then men could discover the real sources of their problems and the real solutions to them.[20] For Napoleon, who had at first supported the Institut and its study of "ideology," the concept came to represent the incorrect ideas that arose as a result of an ignorance of political practice. Thus the term that had a positive connotation for the members of the Institut acquired a negative connotation under Napoleon; but in both cases, incorrect ideas were assumed to be the basis of human limitations. Though Marx never gave the term a strict definition, he used it in this negative sense. For Marx, ideas were, like all other forms of cultural activity, the product of "the material activity and the material intercourse of men."[21] When these ideas are cut off from the historical circumstances that produced them and given the appearance of timelessness and universality, they become objects of false consciousness. This development is encouraged by the dominant class, which controls the production of these apparently timeless and universal ideas and shapes them into an instrument that reinforces its own hegemony. The ideology of the dominant class represents the existing material relations as natural and unchangeable; the ideology of a class that competes for power with the dominant class stresses the separability of powers, the need for mobility, growth, and so forth.[22] Marx did not see ideological struggle as a competition between true and false ideas; on the contrary, he rebuked the Young Hegelians for attempting to change consciousness merely by interpreting it another way. All ideological interpretations of reality are fictions for Marx because all of them raise ideas out of their material/social context and enshrine them in a system that pretends to universal and timeless validity.

The greatest difficulty in applying this orthodox Marxist definition of ideology to the early eighteenth century is that, at least until the emergence of a stable ministry under Robert Walpole in 1722, no single class that could have controlled ideological production was in a position of absolute dominance. Rather, as we have seen, it was a period of gradual transition of power from landed to moneyed interests in which the moneyed interests bought, negotiated, married, and forced their way into the dominant class formerly composed only of landed men. The landed interests resisted this invasion by defending the traditional sources of their dominance, including the concept of divine and hereditary sovereignty, the episcopal structure and state establishment of the Church of England, and the ownership of property as both a source and a test of civic virtue; but the ideological defenses were not enough to counter the declining value of land and the growing power of the financial sector.[23] The moneyed interests, on the other hand, recognized that their entrance into the dominant class would be eased by the settlement in Parliament of the successor to Anne, the toleration of a limited right to dissent from the church structure and liturgy, the recognition of money as a legitimate standard of value and merit, and the preservation of access to the peerage for their most deserving members—though their rhetoric seldom went so far as to challenge the hegemony of the dominant class to which they desired access. This clash of interests was fought out, in part, by ideological examinations of the major issues of the time—that is, by books, pamphlets, newspaper articles, and speeches in Parliament that defined the issues in terms which, though claiming to be guided by the light of reason alone, actually served one interest or the other. While the intentions of an individual writer were often no more than to please a particular patron, rather than to take part in an ideological conflict, the surest way to please a patron was to define and represent ideas in ways that were consistent with the patron's interest.[24] The production of ideology was not, therefore, a free intellectual competition that preceded the formation of classes; on the other hand, neither was it (as in the words of one recent Marxist writer) merely "a consciousness which conceals contradictions in the interest of the dominant class."[25] It was an instrument that served both landed and moneyed interests in a struggle not by a dominant class to subordinate others, but rather over the composition and values of that dominant class.

The orthodox Marxist theory of class dominance was recently reexamined by Raymond Williams in his *Marxism and Literature.*Drawing upon the earlier work of Antonio Gramsci, Williams distinguishes between *dominance* and *hegemony,* the latter term implying a more pervasive form of influence than the formal social controls implied in class dominance. *Hegemony* is for Williams "an inclusive social and cultural formation" that casts "a whole body of practices and expectations, over the whole of living: our senses and assignments of energy, our shaping perceptions of ourselves and our world."[26] In other words, the concept of hegemony includes, in terms of the eighteenth century, not only the power to decide places and preferments, to establish and enforce laws, and to raise or lower the tax on land or the interest on credit, but also the power to affect the "whole area of lived experience" through literature and other cultural formations. Ideology, then, is a systematic organization of ideas, experience, traditions, and expectations that is intended to establish, preserve, or extend the hegemony of a particular interest—whether that interest is, at the time, dominant, alternative, or directly oppositional—in the culture at large.[27] Thus the Whig and Tory parties, which the Namierite historians were reluctant to accept as self-conscious political organizations with articulated ideologies, may be more easily seen as alternative cultures competing for hegemony in a rapidly changing society.

Not only does Williams's notion of hegemony explain how the clash of interests between landed and moneyed men found its way into the political and cultural life of eighteenth-century England, but it broadens the terms of that clash beyond mere land/money or city/country dichotomies. In the broadest sense, the clash was between one culture that was receding and another that was emerging. According to Williams, an emerging culture does not entirely displace the culture that was formerly dominant, but rather incorporates residual elements from it to form a new dominant culture. These residual elements are cultural formations that are still active in the present, though no longer possessing their original social reason for being, while the emergent elements are those that are justified by new material conditions but are not yet established in consciousness. Thus the landed interest struggled to maintain the whole range of traditions and values that supported the value of the land, and the moneyed interest, while emphasizing emergent ideas such as mobility and investment, sought to incorporate many residual elements into its ideology. As Nick Rogers has shown, an alderman of London, the "crème de la crème" of the bourgeoisie, was likely to acquire a modest riverside villa or suburban mansion as a symbol of his prosperity, while keeping most of his money in trade or public securities.[28] From his villa he commuted to London, which was the center of his social and business world and the real source of his claim to

a place in the dominant class. At his death, the villa was frequently sold or let rather than passed down to his progeny. The
ideological consciousness of the London alderman, then, remained primarily that of the "urban genteel culture" from
which he derived his wealth, but included, as a legitimizing
device, some residual elements of the landed aristocrat he displaced.

This description of the formation of ideological consciousness is not intended by Gramsci or Williams as merely another
way to dismiss ideology as a superstructure imposed on consciousness. Rather, the intent is to define ideology in such a way
that it is implicit in consciousness and inseparable from it; in
Gramsci, there is even a suggestion that certain types of "historically organic ideologies" are "necessary to a given structure." To the extent that ideologies are historically necessary,
they have at least a psychological validity in that they serve as an
organizing principle around which men may "move, acquire
consciousness of their position, struggle, etc."[29] If an ideology
is historically necessary, the reason must be that the emergent
culture requires it in order to fulfill the material possibilities
that new developments in technology, exploration, or knowledge have opened up. Ideology in this instance becomes
neither false nor feigned nor superimposed consciousness, but
a projected or intentional form of consciousness that may be
used to assist the emergence of an interest which can achieve
hegemony on the basis of these new material realities. Since it is
an *intentional* form of consciousness, rather than a consciousness of "real" objects, it bears a resemblance to fiction, which is
a consciousness of reality as it might be or might have been.
With increasingly frequency during the second decade of the
eighteenth century, Defoe turned to fiction as a way of demon-
strating the historical necessity of emerging cultural formations
and a way of reconciling the contradictions between the various
factions competing for hegemony in the wake of the Glorious
Revolution of 1688.

2. Defoe and the Uses of Ideology

One way of approaching the origins and uses of ideology in
British politics in the early eighteenth century, then, is to regard it as the product of clashes of interest, such as those be-

tween landed and moneyed men, manufacturers and
merchants, or High and Low Church, since each of these factions attempted to establish its hegemony in the culture
through the production of ideas favorable to itself. But ideology could also be used negatively, as Defoe's patron and political mentor Robert Harley, earl of Oxford, was the first to
realize, to manipulate public opinion in order to prevent any
one interest from arriving at a position of dominance. As Alan
Downie has recently shown, Harley's first loyalty was to that
"Old Whig" or Country party that had developed its principles
through opposition to the Stuart court before 1688. By the time
Harley finally came to power, therefore, his policies were based
on "an anachronistic ideology stemming from the political
world of his earlier and much younger days." The result was a
sensitivity for the liberties of the independent country gentry
against all manner of court or church encroachments and a
disavowal of all ideological attachments, particularly after it
became clear to him that "the whigs notoriously did not make a
determined effort to implement the ideas of the party theo-
rists."[30] Harley's well-known "moderation" was really an attempt to manage political factions by balancing them against
each other while he attempted to keep himself and the queen
above the ideological struggle by a judicious use of the press.
Defoe assisted Harley in this task by extinguishing ideological
fires all over England for the better part of a decade. Even his
defense of the Treaty of Utrecht was conducted on this anti-
ideological basis, according to which it was assumed that all
good men wanted peace unless their natural inclinations were
diverted by their attachment to an interest.[31] Defoe's tendency
to balance contradictory ideas by setting them against each
other and to discredit the opposition by revealing how their
ideas served the interest of a specific faction were legacies from
Harley that Defoe carried to the end of his writing career.

At the same time, however, Defoe was deeply frustrated by
the lack of ideological direction in Harley's ministry. It is probably Defoe's own experience as Harley's agent that is reflected
in his pretended memoirs of Monsieur Mesnager, the French
diplomat charged with negotiating the preliminaries of the
Peace of Utrecht, in which Mesnager laments that "it was much
easier to talk long with [Harley] upon trifling and common
Occasions, than to obtain a Moment in serious Business; in so
much, that I have heard of some who have waited upon him, by

his own appointment, on Business of the Greatest Consequence, and have been entertained by him, from one Hour to
another, on some Trifle, 'till at last the main Affair has been
confined to a Minute or two, or perhaps deferred to another
Occasion."[32] In his letters to Harley in 1713 and 1714, Defoe
frequently begged the treasurer to strike back at his enemies
and establish the dominance of the queen's interest at the head
of state.[33] Defoe's involvement in the campaign to pass the
Treaty of Commerce—which Harley regarded as a matter to be
settled between the merchants and the manufacturers—may
have grown out of his frustration at Harley's refusal to assume
the ideological leadership of his government. As Harley's
"moderation" passed from balancing ideological factions into a
deliberate avoidance of doing any business at all, it became
apparent to Defoe that some stronger hand at the head of
state—one capable of using state power not to keep competing
interests from achieving hegemony, but of uniting these interests into a truly dominant government—was necessary. This
awareness shaped his first enthusiastic welcomes to the elector
of Hanover, his imperious summonses to the people of England to do their duty by the new king, and his virulent attacks
on the Jacobites during the rebellion of 1715–16.

   In this same period, Defoe began using fictions in his writing
not merely to illustrate moral or political ideas—as he had done
for years in the *Review*—but rather as the very *form* of those
ideas. Maximillian Novak has combed Defoe's writing for his
allusions to literary theory and concluded that, while Defoe was
"severely hampered by the lack of an adequate critical theory,"
his professions that his fables were written to advance moral
and political ideas must be taken seriously.[34] Moreover, Novak
argues that Defoe's successful integration of ideas and fictional
forms was one of the chief accomplishments of his career and
one of his most important contributions to the development of
the novel.[35] This integration—which occurred gradually in the
five years that separated Harley's fall from power to the publication of *Robinson Crusoe*—was the result of Defoe's use of persons as emblems—or, ultimately, as symbols—of the ideas with
which he was engaged. In the early stages of this development,
the link between person and idea was a simple and direct one,
and the technique amounted to little more than personification,
as in Defoe's *Memoirs of Count Tariff &c.* In the later stages, as in
the *Minutes of the Negotiations of Monsr. Mesnager,* the persons

and the relations between them are complex, and the ultimate meanings of the work are symbolic; Harley appears in that book, for example, both as a model of the faithful minister of the queen's interest and as a symbol of the Old Whig ideology that has been sacrificed by the modern Whigs for their private interests. The integration of idea and fictional form was furthered by Defoe's limitation of the narrator to a specific ideological or political point of view—for example, that of Mesnager, who suspects that Harley's dilatory behavior is a negotiating tactic, or of the rebel soldier of *A True Account of the Proceedings at Perth,* whose admission of defeat is tempered by his resolve to fight another day. This strict limitation of consciousness to one (though sometimes very complicated) ideological intention—which numerous critics have used to compare Defoe adversely to novelists who succeeded him—is the means by which Defoe was able to make ideas inhere in fiction. In Defoe's more memorable pamphlets, the idea becomes a perceiving and intending subject, a persona who imposes on the reader an imagined world similar to the world of the epic, novel, or short story; the persona makes us see the world as he sees it while additionally asking us to accept him as a model of civic virtue. Our acceptance of this fictional world facilitates, even necessitates our acceptance of the ideological intention that lies at the center of it.

Though Wayne Booth specifically ruled "fiction used for propaganda or instruction" (and, by implication, ideological ends) out of bounds in his *Rhetoric of Fiction,* the ruling is arbitrary and, in the case of Defoe, impossible to maintain.[36] The purpose of this study is to show that rather than applying formal or generic definitions of "fiction" to some of Defoe's work and not to the rest of it, we need to understand that, in Defoe's hands, ideology and fiction were related and interdependent forms of knowledge. Though neither ideology nor fiction is usually thought of as "knowledge," they were for Defoe a way of knowing and, finally, of changing the world. By writing about ideas not as objects, but rather as the subjects of consciousness, Defoe achieved the "psychological validity" which Gramsci allows to ideologies that are "historically organic" and "necessary to a given structure." Defoe was not universally successful in choosing fictions that had historical necessity behind them; his most notable failure, perhaps, was the Treaty of Commerce, whose free-trade economic basis was contradicted

by the needs of the developing English woolen and silk manufactures. But his decision to defend Harley as the emblem of
civic virtue in the period after the Hanoverian succession had a
high degree of psychological, if not historical, validity: the
country needed to believe that the transition was not a radical
one and that there was room in the new reign for men who had
acted a part in the old. His support of the Septennial Act and
the other consolidating actions of the new regime drew psychological validity from the continuing threat of the Pretender,
whose cowardly betrayal of his soldiers was more than made up
by their resolve to prevail for him some day. His portrait of the
Old Whig, first in the person of Harley, then in Shrewsbury,
achieved a psychological validity when contrasted with the
quarreling schoolboys who made a mockery of the king's ministry after the rebellion of 1715 had been suppressed. And as a
result of these earlier struggles, through which Defoe encountered the bankruptcy of the modern Whig ideology and the
need to reconstruct it as a new subject of consciousness, he
created the first "fiction based on a Whig myth of open opportunity," *Robinson Crusoe*.[37] In each of these cases, Defoe took
what many people in the emerging culture wanted to believe
was true of themselves and combined it with the best values
offered by the residual culture. His fictions served, more or less
successfully, as organizing principles around which men and
women became aware of themselves in relation to the dominant
and emerging ideas of their times. In accepting these ideas and
acting on them, Defoe's readers imposed on themselves the
hegemony of the new Whig culture and, at the same time, the
restraining virtues of moderation, experience, and tradition,
thus contributing to the stability of the new order.

Notes

1. James Sutherland, "Mist's Man," chap. 10 in *Defoe: A Biography* (Philadelphia:
Lippincott, 1938); John Robert Moore, "Pamphleteer and Public Servant," chap. 16 in
Daniel Defoe, Citizen of the Modern World (Chicago: University of Chicago Press, 1958).
See also the longer, but now outmoded discussion of this period in William Lee, *Daniel
Defoe, His Life and Recently Discovered Writings*, vol. 1 (London, 1869), chaps. 9–11.

2. Isaac Kramnick, *Bolingbroke and His Circle* (Cambridge, Mass.: Harvard University
Press, 1968), p. 191.

3. See Frank O'Gorman, "Fifty Years after Namier: The Eighteenth Century in
British Historical Writing," *The Eighteenth Century: Theory and Interpretation* 20 (1979):
99–120.

4. H. T. Dickinson, *Liberty and Property: Political Ideology in Eighteenth-Century Britain* (New York: Holmes and Meier, 1977), p. 2.

5. G. S. Holmes, *British Politics in the Age of Anne* (New York: St. Martin's Press, 1967), p. 170. See also Dickinson, *Liberty and Property*, p. 51, and W. A. Speck, "Conflict in Society," in *Britain after the Glorious Revolution*, ed. G. S. Holmes (London: Macmillan, 1969), pp. 135–54.

6. Dickinson, *Liberty and Property*, pp. 18 ff.

7. Holmes, *British Politics in the Age of Anne*, p. 185.

8. J. G. A. Pocock, *The Machiavellian Moment* (Princeton, N.J.: Princeton University Press, 1975), p. 427.

9. Ibid., p. 446.

10. Willson H. Coates, Hayden V. White, and J. Salwyn Schapiro, *The Emergence of Liberal Humanism*, (New York: McGraw-Hill Book Co., 1966), 1:29–31.

11. Pocock, *Machiavellian Moment*, p. 446.

12. Ibid., pp. 458–59.

13. Dickinson, *Liberty and Property*, p. 91.

14. Ibid., pp. 52–53; 171.

15. Joyce Oldham Appleby, *Economic Thought and Ideology in Seventeenth Century England* (Princeton, N.J.: Princeton University Press, 1978), pp. 168–69.

16. Ibid., pp. 14, 11.

17. Ibid., pp. 4–5.

18. Ibid., pp. 11–12.

19. For an account of this process, see Geoffrey Holmes, "Harley, St. John and the Death of the Tory Party," in *Britain after the Glorious Revolution*, pp. 216–37.

20. Jorge Larrain, *The Concept of Ideology* (London: Hutchinson, 1979), pp. 26–27. See also Homa Katouzian, *Ideology and Method in Economics* (New York: New York University Press, 1980), pp. 149–50.

21. Karl Marx and Frederick Engels, *The German Ideology*, ed. R. Pascal (New York: International Publishers, 1947), p. 14. See also Larrain, *Concept of Ideology*, p. 47; Ralph Miliband, *Marxism and Politics* (Oxford: At the University Press, 1977), p. 32; and George Lichtheim, "The Concept of Ideology," *History and Theory* 4 (1965).

22. Marx and Engels, *German Ideology*, p. 39.

23. Speck, "Conflict in Society," pp. 138–41.

24. See the discussion of Pope's early career in D. H. Stevens, *Party Politics and English Journalism, 1702–42;* reprint ed., (New York: Russell and Russell, 1916, 1967), pp. 19ff.

25. Larrain, *Concept of Ideology*, p. 60.

26. Raymond Williams, *Marxism and Literature* (Oxford: At the University Press, 1977), p. 110. See also Antonio Gramsci, *Selections from the Prison Notebooks*, ed. Quintin Hoare and Geoffrey Nowell Smith (New York: International Publishers, 1971), pp. 55–57n, 245–46; E. P. Thompson, *The Poverty of Theory and other Essays* (New York: Monthly Review Press, 1978), pp. 283–84; Gwyn A. Williams, "The Concept of 'Egemonia' in the thought of Antonio Gramsci," *Journal of the History of Ideas* 21 (1960): 586–99. For a criticism of Williams's use of Gramsci, see Terry Eagleton, *Criticism and Ideology* (London: Verso Editions, 1978), pp. 32, 42.

27. Williams, *Marxism and Literature*, p. 113.

28. Nicholas Rogers, "Money, Land and Lineage: The Big Bourgeoisie of Hanoverian London," *Social History* 4 (1979): 448–49.

29. Gramsci, *Selections*, pp. 376–77.

30. J. A. Downie, *Robert Harley and the Press* (Cambridge: At the University Press, 1979), pp. 21–23.

31. See, for example, Defoe's *The Conduct of Parties in England* (London, 1712).

32. Defoe, *Minutes of the Negotiations of Mons. Mesnager* (London, 1717), p. 183.

33. G. H. Healey, ed., *The Letters of Daniel Defoe* (Oxford: Clarendon Press, 1955), pp. 428–39.

34. Maximillian Novak, "Defoe's Theory of Fiction," *Studies in Philology* 61 (1964): 662–66.

35. Maximillian Novak, "Fiction and Society in the Early Eighteenth Century," in *England in the Restoration and Early Eighteenth Century*, ed. H. T. Swedenberg (Berkeley: University of California Press, 1972), pp. 63–68.

36. For the reference to Booth's *The Rhetoric of Fiction* (Chicago: University of Chicago Press, 1961), p. i, I am indebted to Alan Downie's review article "Political Literature As Literature," *The British Journal for Eighteenth-Century Studies* (1979): 71, and I use the concept of fiction Downie describes there.

37. The phrase is Novak's, in "Fiction and Society," p. 63.

2

A Fiction That Failed: The Treaty of Commerce with France

The letters received in the Spring of 1713 by Jean de Robethon, private secretary to George, elector of Hanover, reveal that two questions dominated the thoughts of his correspondents in London.[1] One question was the health of Queen Anne, whose death would set in motion the untested machinery of the Act of Settlement, by which the monarchy was to pass not to her brother the Pretender, but to her distant cousin George. The other was a bill proposed by the Tory ministry that would make effectual the eighth and ninth articles of the Treaty of Commerce with France, recently negotiated by Bolingbroke as the second step, after the Treaty of Utrecht, in normalizing relations between the two nations. It had been the queen's prerogative to sign the Treaty of Utrecht without seeking the ratification of Parliament, despite the resolution offered repeatedly by the Whigs that there should be no peace without safeguards against Bourbon influence in Spain. But the eighth and ninth articles of the commercial treaty, which lowered duties on French imports and raised them on some goods from other nations, gave the Whigs an opportunity to express their bitterness, to demonstrate their loyalty to the Hanoverian succession, and to make a dramatic show of their party unity. Though a minority in the House of Commons, they rejected the bill there by nine votes, assisted by a split in the Tories and an effective propaganda campaign. The propaganda on behalf of the treaty was almost entirely in the hands of Daniel Defoe, who undertook it because of his conviction that England ought not to shut itself out of the French market, even though he had reservations about the treaty itself. A close examination of Defoe's writings on the treaty reveals that it was as spirited and effective a defense as was possible to make of what Bolingbroke himself admitted was "a bad game."[2] But for historians of the novel, the examination reveals an unexpected bonus in the form of clues about the process through which Defoe arrived at a workable method of writing fiction. After plumbing the moral and ideological issues involved in the treaty in at least five pamphlets and better than sixty numbers of the *Mercator*, Defoe published a novel-length pretended biography of Count Tariff, whose misfortunes allegorized those of the idea of free trade in English politics.[3] Whether the result should be considered a fiction or not, it provides us with a clearly defined instance of Defoe's use of fictional techniques to put forward an ideological argument, from which we may trace Defoe's subsequent development as a maker of fictions.

1. Defoe's Propaganda for the Treaty

Defoe's first pamphlet on the subject of the Treaty of Commerce appeared on 23 May 1713, almost simultaneously with the first issue of his new journal, the *Mercator*. The front matter of the pamphlet seems to betray the author's apprehensions about the opposition that the treaty will meet with from the book's readers: the title page prominently displays the proverb "He that Judgeth a Matter before he Heareth it, 'tis Folly and Shame unto him," and the opening pages contain a plea that the members of Parliament should consider the treaty without recourse to partisanship. Appealing to them as individuals and as Protestants, the author expresses the hope "that things being set in a true light, every Man may Reason with himself calmly in this Matter."[4] The Whig opposition to the bill had already drawn itself up into ranks, which to this author's mind was the political equivalent of Popery. Both Defoe and his audience knew that his words on this head reflected the feelings of the queen, whose opposition to the rule of the parties had, in part, prompted her to put the moderate Harley at the head of the ministry. But neither the wishes of the monarch nor the stigma of political Popery could break the Whig solidarity on this issue; when the division came, only eight Whigs, most of whom held offices at court, voted for the treaty.[5] Afterwards, in an apparently fictitious letter to himself as the editor of the *Mercator*,

Defoe took himself to task for having wasted his time attempting to defend the treaty with "Trading Arguments." "Arguing about Trade is but an Amusement with these Men . . . the Peace and the Ministry is their Quarrel." He cited as their "general Maxim" the proposition "*That without a Treaty of Commerce the Treaty of Peace could not be lasting*," and then "*Hey boys up go we, &c. is the next Step*," referring to the ministerial ambitions of the opposition leaders.[6]

The Customs House, London. From Stow's *Survey* (1722).

Nevertheless, though the cause of the treaty may have been lost from the start (and the narrow margin of defeat suggests it was not), Defoe did attempt to defend the treaty on economic and ideological grounds. His efforts to do so were hampered not only by the general antipathy toward the French, who were so recently England's enemy and who still harbored the Pretender, but also by the fact that commerce with France was a prospect whose dangers and benefits were entirely unknown. As he pointed out in an effort to turn the fact to his advantage, England had never had a treaty of commerce with France; there had been at most treaties of navigation and duties imposed unilaterally by both sides. These duties had begun with a tariff of fifty sols per ton laid by the French on all shipping in 1664, to which the English had responded with a tariff of five shillings per ton upon all French ships; in the ensuing commerce, it was widely believed, England had suffered a declining balance of trade, importing more wine and brandy than it had exported in woolen goods to France.[7] Additionally, English manufactures in silks, linens, paper, glass, and other goods had suffered from French competition.[8] War with France had brought some relief in the form of high duties imposed on French goods, and at the Peace of Ryswick in 1697 the English had showed little interest in negotiating a treaty of commerce with France. As a result, Louis XIV had responded with a new tariff that prohibited certain English goods, such as red herrings, and laid high duties on English woolens. Because of these high duties on both sides, trade came to a standstill; in the articles of wine and brandy, the duties "amounted to a meer Prohibition," and the English developed a taste for the stronger wines of Portugal, which became "our general Draught all over England."[9]

Between the treaties of Ryswick and Utrecht, however, the situation had changed radically. The Treaty of Union with Scotland had eliminated a prospective economic rival, while the end of the war with France had left English shipping in far better condition to carry on a commercial trade than the French.[10] The export of raw wool from Great Britain to France had almost entirely stopped, thus shutting off an important supply of materials for French manufacturers and holding down prices at home. The settlement of the Huguenot refugees had brought an influx of skilled labor to the textile industry, and the development of financial institutions such as the Bank of England had increased the credit resources of English merchants.[11] Furthermore, there was substantial evidence that prohibitions did not work. During the war, the English had prohibited trade with France in materials of military importance, to which Defoe had objected at the time that the trading nations to whom the English sold its strategic materials resold them to the French at double the price, "so that the Enemy got our Lead and our Corn for Bullets and Magazines, and we only cheated ourselves of the profit."[12] In spite of the prohibitions, Defoe alleged, the French market was so great that the trade produced a surplus of £ 90,000 per month, which had to be made up in French money. Though he overlooked the artificial demand raised by the war itself, Defoe was able to point to this favorable balance of trade as evidence that England could profit from commerce with France. When the treaty opened French ports to English ships, Defoe argued in the *Mercator,* goods that were currently prohibited could be sold at duty levels significantly lower than those in effect before the Treaty of Ryswick, in some cases not much more than in 1664, thus opening a lucrative market to English merchants.[13]

Defoe chose to argue the case for the treaty on the basis of a favorable balance of trade not because, as Joyce Appleby has suggested, he found it impossible to defend the social values implicit in the Tory ideology of the free international market-place,[14] but rather for the much more practical reason that his antagonists were disseminating false information which purported to show that England would lose heavily in the trade with France. The information appeared primarily in the pages of the *British Merchant,* a Whig newspaper edited by Henry Martin. Martin raised anew the rumor that England's trade with France in the 1660s and 1670s had been conducted at a deficit of more than £ 1,000,000 per year, with the implication that a renewal of trade upon the old footing would be equally disastrous. His information was drawn from a report submitted to Parliament in 1675 entitled "A Scheme of Trade, as it is at present carried on between England and France"; the "Scheme," as it was known, had since been so widely circulated and quoted that its conclusions were received as common knowledge.[15] In the words of a modern historian, the Scheme was still "a powerful instrument in the moulding of anti-French opinion" in 1713.[16] But the Scheme had been the product of a specific interest group, the City merchants—fourteen of whom had signed it—with the specific intent of obtaining protectionist legislation in the form of higher duties on imported goods from France. Defoe himself had accepted the conclusions of the Scheme and had quoted from it in earlier times; in the less than four weeks between the commencement of his writing on the treaty and the division on it in the House of Commons, he was unable to refute the Scheme and was considerably embarrassed by the necessity of writing against what was generally regarded as the truth.[17] Charles Davenant, the inspector-general of the Customs, was also taken in by the Scheme; when asked by the House of Lords to deliver a report on the French trade on short notice, he had "found" the Scheme and delivered it to the Peers without checking it for accuracy.[18] But

shortly before the vote on the treaty in the Commons, the commissioners of the Customs House examined the Scheme and
found it to be inaccurate, which Defoe immediately reported in
the *Mercator*.[19] The inaccuracies were the result of inflated estimates of French imports, especially linens and silks, through
the "outports" (i.e., not London), which all together took in less
than one-third of the goods entering England, though the
Scheme estimated their volume at more than double that of
London's.[20] Further inaccuracies occurred through the omis-
sion of certain exported goods and the valuation of imported
goods at their retail prices, rather than their prime cost. It was
Defoe himself who eventually discovered that the "balance"
shown in the Scheme in fact set the exports of 1668, a "low"
year, against the imports of 1674, "the 'highest' year they could
find."[21] After the findings of the commissioners of the Customs
regarding the Scheme had been published in the *Mercator*, Martin continued to use the Scheme as a basis for discussing trade
and for libeling the *Mercator*, which so antagonized Defoe that a
personal vendetta began between the two men that lasted long
after the treaty was a dead issue. Meanwhile, Defoe tried un-
availingly to counter the belief that England had suffered in the
balance of trade. He printed a letter from Davenant in which
the inspector-general declared that he no longer believed the
reports either for or against an "overballance" in trade with
France, since all the reports were written for political ends,
though he now did believe that "England was every year a
Gainer in its universal Trade," that is, taking all trade together.[22] Provoked by the repeated allegations of the *British
Merchant*, Defoe published a special edition of the *Mercator* that
gave a complete analysis of the French trade for the year 1685–
86, showing that England exported goods valued at more than
£ 742,077 directly to France, and another £ 300,000 indirectly
through the Dutch that went to France, while importing approximately £ 880,000, for a clear gain of over £ 160,000.[23]

For Defoe, then, the most difficult economic question posed
by the treaty was not whether the French market was worth-
while, but whether the treaty established sufficient protections
for English manufactures; and in this respect, he was forced to
admit that it did very little. It repealed the duties and prohibitions that the two countries had imposed on each others' goods
since 1699, which had sheltered and encouraged the growth of
the fledgling English linen and silk industries.[24] In no case were

French imported goods to pay a higher duty than comparable goods imported into England from another country. Thus, French brandy, which in 1713 paid a duty of £ 81 14 *s.*, would pay no more duty than Spanish brandy, which paid £ 51 14 *s.* per tun; and French wrought silks, which paid £ 27 duty per 20 pounds of merchandise, would pay no more than the Dutch, or £ 13.[25] The lower duty on brandy created no problems, but the lower duty on silks was seen by English silk manufacturers as the ruin of their trade.

To his credit, Defoe did not try to hide the threat to the silk industry in his writings on the treaty. He admitted that "some part of Trade, some particular Persons and Interests in Trade may be touched, may be shortened in their present Advantages and future Prospects," though he asserted at the same time that the "General Interest of Trade in Britain shall be bettered very much by the Treaty."[26] The damage to the English silk industry caused by the import of French silks at lower duties would be more than offset by the increased exports of English woolens to France. "Every one agrees," Defoe claimed, "that our Woolen Manufacture is the Life and Soul of our English Trade, and if this is but forwarded and promoted, whatever other Trade suffers, it is able sufficiently to make amends for that Loss."[27] The silk trade is "useful and advantageous," but only "as it is a Return for and encourages the Exportation of the Woollen Manufacture, and no otherwise."[28] To show how the purchase of French silks benefited the English woolen industry, Defoe explained that raw silk bought in Turkey with English woolen cloth was sold to the French for money that covered the cost of the woolens. After being woven into cloth in France, it was purchased from them with more English cloth, with the result that "the said Silks, when wrought, not only consumed the Growth of England, but employed above Sixteen times the Number of People in their making, &c. more than the Bale of wrought Silks would have done, if they had been made in Spittlefields."[29] Giving up the effort to manufacture silk, and instead using the trade to stimulate the foreign purchase of woolen goods, was an economically defensible plan that would accord with "the undoubted Rule of Trade, that the Employment of our own Poor, and Consumption of our own Growth, is the first Principle of Commerce, and should be the last End of all our National Improvement."[30] When this argument proved unacceptable to the silk manufacturers, Defoe was forced to fall back on the fact that the treaty required only that French silks should pay no more duty than the silks of any other nation.[31] The level of duty, after all, was not set by the treaty, but by a board of commissioners subject to Parliamentary approval, with the proviso that the duty should be no greater on French goods than on any other. If English ladies will insist on wearing goods of foreign manufacture, Defoe suggested, and they are now able to pay twelve shillings in the pound duty, then they can afford "a Shilling, Two or Three in a Yard" more, which would be enough to insure the survival of the domestic industry.[32]

The threat to the English woolen industry was an even more serious problem, and while Defoe was duly ingenious in inventing reasons for confidence, it is here that he most resembles a man grasping at straws. The case was made difficult for him by the fact that though England, like France, was to enjoy most-favored-nation status in the setting of rates on goods, the French were prepared to impose the high rates of 1699 on all imported woolens in order to protect their own industry. Furthermore, as Defoe admits, the French no longer lagged behind the English in their ability to manufacture woolens; they are "a Nation arrived to such an Improvement, that they are really our Rivals" in the trade. The people of France are "Poor, Industrious, and work very low," for which reason "they are sure to underwork and undersell us."[33] The possibility of slowing the growth of this rival is one reason, said Defoe, for the immediate opening of trade with France, even upon unfavorable terms. A better reason is that French production is limited by the difficulty of obtaining wool, which the English have in abundance; indeed, the French woolen industry is only able to compete through the "Baseness and Treachery of our own Peoples, who for Private Gain will set their Hands to the Ruin of their Country" by smuggling raw wool over to France.[34] Thus a necessary corollary to the treaty was strict enforcement of the laws prohibiting the export of raw wool.

But the ultimate protection for the English woolen industry, Defoe asserted, was the excellence of English labor; taking into account the value of the goods produced, "neither the French, or any Nation in the World do, or can, Work Cheaper than the English both can and do."[35] Though English goods may have cost more in foreign markets because of the higher wages paid in England, there would always be a market for the superior

English goods. The superiority of English goods lay mostly in the talent of English women for spinning, a talent which was as endemic to a specific region as an accent in speech, and which could only be learned by a child at her mother's side: it was transmitted "from Mother to Daughter, as Birds Learn to Sing; Cocks to Crow; and little Children to Speak, (viz.) by Immediate Imitation."[36] This process was so mysterious that even those who know the art could not teach it, and so the skill would never be stolen away by the French. The undoubted charm of Defoe's evocation of the cottage wool-spinning industry, however, was not proof against the fears of English manufacturers that cheap French woolens would steal the domestic market while they faced high French import duties.

The provision in the treaty that France should pay no more duty on its goods than would be charged on comparable goods from other nations created the final serious difficulty for Defoe. At the beginning of the war ended by the Peace of Utrecht, Portugal had been persuaded to ally itself with England on the promise that, after the war, Portuguese wine would always be admitted into England at a lower duty than that paid by French wine. The Portuguese agreement, negotiated by John Methuen in 1703, also stipulated that the Portuguese should remove all prohibitions on the import of English woolen cloth into Portugal. Under those favorable conditions, trade with Portugal had come to represent a significant portion of the English commerce. The balance of trade with Portugal was not nearly as favorable to England as Defoe had been led to believe it was by his opponents in the debate.[37] But it was true that, in 1713, the Portuguese took off about 628,000 pounds sterling in goods—mostly woolens, much of it for reexport—while selling the English only £ 196,000 in goods, mostly wine, for a surplus to England of £ 432,000.[38] This surplus was made up in bullion from Brazil, which English merchants then used to pay off their chronic deficits in less lucrative markets. The Portuguese trade thus functioned not only as an outlet for woolens, but also as a source of capital to finance other operations. Equally important was the fact that the English merchants enjoyed a near monopoly over the Portuguese trade, which obliged Dutch, German, and other Continental merchants to accept the pound sterling as an international currency and to accept London as an international payments center, and which also made the Portuguese dependent on the English for credit.[39] But the weak link in this golden chain that stretched from London to Brazil was the differential duties on wine: a tun of French wine paid, in net duties, over £ 56, while a tun of Portuguese wine paid less than £ 28; the new treaty would allow French wines to be imported at the same duty as the Portuguese.[40] The merchants feared that the lowering of the duties on French wine would be resented by the Portuguese so much that they might be moved to prohibit English woolens again—or such was the fear raised by the merchants to bring the woolen manufacturers into opposition to the treaty.

Posing as a disinterested historian of the Portuguese trade, Defoe endeavored to point out the groundlessness of these fears: all English woolens had never been prohibited, only some of them, thus it was nonsensical to talk of the Portuguese "returning" to a policy that had never existed; the market for Portuguese wines might be reduced by half, but not entirely destroyed, because the English had acquired a taste for the stronger Port wines; Portugal needed English woolens and credit to carry on its Brazilian trade far more than it needed England as a market for its wines.[41] To these economic arguments Defoe added a compelling political one: the agreement negotiated by Methuen in 1703 had been signed by the king of Portugal, but was never submitted to the English Parliament, though it established duty levels.[42] Rather than a sacred obligation, then, the agreement with Portugal was an encroachment on the Constitution and parliamentary authority, and therefore null and void, "or else we give up Parliaments to the Prerogative, and revive that fatal Exercise of it, the DISPENSING POWER, which I hope never to see done in Britain, especially by those who Espouse the Revolution Principle."[43] What would the Whigs have to say, Defoe wonders, if the Harley ministry had negotiated a commercial treaty with France without consulting Parliament, citing the Methuen agreement as a precedent?

Defoe's use of the "Revolution Principle" petard in an effort to embarrass the Whigs lays bare the fact that the battle over the treaty was a political one with a basis in economic interests rather than in principles. It was contradictory of the Whigs, he pointed out, to prefer a trade agreement with Portugal that had never received the consent of Parliament over an agreement with France, which was both properly submitted to Parliament and of potentially greater benefit to the middle class than the

Portuguese trade was.[44] The contradiction suggested that the Whig commitment to constitutional republicanism as the heritage of the Glorious Revolution would be sacrificed when the interests of the landowners, many of whom were Whigs, were threatened. Another suspicious circumstance was the remarkable suspension of ideological differences between merchants and manufacturers, which had been brought about by the Whig propaganda that forecast an imbalance of payments in favor of France.[45] As Professor Appleby shows, there was normally an antipathy between merchants and manufacturers because of their divergent economic roles; in this instance, however, the manufacturers were induced to send petitions to Parliament protesting the treaty, even though stable relations with France would bring relief from land taxes and arrest the slide in land values, thus lowering the cost of producing wool.[46] Recognizing in these contradictions the fact that ideological arguments could be used to sway men from their longterm economic interests, Defoe attempted to separate the question of trade from the political and ideological considerations that interfered with it. Trade, he argued, was the common interest of all parties, and ought to be removed from the political arena entirely. Even when he had supported the war in the early years of the *Review,* he said, it had been his position "that we ought to have kept open our Trade with France, (viz.) Because we could get by the Trade; and that we ought to Trade with every Nation we can get Money by."[47] Not the balance of payments, but the continued growth of manufacturing capacity and extension into new markets was the real objective, and in this both landed and moneyed men were concerned:

> We are a nation which Depends upon our Commerce, and our whole Prosperity, Wealth and Subsistance depends upon it, the Landed Interest not excepted, whose Rents would soon be reduced to such a Condition as to starve the Landlords as well as the Tenants, a few of higher Dimensions than Ordinary excepted, if our Commerce should fail: This Commerce is supported and maintained principally by our Woollen Manufacture, which is so Considerable and Essential to it, that should we have no more a free Export, or a Vent Abroad for our Manufactures, the Import we make from Abroad would so overballance us from all our Specie, and the other Produce of our Country would scarce feed us: for this Reason, nothing but a blindness, which no Nation but ours was

ever possessed with, would have led us to be accessory to the
stopping the Exportation of our own Manufactures, as has
been done by Prohibitions of Trade whether to France, or to
any other part of the World.[48]

The "blindness, which no Nation but ours was ever possessed
with" to which Defoe refers is the protectionist ideology that
the Whig merchants were using to draw the manufacturers into
their opposition to the treaty. But Defoe's metaphor carries a
second, related meaning: it was a "blindness" to use trade as a
pawn or weapon in the struggle between parties, or, in a larger
sense, as an instrument of state power internationally. Though
not committed unreservedly to the idea of free trade—as is
shown by his insistence on duties in the proposed treaty adequate to insure the survival of threatened English manufacturers—Defoe shared with many Tories the suspicion that the
most partisan of the Whigs were not concerned about trade for
its own sake, but instead regarded it as a political means to
punish their enemies and reward their friends. Defoe himself
was a Whig to the extent that he favored a strong central government capable of encouraging trade, but to restrain trade for
political ends was another matter. Trade was an "Affair of
Peace" that ought not to be dragged into quarrels between
nations; on the contrary, "to stop our Trade, is to make war
against ourselves."[49] It is possible that the separability of trade
from politics was a deeply held conviction on Defoe's part, but
it seems unlikely that he could have seriously expected the idea
of the separability of trade and politics to be a telling point in
Parliament at the close of a war with France that had lasted for
better than thirty years, taking at various times commercial,
political, and military forms. Thus the "blindness" metaphor
constitutes an instance of Defoe's frustrated, perhaps impotent
rage at a value system of partisanship, nationalism, and power-
broking that he had come to equate with "modern" Whiggism,
and that he hoped the Treaty of Commerce, with its moderate
free-trade spirit, might help to counteract.

2. The Politics of the Treaty

Besides the economic and ideological questions behind the
proposed treaty, however, there was another entirely separate
set of considerations, which was ultimately to decide the issue.

The proposed treaty enjoyed the favor of the reigning monarch, but her failing health was the subject of regular reports from London to Hanover, the seat of the designated successor. Along with the reports of the queen's health went estimates of the strength of the opposition to the treaty. As a general officer of the Empire, George had made his reputation for bravery in the wars against the French; as a Lutheran, he had learned anti-Catholicism among the first principles of his education. The attitude of the Hanoverian court toward the treaty was well known in London, and men who valued their political futures were endeavoring to measure the effect of a vote for the bill. For the Whigs (except for those few who held office), there was little reason to vote for the treaty and good reason to expect a fair return for their opposition when the succession took place. For the Tories, the benefits of loyalty to the court had to be set against the mood of the electorate in the parliamentary elections, due to be held in the fall, and the possible repercussions that might follow the death of the queen. From 11 April 1713, when he first discussed the treaty in the *Review,* to 18 June, when the bill received its third reading in the Commons, Defoe never mentioned the succession as a factor in the debate—perhaps because he believed in the separability of politics and trade, but more likely because there was no way he could turn it to his advantage. As soon as the defeat of the bill was known, however, he promised to make the political motivation of its opponents his main subject; the purpose of the *Mercator* would henceforth be to "detect the Folly . . . of those who make this Debate, which is a Matter of meer Trade, to be a Party-Cause."[50] Bitterly, Defoe remarked that the defeat of the treaty meant that trade would go on now on the basis of Louis XIV's edict of 1701, which prohibited almost all English, Scottish, or Irish goods, and imposed heavy duties on those permitted to enter France. French goods would still be imported into England, though under high duties; but since those duties would be drawn back when the goods were reexported, those colonies and foreign nations that traded through England would be able to buy French goods cheaper than English. The only explanation Defoe could see for the outcome was that trade had been sacrificed to the interest of parties: "But the Divisions among us having extended so far, as unhappily to reach this Affair; which in Truth has not, nor ought to have any concern with the Parties into which we are so fatally Divided: It leaves us no longer in doubt, or to seek for the

Reason why some People are against this Treaty, who, there is good Cause to believe, had they been concerned in the making it themselves, would have discovered other Thoughts about it."[51]

The long shadow of Hanoverian influence did not, however, touch only the Whig party. Had the voting gone strictly according to party lines, the treaty would have passed the Commons. It was rejected by a vote of 194 to 185, with fully two-fifths of the opposition coming from Tory members.[52] Of the approximately eighty Tories who voted against the treaty, Defoe regarded nearly half as "very Whimsical indeed," and he marked their names with a "Wh" in the division list; the names of the other Tories were not marked, though listed against the bill. The intent was, as he said, to distinguish between "the Sheep and the Goats," the former being "good natured Gentlemen whose Reasons for voting as they did were apparently foreign to the Question." Unlike the Whimsicals, who had shown their opposition to the ministry on previous occasions, these independent Tories "are very far from lost Sheep, which were hardly ever known to straggle from us but this once, and I hope never will again." Some of the independents had voted against the treaty because they were "falsely amused and terrified with the Loss of their future Elections," and some because they were "personally piqued at the Ministry," but others voted against it because they were "either by Interest or relation, strongly attached to one or two Lords, who took the liberty to sollicit against it."[53]

It was these "one or two Lords" whom Defoe blamed most for the loss of the treaty, though Geoffrey Holmes has recently estimated their influence at only one-fifth of the total Tory opposition.[54] Defoe published a devastating character of these two lords—the earls of Anglesey and Abingdon—and of the "declamatory Commoner," Sir Thomas Hanmer, as well as a libelous description of their conduct in his brief analytic history of the defeat of the bill, which appeared within a month after the division. Defoe's version of the defeat has been largely ignored by historians, who have tended to follow the contemporary reports by Swift and others that the defeat was due to Harley's carelessness and mismanagement, including the public statement that he did not care whether the bill passed this session or the next.[55] Holmes, however, has shown that Harley took care to estimate the strength of the opposition to the bill in

the Lords, as if he were concerned about its passage; and
Holmes has also remarked that the information in Defoe's book
"is exceptionally accurate as far as it can be cross-checked."[56]
Perhaps more important for our purposes, the character of the
two earls and the narrative of their political maneuvers marks
the first time in his writing on the treaty that Defoe unleashed
his considerable ability to associate character with action in the
reconstruction of a historical event. If Defoe's account is at
variance with the rest of the available evidence, then it is more
interesting, rather than less, as a starting point from which to
trace Defoe's ability to weave fictional elements into his narrative in order to answer ideological ends. Defoe's account of the
defeat, written from the perspective of a member of the House
of Commons, runs as follows:

> . . . the chief fomenters of the Opposition to this Bill were not
> Members of our House, but two noble Peers, who have all
> along hitherto been of the Church Party, and I hope for their
> own sakes will, notwithstanding this Slip, continue so. They
> are both in Her Majesty's Service: The one [Anglesey] enjoys
> a very profitable, as well as honourable, Post in *Ireland;* the
> other [Abingdon], besides a Post a great Honour on this Side
> [of] *Trent,* and his Wife's being of the Bedchamber, has a very
> considerable Pension of 1200 *l. per Ann.* which, I dare say, in
> every Body's Opinion, besides their own, is at least equal to
> any Services they have, or hereafter can do the Crown. The
> former indeed is a Man of lively Parts, such as are fit, and
> have carried him through the first Scenes of Life with some
> Sort of Reputation: They were Funds sufficient to enable
> him at the University to argue with the Sophs, and pun with
> the young Masters of Arts with Success, as they did
> afterwards to wrangle with *Walpole* in the House of Com-
> mons; but now being unfortunately come to have a Seat in
> the other House, upon the Strength of this unpolished Wit
> he sets up for a deep Politician, would fain be in the Secret,
> and fancies himself equal to the first Posts in the Govern-
> ment, though nothing can be more apparent, than that
> whenever any Thing that can be called Business is stirring in
> either of the Houses, let the Waters that are moved be ever so
> shallow, he always contrives to get himself out of his Depth in
> them, and plunge some few of his implicit Followers along
> with him. The other, though a Lord, were it not for his
> numerous Relations, would never be considered any further
> than his Title. As to his personal Qualifications: his Pride and

Self sufficiency, whilst his Cousin the Duke of L[ee]ds was alive to point them right, have been useful to the Publick; but now they are left to his own Management, we must take our Chance, it seems, whether they are to do Good or Hurt for the future. To these two Lords a declamatory Commoner [Hanmer], having chose for his Supporters two Lawyers, (Persons of as little Interest, and as ill heard in the House as any that ever opened their Mouths there), was pleased to join himself: And this Detachment of the two Houses, o'their own Heads, without consulting their Friends, undertook to acquaint the Men in Power, that it was the united Opinion and Desire of the whole Church Party, that this Bill might be dropped for this Sessions, and revived in the next; which they believing to be a real Embassy from the whole Body of their Friends, were prevailed with to give their Consent to; and accordingly this wise Scheme of dropping it was for some Time handed about the House, but very ill relished by Men of Sense and Spirit.[57]

Defoe's version of the defeat of the treaty is consistent with some of the facts available in other versions, notably that the treaty was torpedoed by the Abingdon-Anglesey-Hanmer factions of the Tory party (thereafter known as the "Hanoverian Tories"), who took the independent Tory members into opposition with them. [8] What is missing is any statement of Harley's role in the event. While other versions suggest that Harley may have encouraged the Hanoverian Tories to defect, the blame here is laid entirely on the incompetance and ambition of the two noblemen, whose characters are drawn in such a way as to make credible the action attributed to them. Facts that cannot be denied, being public knowledge—such as Hanmer's next-day conversion back to the Tory fold—are incorporated into the narrative in such a way as to support the appearance of treachery and betrayal in the main actors: "our Commoner, who I think acted only weakly, and was drawn in by the Lords . . . made the best and earliest Retreat from it he possibly could, by moving within a Day of two for that Address to the Queen which thanks her Majesty for the Care she had taken of us in Her Treaty of Commerce."[59] The weakness of the Hanoverian faction, together with the anger of the independent Tories when they found how they had been tricked, suggests that the same division in the party will not occur when the treaty comes up again.

Defoe's efforts to rewrite the history of the failure of the treaty were probably undertaken not merely to shield his old patron, but also to prevent the complete breakup of the party. There were, of course, abundant rumors that Harley had spiked the treaty at the last minute to embarrass Bolingbroke, who had become his rival, and would be more powerful still if the treaty he had negotiated became effectual; the purpose of Defoe's *Letter from a Member* might then have been to heal the divisions between Harley and Bolingbroke by laying the blame on the Hanoverians. Another purpose of the book, however, appears to have been to influence the votes of Country Tory readers in the upcoming parliamentary elections by publishing both the full text of the treaty itself and a division list revealing the votes of the members, with the independent Tories clearly distinguished from the Whimsicals. The enemies of the treaty were in fact disappointed with the results of the election,[60] and letters from Defoe to Harley in October of 1713 suggest that Harley should propose separate money bills that would set duties on Portuguese wines and Dutch silks at levels established by the treaty, thereby making the complete treaty easier to pass. Harley was advised, however, to introduce these bills "Silently Among Other Things" and to appear indifferent to the treaty itself, so that it might not become a political issue again.[61]

If the intent of the *Letter from a Member* was merely to return a majority favorable to the treaty to Parliament, it may be considered a success; but if the purpose of laying the blame on Anglesey and Abingdon had been to unite the rest of the party behind Harley's leadership, there is evidence that the strategy backfired. A letter from a Whig correspondent in London to the court at Hanover testifies that Defoe's libels created further dissension among the Tories, rather than isolating the two noblemen from the rest of the party as Defoe had hoped:

Le Parti de la Court desavoue hautement Le Livre dont je vous ai parlé par L'ordinaire dernier, dans lequel Les Comtes d'Anglesea et d'Abingdon et le Chevalier Hanmer sont si rudement attaqués, et ils disent, que ce son les Whigs qui L'ont ecrit pour irriter d'autant plus les trois Messieurs et pour mettre la division de plus en plus parmi Le Tories. Quoiqu'on ne peut pas disconvenir, que Le Parti succombant ne se serve quelques fois icy de ces ruses, cependant il me paroit, qu'il a esté veritablement ecrit par un Tori et qu'on le

desavoue a cette heure apres qu'on voit le mechant effêt qu'il
fait. Ce que ces trois Messieurs en disent, ou en croyent, je ne
le scay pas, puisque Md. Anglesea est en Irlande et les deux
autres à la Campagne.[62]

By all accounts, the failure of the Treaty of Commerce had so
divided the Tories that even the talents of a maker of fictions of
Defoe's magnitude could not devise a history or a platform that
would bring them back together. The triumph of the Whigs in
having defended the Hanoverian succession by defeating the
French treaty, on the other hand, was the occasion for the
greatest rejoicing seen in London for the past twenty years, if
one will credit another Whig correspondent to Hanover:

La joye sur la rejection du Traité de Commerce avec La
France, se manifest de plus en plus, tant dans cette ville que
dans les provinces. Vendredy au fair il y eut en divers en-
droits de la Ville, des feux de joye, et d'autres marques de
rejouisance et on dit qu'en vingt ans on n'a pas vue une joye si
generale que pour cette fois.[63]

3. The Treaty and the Idea of Fiction

Paul Hunter rightly declares that it was in *Robinson Crusoe*
that Defoe took the "necessary step toward one of literature's
most impressive forms, the symbolic novel."[64] But as Hunter
also shows, Defoe had prepared for that step through a long
and arduous apprenticeship in lesser literary forms. Defoe accepted the idea of fiction only reluctantly, and perhaps never
completely; for him "the Fable is always made for the moral,
not the moral for the Fable."[65] Fictive elements were frequently
present in Defoe's work; only very gradually did they come to
dominate it. Readers of his *Review* are familiar with his
penchant for illustrating a point of trade or politics with an
anecdote or pretended dialogue, but these fictional elements
hardly make the writing a fiction. A fully formed fiction is, in
Henry James's phrase, one that "cuts the string" that ties it to an
external world; writing that is moral in intent, on the other
hand, loses its reason for being if the connection between it and
the world experienced outside the book is severed. Yet the
course of Defoe's writing in the second decade of the eigh-

teenth century reveals a steady decline in the dependence of his work on realities that exist outside the text, and a corresponding rise in his ability to construct a world of persons and ideas that constitutes its own reality. This development may, as Hunter suggests, have been a logical outgrowth of Defoe's Puritan background, which was rich in emblematic potential; but the motivation that prompted the growth to take place is still unexplained. The history of the Treaty of Commerce suggests that his motivation may have been the failure of his efforts to attain his goals through normal expository genres of expression.

After the backfiring of Defoe's attempt in the *Letter from a Member* to pin the blame for the treaty's defeat on the Hanoverian Tories, he wrote no more pamphlets arguing the case on economic or ideological grounds. The *Mercator* continued to appear three times a week, although by the end of the year it was almost entirely taken up with the running feud between Defoe and Henry Martin, and with Defoe's discovery that many ships which the Customs House books vaguely described as bound for the "Streights" were in fact headed to Marseilles, laden with prohibited goods, which proved to Defoe that the French were eager enough for English goods to run the risk of smuggling them, and that English merchants were part of the scheme.[66] His only other known production on behalf of the treaty was a 95-page book called *Memoirs of Count Tariff &c.* While not a "fiction" properly considered, the *Memoirs* is a stage on the way, and its mixed generic pedigree offers some interesting clues to the derivation of Defoe's idea of fiction. Its debt to satire is evident from the epigraph, the famous first four lines of Juvenal's tenth satire, which Johnson was to render as a comment on the vanity of human wishes. The *Memoirs* thus takes its intent from Defoe's concept of satire, which for him was a description of things as they are rather than as they seem.[67] But generically it owes much more to allegory, in that the characters who are satirized in it are not so much disguised portraits of real persons as they are social types or categories of thought—the city merchant, the country manufacturer, the Whig politician, the Dutch trader. In this respect the book clearly derives from what Hunter has called the "emblematic method," according to which contemporary events became for Puritan writers "emblems of concepts, and the contemporary world itself became emblematic of the spiritual or conceptual

world which was the ultimate referent for all creation, the ultimate reality."[68] But the *Memoirs* differs from the Puritan tracts
in that its intent is not to reveal a spiritual world of which the
visible world is a mere emblem, but rather to reveal the moral
or ideological significance of those emblems for the secular
world. If Defoe's main contribution to the development of
fiction was, as Hunter says, taking the step from the emblematic
method to the symbolic novel, then the step began with Defoe's
perception of moral and ideological categories in such material
and practical matters as the Treaty of Commerce.

There is, however, another equally important generic strain
in the *Memoirs:* the historical biography written for the defense
of a prominent person's character. Defoe had had the historical
biography in his repertory at least since 1703, when he had
written a defense of King William's affection for the Church of
England; in 1711, two years before the *Memoirs,* Defoe had
composed a *Short Narrative of the Life and Actions of His Grace
John, Duke of Marlborough.* In the next four years Defoe was to
use the historical biography to defend the conduct of Queen
Anne, Harley, Townshend, and Walpole in books that contrib-
uted significantly to his development as a maker of fictions. The
occasion of these books was invariably the public besmirching
of the subject's character through misrepresentations by the
mob and the popular press, which it was the biographer's duty
to correct. The means of correction was generally a narrative of
the "secret history" behind the public events—that is, the facts
which, if known, would tend to exculpate the subject of the
biography from the most serious charges. The *Memoirs of Count
Tariff,* however, was to be the secret history not of a real person,
but of a concept in the shape of a person, one "who has been so
much represented among us, and painted in such monstrous
shapes," that it is only "Justice to a Stranger to rescue his
Character from the Mob."

The character of Count Tariff is quickly traced. He comes
from a family of quality and antiquity in France, a family that
appears "equal in Birth to Commerce it self, whose Antiquity
no Body doubts of." The count has the esteem of all the nations
of Europe because he has shown himself to be "a Friend to
universal Commerce," though at the same time "he was a particular Friend to the English Trade." He clothed his countess,
his daughters, and their attendants in East-India silks, furnished his houses with English goods, and covered his roofs

with English lead. This favoritism created such animosity in his own country that he was "obliged" to reduce his imports from England by degrees, upon which his English friends "acted the weakest part that ever was known among Trading Men and Merchants," that is, prohibiting the trade. The depiction of the count's character, then, admits his role in the mutual suspension of trade between the nations, but with the difference that, while he was "necessitated . . . to lay aside all Correspondence with his English Friends," it was they who "cut off their own Trade . . . by which piece of Wisdom they lost their Country, the Exportation of above Six hundred thousand Pounds a Year, in Goods of their own Growth or Manufactures."[69]

At the cessation of trade between the Count Tariff and his English friends, the French commerce was eagerly taken up by "Mynheer Coopsmanschap, an old Carrier, and a cunning, tricking, circumventing sharping Dutch broker." Defoe hangs on the neck of his old Dutchman all the cumulative ill feeling produced by more than a century of Anglo-Dutch competition for the shipping trade: "It was he who made that famous Voyage to Japan, where when he was asked by the Emperour, whether he was a Christian or not, he answered, he was a HOLLANDER." Count Tariff was aware of the "Subtilty and Knavery of this Tricking Dutchman," but the cessation of the English trade left him no commerce except with Coopmanschap, who then sought to monopolize the trade. Coopmanschap "bubbled" his two English suppliers of woolen goods, Alderman Traffick, "an eminent Merchant and Alderman of London," and Harry Woolpack, "a famous Clothier in the West," into thinking that he was the only man who would take off their goods. But Traffick and Count Tariff, realizing that "this subtle Dutchman had only been a Pick-Pocket on both sides," had recently negotiated a partnership by which they were to trade directly, which they were "undoubtedly impowered by their own Natural Right to engage in," but which Tariff was willing to submit to a jury of Englishmen because he had no fear that justice would be done "in such a Religious Nation as this was famed to be."

The emblematic types employed by Defoe in this history do not have the complexity of fictional characters and are clearly not intended to be understood as real in themselves, but they do have moral and ideological significance. The antiquity of the count's pedigree and the universal good that he does legitimize him, while his goodness disables him from counteracting the knavery of his enemy. Mynheer Coopmanschap, on the other hand, whose character is described in terms drawn from the literature of roguery, is an interloper in English trade and politics who looks out for no one's interest but his own. Alderman Traffick is an intelligent and sophisticated man, knowledgeable enough so that, left alone, he might be "steady as to his old Notions of the Liberty of Trade"; but Traffick is considerably under the influence of Woolpack, a well-meaning but loud and ignorant man who is easily outwitted by Coopmanschap. Defoe uses Traffick and Woolpack to show that the clash of interests between merchants and manufacturers was not a natural one, but was fomented by the enemies to the treaty, who found it "absolutely necessary to separate Harry Woolpack from him [Traffick], *that is,* to sow such Jealousies and Misunderstandings between the Country Manufacturers and Merchants, that they may not join together in this Partnership." The conspirators against the treaty agree that Woolpack has "a prodigious Interest in the Country; as well *Landed-Men* and *Trading-Men,* as *Monied-men,* they are all of his side," so that whoever controls Woolpack's voice wins the contest. The notion that the clash of interests that defeated the treaty was the work of a political conspiracy underscores Defoe's insistence, in *Some Thoughts Upon the Subject of Commerce with France,* on the necessity of separating trade and politics.

The evil design of this conspiracy emerges in Defoe's reconstruction of the process by which Woolpack was seduced into opposing the treaty. Coopmanschap was aided by "a certain CLUB or Society of Men" who had "certain private-wicked Projects of their own to carry on by his Assistance." These gentlemen sit about drinking port while they listen to their chairman, Sir Politick Falshood, present the case for Mynheer Coopmanschap. In his description of these meetings, Defoe exercises his talents both for humor and for narrative: for example, when Sir Pol informs the club that the French have invented a way to make fine woolen cloth out of coarse wool and are working on a way to make woolens without using wool at all, a club member is observed to shake his head and sigh, "LAURD! . . . What will become of poor *England!* This will ruin us all with a Witness! *What!* The *French* Manufacturers *without Wooll! good lack!* This is the effect of making Peace with the *French!* This is a *French* Popish Project indeed! I'll warrant the

NEW MINISTRY have a Hand in it! We shall be all undone! alas! por *England.*"⁷⁰ In an aside that presages Fielding's authorial intrusions, the narrator confides that "History has made mention of no more than what is hinted above, which Silence has been a sensible loss to Posterity, who are thereby deprived of the many weighty Sentences dropt on that Occasion."

The mixture of fictional and allegorical elements persists throughout the *Memoirs.* The members of the club are clearly intended to represent the modern Whigs, whose objectives are to obstruct, for their private advantage, the designs of their landlady, "however laudable and useful for the good of her Tenants" her designs are. But though Anne is the landlady, no certain identity can be fixed on Sir Pol. The closest Defoe comes to a specific description is to say that he was a "tall, black, passionate, hangman looked Fellow," which puts one in mind of Daniel Finch, earl of Nottingham, who was popularly dubbed "Dismal" and who was perhaps Defoe's and Harley's worst enemy. But it is unlikely that Nottingham, though a Hanover Tory, was ever admitted to the inner councils of the Whigs, much less the leadership. Sir Pol is probably not an actual person, but an emblem of the advancement of political interests over trading interests that Defoe felt dominated the Whig party at that time. His assistant is even more frankly a political construct: it is "Old Scheme," who has "misled the City these thirty Years with such Dexterity and such admirable Success, that no Body has discovered or detected him yet, having thirteen or fourteen Hands of the principal Merchants of London, to a Certificate of his Integrity in the year 1674." It is Scheme, who has "lived several Years by Cheating, and Counterfeiting Names, making false Accounts, forming Abstracts of the Custom-House Books, and the like," who now charges Count Tariff with being a cheat, occasioning the trial by a jury of Englishmen.

The critical moment of the *Memoirs* comes after a member of the club who is not let into all the secrets asks Sir Pol to recruit Merchant Fact to their cause, to which Sir Pol replies that he has attempted in vain to enlist Merchant Fact; he will, however, "set up a Counterfeit Merchant Fact in his room." At the trial, the beard of this counterfeit Merchant Fact falls off, revealing the face of Sir Pol himself beneath it, but even this exposure does not convince the court, which is swayed by the petitions from Woolpack and the tumult of the mob outside. At length "a

certain Suffolk Gentleman"—who would be Sir Thomas Hanmer—proposes that in the interest of discovering the truth, the
matter be tabled until the next sitting of the court, which was
carried by nine votes.[71] The members of the club find out soon
after how false a friend Coopmanschap is, and Woolpack's outraged discovery that he now has no market for his woolens
bodes well for the eventual passage of the treaty.

4. Truth and Fiction in a "Bad Cause"

The *Memoirs of Count Tariff &c.* brought Defoe only part of
the way toward the symbolic novel, but the importance of that
book—and of the whole controversy over the Treaty of Commerce—cannot be discounted. Surely Maximillian Novak is correct in saying that "Defoe did not enjoy defending the
commercial treaty," and perhaps also in suggesting that Defoe's
effort was compromised by the treaty's obvious defects in the
important matters of the protection of the silk and linen industries and the assurance of a satisfactory balance of trade.[72] But
it is difficult to discount Defoe's practical recognition that the
treaty was an agreement between nations in which neither side
could expect to get everything it wanted;[73] and the several
admissions in Defoe's later writing that the treaty was "a bad
Cause to handle" must be interpreted in the context of a Whig
hegemony to which Defoe was attempting to accommodate
himself.[74] Modern historians who have examined the issue are
generally agreed that the major flaw in the treaty was that it was
too far ahead of its time.[75] But even if one grants Novak's
conclusion that "Defoe did not approve of the commercial
treaty"—or perhaps, especially if one grants it—the *Memoirs of
Count Tariff &c.* is a remarkable accomplishment. It proves that
Defoe was by 1713 in possession not only of the allegorical
method—which he had shown in 1705 with *The Consolidator*—
but of a method that allowed for significant interaction between
characters and made the connection between events and their
origins in character, features usually wanting in allegory. Furthermore, the characters in the *Memoirs* were not empty categories, but were distillations of specific moral and ideological
types, however much they may have been lessened and distorted by Defoe's propagandistic objectives in writing the book.
The *Memoirs* also suggest that Defoe was well along in that
process of generic recombination that would eventually unite

the emblematic tract with the historical biography in the symbolic novel. Whether Defoe wrote the truth regarding the desirability of opening commerce with France is arguable; what is certain, however, is that he came very near to writing fiction.

Notes

1. Jean de Robethon, Letterbook of Correspondence, 1713. Huntington Museum, HM 44710. Letters from Baron Von Bothmer, L. J. Schrader, Daniel Pulteney, [?] Martines, [?] Gatke, C. F. Kreienberg, John Churchill duke of Marlborough, William Cadogan, James Jefferyes, Arch. Hutcheson, George Ridpath, and Robert Goes, from London and other cities. Quoted by permission of the Huntington Library, San Marino, California.

2. HMC Portland, v, 299–300, cited in J. A. Downie, *Robert Harley and the Press* (Cambridge: At the University Press, 1979), p. 171.

3. The pamphlets referred to are *An Essay on the Treaty of Commerce with France* (London, 1713), *Considerations Upon the Eighth and Ninth Articles of the Treaty of Commerce and Navigation* (London, 1713), *Some Thoughts Upon the Subject of Commerce with France* (London, 1713), *A General History of Trade, Part IV, A Letter from a Member of the House of Commons* (London, 1713), and *Memoirs of Count Tariff, &c.* (London, 1713). The *Mercator* was published between 26 May 1713 and 20 July 1714.

4. Defoe, *An Essay on the Treaty of Commerce*, p. 4.

5. Geoffrey Holmes, *British Politics in the Age of Anne* (New York: St. Martin's Press, 1967), p. 40.

6. Defoe, *Mercator* #108 (23 January 1713/14).

7. Defoe, *An Essay on the Treaty of Commerce*, p. 9.

8. Ralph Davis, "The Rise of Protection in England, 1689–1786," *Economic History Review* 19 (1966): 306–7.

9. Defoe, *An Essay on the Treaty of Commerce*, p. 16.

10. Ragnhild Hatton, *George I, Elector and King* (Cambridge, Mass.: Harvard University Press, 1978), pp. 116, 118.

11. Ralph Davis, *The Rise of the Atlantic Economies* (Ithaca, N.Y.: Cornell University Press, 1973), pp. 248, 302.

12. Defoe, *Some Thoughts Upon the Subject of Commerce with France*, pp. 4–5.

13. Defoe, *Mercator* #6 (4 June 1713).

14. Joyce Oldham Appleby, *Economic Thought and Ideology in Seventeenth-Century England* (Princeton, N.J.: Princeton University Press, 1978), pp. 269–70.

15. Patience Ward et al., *A Scheme of the Trade, as it is at present Carried on between England and France . . .* (London, 1674). Collected in *Somers Tracts*, ed. Walter Scott (London, 1809–15), 8:32; Charles Woolsey Cole, *Colbert and a Century of French Mercantilism* (New York: Columbia University Press, 1939), 2: Appendix 1, 562–69, and William Cobbett, *Parliamentary History*(London, 1806–12), 4: Appendix 11, cxv–cxviii. For its use by the *British Merchant*, see D. A. E. Harkness, "The Opposition to the Eighth and Ninth Articles of the Commercial Treaty of Utrecht," *Scottish Historical Review* 21 (1924): 220.

16. Margaret Priestly, "Anglo-French Trade and the 'Unfavorable Balance' Controversy, 1660–1685," *Economic History Review*, 2d ser. 4 (1951): 40.

17. Defoe, *Mercator* #2 (26–28 May 1713).

18. Ibid., #98 (5–7 January 1713/14).

19. Ibid., #11 (16–18 June 1713).

20. Priestly, "Anglo-French Trade," pp. 48–49. See also Ralph Davis, "English Foreign Trade, 1700–1774," *Economic History Review*, 2d ser. 15 (1962): 156–58.

21. Ibid., p. 49n.

22. Defoe, *Mercator* #98 (5–7 January 1713/14).

23. Ibid., #63 (15–17 October 1713).

24. Davis, "The Rise of Protection in England," p. 316.

25. Defoe, *A General History of Trade, Part IV*, pp. 10–11, 13.

26. Defoe, *Essay on the Treaty of Commerce*, p. 37.

27. Ibid., p. 39.

28. Defoe, *Mercator* #8 (9 June 1713).

29. Ibid.

30. Ibid.

31. Defoe, *Considerations Upon the Eighth and Ninth Articles*, p. 15.

32. Ibid., p. 38.

33. Ibid., p. 16–17.

34. Ibid., p. 16; see also *A General History of Trade, Part IV*, p. 36.

35. Defoe, *Some Thoughts Upon the Subject of Commerce with France*, p. 37.

36. Ibid., p. 39; see also *Mercator* #143.

37. Defoe, *A General History of Trade, Part IV*, p. 30.

38. H. E. S. Fisher, *The Portugal Trade: A Study of Anglo-Portuguese Commerce, 1700–1770* (London: Methuen, 1971), p. 142.

39. Ibid., p. 133.

40. Defoe's statistics, in *A General History of Trade, Part IV*, pp. 8–9, confirmed by Fisher, *The Portugal Trade*, p. 27.

41. Defoe, *A General History of Trade, Part IV*, pp. 8–9; 17–32.

42. Ibid., p. 20 ff.

43. Defoe, *Some Thoughts Upon the Subject of Commerce with France*, p. 23.

44. Defoe, Ibid., pp. 26–27.

45. Appleby, *Economic Thought and Ideology*, pp. 168–69.

46. For the political implications of the decline in land values, see W. A. Speck, "Conflict in Society," *Britain after the Glorious Revolution, 1689–1714*, ed. Geoffrey Holmes (London: Macmillan, 1969), pp. 135–154. For the petitions from British manufacturers, see Harkness, "Opposition," pp. 221–22.

47. Defoe, *Some Thoughts Upon the Subject of Commerce with France*, p. 27. See also Maximillian Novak, *Economics and the Fiction of Daniel Defoe* (New York: Russell and Russell, 1976), p. 24.

48. Defoe, *Some Thoughts Upon the Subject of Commerce with France*, pp. 27–28.

49. Defoe, *Mercator* #27.

50. Ibid., #12 (18–20 June 1713).

51. Ibid., #14 (23–25 June 1713).

52. Holmes, *British Politics in the Age of Anne*, p. 39. Holmes and other historians recorded the vote as 194 to 185, though Defoe's division list in *A Letter from a Member of the House of Commons*, pp. 25–42, gives the totals as 196–187. Defoe's totals include the tellers.

53. Defoe, *A Letter from a Member of the House of Commons*, p. 24.

54. Holmes, *British Politics in the Age of Anne*, p. 40.

55. J. A. Downie, *Robert Harley and the Press* (Cambridge: At the University Press, 1979), p. 171; Sheila Biddle, *Bolingbroke and Harley* (London: George Allen and Unwin, 1975), p. 251; I. S. Leadam, *The History of England, From the Accession of Anne to the Death of George II* (London: Longmans, Green, 1909; 1969), p. 208.

56. Holmes, *British Politics in the Age of Anne*, pp. 422, 501 n.

57. Defoe, *A Letter from a Member of the House of Commons*, pp. 43–44.

58. Holmes, *British Politics in the Age of Anne*, pp. 280–81.

59. Defoe, *A Letter from a Member of the House of Commons*, pp. 45–46. A letter from C. F. Kreienberg to Robethon dated 4 July 1713, however, passes on the rumor that Hanmer's reversal was part of a bargain he made by which he was to become secretary of state in Bolingbroke's place when Bolingbroke was promoted. Since Harley had no intention of promoting Bolingbroke, this offer might have come from Bolingbroke himself. Robethon Letterbook, folio 28.

60. "En gros il faut dire, que la Rejection du Bill de Commerce n'a pas en cet effêt dans Les Elections comme Les Ennemis du Ministère s'en sont flattés, et La poignée de laine que les Whigs mettent à leurs chapeaux dans toutes les Elections contestées pour le distinguer des autres, ne leur sert gueres." Kreienberg to Robethon, 8/19 September 1713. Letterbook, folio 217.

61. G. H. Healey, ed., *The Letters of Daniel Defoe* (Oxford: Clarendon Press, 1955), pp. 417–21.

62. Kreienberg to Robethon, 31 July/11 August 1713. Letterbook, folio 143.

63. Gatke to Robethon, 23 June/4 July 1713. Letterbook, folio 26.

64. J. Paul Hunter, *The Reluctant Pilgrim* (Baltimore, Md.: Johns Hopkins Press, 1966), p. 124.

65. Defoe, *Serious Reflections of Robinson Crusoe*, ed. Maynadier, III, ix.

66. Defoe, *Mercator* #144 and following numbers.

67. Defoe, *Conjugal Lewdness: Or, Matrimonial Whoredom*, ed. Maximillian Novak (Gainesville, Fla.: Scholar's Facsimiles, 1967), p. 403.

68. Hunter, *Reluctant Pilgrim*, p. 102.

69. Defoe, *Memoirs of Count Tariff &c.* (London, 1713), pp. 7–8. Defoe's version of the enactment of prohibitions should be corrected by reference to G. N. Clarke, *The Dutch Alliance and the War against the French Trade, 1688–1697* (New York: Russell and Russell, 1923 and 1971), pp. 63–71.

70. Defoe, *Memoirs of Count Tariff &c.*, p. 43. The italics appear in the original, but reversed.

71. Ibid., pp. 74–76. The identification of Hanmer as the Suffolk gentleman is based on Romney Sedgwick, *The House of Commons, 1715–1754* (London: The History of Parliament Trust, 1970), pp. 107–8.

72. Novak, *Economics and the Fiction of Daniel Defoe*, p. 25.

73. Defoe, *Some Thoughts Upon the Subject of Commerce with France*, p. 20.

74. Novak, *Economics and the Fiction of Daniel Defoe*, p. 25, who cites the *Manufacturer* #10 (6 November 1719).

75. Ralph Davis has said that the treaty was thrown out because of "political attitudes to French power," and that the protectionist duties that were preserved by the failure of the treaty were withdrawn in 1786 when the Anglo-French wars ended "with honours even enough to abate the motives of fear and hatred which had blocked it before" ("The Rise of Protection in England, 1689–1786," *EHR* 19 [1966]: 309–10.

3

Fiction and the Faithful Minister: The Tragedy of Robert Harley

Defoe was, as Maximillian Novak has suggested, a hero-worshipper. Believing in the efficacy of the individual and in the existence of a direct relation between character and action, he admired men like Gustavus Adolphus and William III for their seeming ability to overcome the most difficult circumstances, often by military means, without losing their integrity or sense of justice.[1] But there was too much of the Whig in Defoe for this hero-worship to become the basis for his philosophy of the modern state, as it was for many Tories. The disastrous military reverses suffered by Charles XII, the apparent peculation and insubordination of Marlborough, and the abuse of Anne by her own courtiers were all lessons for Defoe in the declining power of heroism. Defoe continued to believe in the concept of the hero after the Peace of Utrecht, but he believed in it and wrote about it *as* a formal concept, rather than with the expectation that such a hero would actually be England's salvation. The monarch was, with the Lords and Commons, a necessary part of the Constitution; in order to keep the monarch above the petty strife of parties and factions as a symbol of national unity, the monarch must be a hero, or at least considered and addressed as such. It was also necessary to believe that the king's ministers were nothing more than an extension of the king's will, having no independent shaping force of their own in government. For this reason, Novak is also correct in saying that Defoe never regarded Harley as a hero—if Harley were no more than an instrument of the monarch's authority, as it was his place as a minister to be, then how could he be a hero himself? But Defoe was becoming sharply aware that these men who were nominally no more than the advisers to kings were, in the modern state, the real makers of policy, out of office as well as in. His formal admiration for the hero was at least equally matched by his respect for the faithful servant on whom the hero's accomplishments depended.

The relationship between monarch and minister received perhaps its ultimate evocation in Defoe's hands shortly after the execution of Baron Goertz, Privy-Councilor and minister of state to Charles XII, in 1719. Defoe's eulogy of the Swedish minister idealized Goertz at the same time that it praised him: "wherever the King was, the Baron always went to him himself; there he communicated to his Majesty, what Steps he had taken in Pursuance of former Instructions, and received new. There he had Occasion to give his Opinion freely in the Points disputed, to expostulate with that generous Prince, who knowing the Goodness of his Judgment, yielded to him in many Things, in which to the Opinion of others he was deaf and unpersuadable. There he took his father Instructions in all Things, and the King's Resolutions to every Question in Debate, viva voce, without the Trouble of written Instructions."[2] While Defoe's ideal of service emphasizes the perfect submission of man to master, it also stresses the dependence of the hero upon his counselor: "So faithful, so capable as Agent, merited well to be entrusted with Things of the highest Moment, and of the greatest Consequence. Matters committed to him, were as dark as Death, and as secure, as if they had been buryed."

No doubt the intensity of Defoe's feeling on this head had more to do with his own experience as Harley's agent than with any direct observation of meetings between Goertz and Charles XII, and there is more than a little fellow-feeling in his description of Goertz's end, when the death of Charles XII had "left him Friendless in the hands of his utter Enemies." Defoe had been similarly abandoned to his enemies after Harley's fall from power in July of 1714. But the fact that Defoe continued to defend Harley's record as the manager of the queen's affairs long after Harley was powerless to repay him—in fact, even after Harley had disowned and rejected the kind of help Defoe was able to give—suggests that Defoe's involvement in the defense of the Harley ministry was more than the fulfillment of a personal obligation. Harley had become for Defoe the emblem of perfect service, a formal concept equally important with that of the hero in Defoe's ideological system, and in the years immediately surrounding the accession of George I, Defoe made the elaboration of this concept one of the main thrusts of his writing. His aim was not, as is usually supposed, the defense of Harley as an individual by means of fathering lies upon distortions and omissions of fact, but rather the defense of the remnants of an ideological system that the Whigs, with their formidable ability at party government, seemed bent on destroying. The history of the Harley ministry became for Defoe one of those fictions in which, as in the struggle over the Treaty of Commerce, the specific historical or economic facts were less important than the concept that the fiction represented: the Commercial Treaty had represented the liberty of trade from political interference; the Harley ministry represented the last effort at nonpartisan government, based on the ideal of service.

1. The Harley Ministry and the Decline of Moderation

That it was truly Harley's aim to have a nonpartisan government after becoming chancellor of the Exchequer in 1710 has been thoroughly documented by Geoffrey Holmes, Angus McInnes, and Alan Downie, among others.[3] The conventional description of Harley as a "moderate" does not really do justice to the problem: he had to act almost as if parties did not exist, while recognizing that party affiliation was perhaps the paramount factor in the choice of men to fill places or the determination of policy. Harley was not free to act in moderation, but rather was obliged to act first in behalf of Low Church and Dissenters, then in behalf of High Church; next in behalf of Court Whigs, then in behalf of Country Tories, in a perpetual round of balances. The only way to preserve a "moderate" stance was to deny that the queen's minister served any party interest, but, in serving the interest of the queen and nation, he served all. Defoe offered just this solution to Harley in his *Essay Upon Credit* when, impelled by the news of Harley's appointment as chancellor, the moneyed interest, mostly Whigs, drove the public credit down by more than fifteen points.[4] Defoe argued that the government's credit "depends upon the Queen and Parliament entirely, and not at all upon the well or ill Management of the Officers, of what kind soever."[5]

But Defoe's main service to Harley in propagating support

The Tower of London. From Stow's *Survey* (1722).

London Bridge. From Stow's *Survey* (1722).

for a moderate policy was in developing the line of thought begun in Simon Clement's pamphlet, *Faults on Both Sides,* said to reflect Harley's own opinions.[6] Writing in the guise of a disinterested patriot, Clement—the first of many writers who, in the year 1710–11, would play on the "fault-finder" theme—endeavored to prove, as Charles Davenant had suggested eight years earlier, that the parties had virtually swapped principles between the time of the Revolution and the present. The Old Whigs, who had earned the nation's gratitude for their resistance to monarchical intrusions upon the church and Constitution, had been replaced by a set of Modern Whigs who threatened to erect a tyranny even worse than absolute monarchy in the form of party government, while the Old Tories, who had once preached nonresistance, now used highflying sermons and street mobs to intimidate Her Majesty's administration. The new Harley ministry proposed to carry on the Old Whig principles upon a Country Tory base—"offering to include all those of the whig party who shall . . . concur in the promotion of the public good."[7] In Defoe's pamphlet, entitled *Rogues on Both Sides,* Clement's admission of faults on both sides became a denunciation of both the Modern Whigs and the Old Tories, reserving praise for the "Trimmer," an honest man who pursued "the Publick Good, and enclined either to the Whigs, or the Tories, as they pursued that End."[8] The Trimmer "has . . . a great while kept a just Balance betwixt the two Parties, whose Violence or Self-Ends would else have overset the Boat." The Old Whig, it is said, has "always the good of his Country in his Eye," and is Zealous against the Mismanagement of the Publick Treasure"; he is "for Non-Resistance of the Laws, and a Legal Administration; for bringing Publick Delinquents to Punishment, sooner than the Private; and general Robbers of the Kingdom, rather than Particular Thieves of Private Goods." Defoe's praise of the Old Whig is intended not only to reflect badly on such Modern Whigs as Marlborough, who had recently been accused of peculation and whose case was the current test of party loyalty, but also to convince the Modern Tories to take up the abandoned Old Whig ideology. By cloaking themselves with these patriotic principles, the Tories may distinguish themselves from the "New High Flyer, or Motly," who commits the "impudence" of preaching principles that must bring in the Pretender, while taking the Oaths of Abjuration intended to keep him out.[9]

Defoe's refinement of the political line begun by Davenant and Clement appears at first to be a mere polemic against all politicians except Harley, who in some respects fits the character of the Trimmer or the Old Whig. Since the Old Whigs no longer existed as a party, but only as a set of neglected principles, it follows that Harley was a minister without a party, or rather a minister whose administration was open to all men of good will irrespective of party; therefore, Defoe's praise of Harley as an Old Whig made any man who would not come into Harley's ministry seem to be either a man of ill will or a factious partisan. But Defoe's pamphlet, unlike Clement's, did not merely extend an invitation to the Whigs to become part of Harley's Tory ministry; rather, it insisted that the price of participation in the Harley ministry was the complete submission of party interest to that of the queen, represented by her prime minister, the treasurer. The lucre of a place in the queen's service was not to be obtained as a reward for party wrangling, but only through the treasurer's power of patronage. Thus from a relatively conciliatory appeal for both sides to admit their faults and work together, Defoe escalated the moderate position into a virulent campaign against the Junto, the leaders of the Modern Whig faction, and the High Church Tories who would not submit themselves to Harley's leadership.

The evil of party government was not a new theme in Defoe's writing, nor was it merely a way of ingratiating himself with Harley by erecting a new party with Harley at its head. It had been a shared belief between the two men that a "Prime Minister" must defeat the influence of any single party over him at least since 1704, when Defoe wrote for Harley a memorandum on the question "How shall you Make your Self Prime Minister of State, Unenvyed and Unmolested. . . . Neither Addressed Against by Parliament, Intreagued Against by Partyes, or Murmured at by the Mob?"[10] Now that Harley had the treasuryship, however, the factionalism of parties became in Defoe's eyes the reason for virtually all the ills of the body politic. Trade was perhaps the most innocent sufferer; even the peace would not bring prosperity, Defoe warned in the *Review*, unless the members of the various parties "come to speaking Terms one with another again . . . that you may draw together all in one Yoke, and push forward the great Article of Trade."[11] Religion was sacrificed to party interests on all sides: the High Church, while professing itself "Zealous to the last degree against Popery," defended the Episcopal Dissenters in Scotland, whom Defoe accused of Jacobitism; the Low Church promised to exempt the Presbyterian Dissenters from the Sacramental Test Act, and then not only forgot the promise, but turned the act against the Dissenters as if they were a threat to the Church; the Dissenters, in their intrigues with James II and their acceptance of Occasional Conformity, have "pursued their Political Interests at the Expence of their Religious Interest" to such an extent that "the Spirit of God has departed from them."[12] Political principle, too, appears to have been sacrificed to party interest: the "New Ministry" (a locution Defoe adopted to avoid referring to Harley's as a Tory ministry) has been forced to cooperate with Jacobites in order to secure a majority in Parliament, which would make them "Traytors to God, to the Queen, and to the Nation" if it were not part of a scheme to bring "*France* and the *Jacobite Interest* to be subservient to the Interest they are carrying on," which is the queen's.[13] Even the fundamental quality of honesty is undermined by the strife of parties: like the plague, the contagion of lying is so universal "that not a Man of us that has the least byass to this or that Party, but is infected with it." In a passage that calls to mind Pocock's description of these ideologues as "trapped" in their own "highly ambivalent rhetoric" that they bemoaned even as they pursued it, Defoe lamented that "the Manufacture of Falsehood, however other Trades may have decayed in this Time of War, has improved to a wonderful degree." That "improvement" would not have been possible, however, without a "dreadful Gust and Inclination in the People all over the Nation, to hear and receive the most palpable Forgeries, a willingness to be Deluded and Deceived. . . . When the Market is quick, the Trash always sells . . . the grossest Lyes that can be brought to Sale, never want a Market."[14]

But worse than all these evils of party strife was the threat they posed to the Protestant succession. To some extent, the succession had always been a party question. Though virtually all members of the political establishment were agreed on the desirability of having a Protestant monarch, the idea of settling the crown on a distant relative of the Stuart line, when a much more direct descendant could be found in the son of James II, had never been easy for most Tories to accept. The vision of the king as a "standing miracle" who ruled by the moral example of his own virtue was peculiar to the Tory ideology and depended largely on his hereditary and divine right to the crown.[15] Parliament could not transfer this right from one individual to another, though—if it were held that James II had abdicated—Parliament could declare the throne vacant and legitimize the new successor, as had happened in the Revolution. For those who held the doctrine of *jure divino*, however, neither abdication nor revocation had occurred, nor had Parliament the right to recognize William III, much less pass the succession to George if Anne died without issue. The *ideological* conflict, therefore, was not over whether George or James should be monarch, but over the legitimacy of a succession established by Parliament out of the normal line of descent. The Whigs, not wishing to confront the Church head-on, preferred to argue that the Pretender was the issue; Defoe's task was to show that if the Whigs truly supported the Protestant succession, their only choice was to join Harley in standing up to the High Church clergy and the doctrine of *jure divino*.

Like the Whig journalists, Defoe raised the cry that the Protestant succession was in danger. Unlike them, however, he claimed that the danger came from the confusion and ideological disunity among the common people aroused by the "thousands" of Jacobite agents who he said were dispersed about the country, "cunningly" distributing printed papers and handwritten letters, as a result of which "the Monster [i.e., the Pretender] begins to seem not so black as he was painted."[16] The ministry was hindered in its efforts to counter this Jacobite propaganda by the fears raised by the Whigs that an invasion was imminent. To illustrate his point, Defoe likened "those People, who talk so much of the Danger of the Pretender" to "Men beseiged in a Populous City, who take care to guard the Walls and Out-works of the Town, but neglect to disable and disarm the Factious Inhabitants within."[17] These inhabitants, being "disaffected to them, and willing to receive the Invader, are far more dangerous than the open Adversary that Assaults them without." As a consequence of their neglect, "in the heat of the next Attack, while all Hands of the Garrison are defending the Out works, the Citizens open a Gate, and let in the Enemy behind them, and thus they are Sacrificed at once." The danger is not a lack of vigilance in the ministry, but the "Party-heats" that cause confusion, disaffection, and ideological disunity among the common people. Making the same point through another anecdote, Defoe tells the story of the town of Alresford in Hampshire:

> In the middle of the Day, whether by Accident or on purpose, God only knows, a small Cottage House was on Fire, at the farthest End of the Town, *I mean farthest from what followed,* the Cry was great, and the Town all in Confusion immediately, and the People run Universally away to that Corner of the Town to the Fire—While they were all thus hurried away, some to help, some to gaze as usual, on a sudden, the Town takes Fire at the very opposite End, and the People being absent, the Flame got a Head, and in the fewest Hours that one would think it possible, the whole Town was laid in Ashes, almost to a House, the Church, Market-House, and all destroyed, and that with such Fury, that tho' the People were all up, awake and at home, as above, yet they had not time to save their Goods.[18]

If the real threat to the succession was not the Pretender, but rather the strife between parties at home, then the proper remedy was to unite behind the ministry in its efforts to hunt down the Jacobites in the countryside. As the miniature, yet highly detailed history of Alresford made clear, the enemy was already with the gates. The enemy was not the common people, though their delusions were dangerous, nor was it the Whigs, though their factionalism helped to undermine the ministry's authority. The enemy was the legion of High Church priests who, whether they swore the Oath of Abjuration or not, still held and defended the doctrine of *jure divino.*

While Defoe was pursuing this line in defense of the Harley ministry—which he surely must have known would soon land him in trouble with the High Church Tories—he was toying with two other dangerous ideas. One was that given the level of party strife in England, it would be wise for the elector of Hanover not to come at all. Those who espoused the cause of the "Prince of Hanover" would not do him any good by fetching him "from that Heaven upon Earth, which he now enjoys, to come to that Hell of Faction and Strife, upon Earth, that he will find here."[19] George was a sensible man, and what man of sense "would thrust in between the two moving Mountains of our Parties? Who ever does, must be sure, either to Overthrow them both, or be buryed in the Ruins, and crushed to Death by the Weight of them both." On the other hand, what was true for George would also be true for the Pretender; if James were to come over, he would be crushed by the parties as surely as George, with the added benefit that the domestic Jacobites would be exposed and destroyed in the process. Defoe experimented with these ideas through several numbers of the *Review*, seeming not to realize the depth of the water he was getting into. On 21 February 1713 he declared that "while the Distemper I speak of continues, and I do not see that it abates—the Pretender, for ought I see, is the only Cure—Desperate Diseases must have desperate Cures."[20] In the same number of the *Review* in which he ironically suggested bringing over the Pretender to cure England of its distemper, he attacked the ministry's most outspoken High Church enemy—Daniel Finch, the earl of Nottingham—and on that day also published the pamphlet which had grown out of his notion that it was not in Hanover's interest to assume the English crown. With more boldness than tact, Defoe thrust himself between the two moving mountains of the parties—exactly as he had warned the elector of Hanover not to do—and was nearly crushed to death for his pains.

2. Defoe's Nemesis: the Earl of Nottingham

The story of the antagonism between Nottingham, Defoe, and the Harley ministry is so important a part of Defoe's development as Harley's ideologist and apologist that it deserves a separate examination. The relations between Nottingham and Defoe go back to the first month of 1703, when the earl, as one of the secretaries of state, sought information about the authors of "Legion's Memorial," an address delivered to the House of Commons which had thwarted the ministry's efforts to prosecute the Kentish petitioners. Defoe was suspected to be one of the authors, though no hard evidence could be proved; the well-known satire, *The Shortest Way with the Dissenters*, however, could be proved upon him, and Nottingham issued a warrant for Defoe's arrest for libeling the ministry and the queen. Defoe was forced to make what he termed in a letter written to a friend "the Lowest Submissions I was Capable of in a Letter I wrott to my Lord Nottingham," and was examined before Nottingham about his coconspirators in the matter of the Legion's

Memorial.[21] Defoe refused to give any useful information, saying that "if my Life were Concerned in it I would Not Save it at the Price of Impeaching Innocent Men . . . for the Freedom of Private Conversation." Despite the intercession of Willam Penn and, eventually, Robert Harley, Defoe stood three times in the pillory and was confined in Newgate from July to November, 1703. If Nottingham had had his way, Defoe would have stayed in Newgate until he died of a fever or made a complete submission; the experience made the earl Defoe's lifelong enemy. Since Defoe regarded Harley as his deliverer and Harley was in the process of establishing himself as the moderate Country Tory alternative to the High Church politics of Nottingham, the two men found a mutual interest in intriguing against "Dismal."[22]

From time to time during Harley's rise—as in his 1705 poem, *The Dyet of Poland*—Defoe took opportunities to ridicule Nottingham. But the quarrel did not heat up again until Harley received the White Staff in 1711, at which time Nottingham came up to London with the apparent intention of causing Harley as much trouble as he could. In a pamphlet written (but not published) in 1711 or 1712, Nottingham or someone writing at his direction described Harley as the hub of "a promiscuous party" of "some renegade Tories and a few Whigs."[23] Under the guise of a moderation that was "wretchedly distorted to evil purposes," Harley's party seemed to Nottingham to be following a course potentially disastrous to both church and state. Nottingham saw the origins of the war against France in the time of his own ministry as a reply by England to the "gross prevarications and unjust usurpations of the Spanish Monarchy"; these original and honorable intentions remain "an obligation upon them [i.e., the Tories] . . . to bring us well out of it." But he predicted that the animosity of the Harley ministry toward the Whigs will "transport them to a scandalous and treacherous peace." Similarly, the Act of Toleration, which Nottingham himself had helped to frame in 1689, was intended to apply only to those who were "truly and conscientiously Dissenters"; Harley's party, however, had stretched the act to include others who joined with them "not from any principle of religion, but for faction and interest," thus resulting in the division of the Church of England into High and Low congregations.[24] In a letter to his wife written about the same time, Nottingham announced his intention to oppose the peace "if Spain and the Indies were to go up to the Duke of Anjou," which were the terms then being contemplated.[25] In the same letter, the earl told his wife that Charles, Viscount Townshend had recently called on him to offer his support for a bill against Occasional Conformity. The Whigs had always counted the Dissenters among their interest; yet, knowing that the Dissenters could expect no help from the High Church party, the Whigs were willing to barter the rights of the Dissenters to hold office through the practice of occasional conformity in exchange for Nottingham's opposition to the Peace. In return for Townshend's support of the bill against Occasional Conformity, therefore, Nottingham attached a rider to the bill expressing thanks to the queen for opening the Parliament, in which rider Parliament resolved aganst "any peace that left Spain and the West Indies to a Bourbon Prince."[26] A week later, the earl brought in a bill against Occasional Conformity, which, with the support of the Whigs and the Earl of Anglesey, passed the two Houses. When Nottingham was charged with fathering an act of religious persecution, a "vindicator" defended him by saying that the penalties "are extremely mitigated from what they were in the Occasional Bill of 1702, and in short [the Dissenters] have no Hardship put upon them" that was not present in the original Toleration Act, which they supported.[27] In a footnote to this passage, the "vindicator" explained that the Bill of 1702 imposed a fine of 100 *l* and 5 *l* a day for persons who continued in offices "after he or they shall have been at Conventicle." The new bill calls for a fine of "only 40 *l*." Perhaps, to a landed aristocrat like Nottingham, that sum was little enough to pay for religious freedom; to a small City merchant or village magistrate, however, it was still a heavy fine; and to Defoe, it was persecution in spirit no matter what the amount.

Defoe could hardly have been any more dependent on Harley than he already was at the beginning of 1712, yet the cynical deal between Nottingham and the Whigs closed off any possibility of a reconciliation between Defoe and the party whose "revolution principles" he still supported. The apostasy of Nottingham from the Tory party, the betrayal of the Dissenting interest by the Whigs, and the political naïveté of the Dissenters who accepted the Whig explanation for the act against Occasional Conformity on the grounds of the necessity of preventing a bad peace left Defoe entirely isolated from Hanover Tories, Whigs, and Dissenters alike. As he expressed it in a letter to Harley from Scotland, "I have my Lord Openly Declared against and Opposed Them, my Own Principle Concur-

ring with my Duty to your Ldpp Therein," with the
consequence that "my Entire Dependence is that I shall not be
left Unsupported in The Prosecution of That Duty."[28] Ideologically, the event cemented Harley in Defoe's mind as the
emblem of the faithful servant, while confirming Nottingham
as the antithesis of obedience and submission. The proper behavior for a displaced minister, or (as in Nottingham's case) for
one who had not been called to the queen's service, was to retire
quietly to private life and await a new turn at court; instead, he
had taken an active role in opposition by forming his coalition
with the Whigs. Nottingham was "the most trifling Ridiculous
Embryo of a Politician in the Nation," Defoe declared in the
Review; the interest of the Dissenters had been squandered on
him, and his use of them for his own purposes more than
justified Harley's use of Jacobites as tools in the queen's interest.[29] In an impassioned paragraph that helps to define the
ideal of service which Defoe accused Nottingham of having
violated, Defoe poured out all his invective on the head of this
most ungrateful of Her Majesty's subjects:

> The Regret of seeing others, in their Turns made use of in
> their Room [referring to Nottingham and those Whigs who
> did not receive a place in the ministry], causes them to break
> out in Bitterness and Indecencies, not to be named, and this
> even to their Sovereign, as if their Duty and Respect found its
> Period at the End of their Employments, and were measured
> only by the Emoluments; like the Shores of the Sea, which
> remain moist no longer than the continued Surges of the
> Ocean wash upon them, but when the Ebbing Water falls off
> from them, they immediately Harden, and turn into Crust
> and Roughness: So while Her Majesty's Bounty watered
> these Mens Avaritious Tempers, and the Profit of the whole
> Kingdom roul'd in upon them, they appeared (tho' it seems it
> was but forced by those Accidents of Royal Goodness) to be
> Pliable, Dutiful, and Subservient to the Just Authority Na-
> ture had made to govern them; but as soon as Justice di-
> rected the Royal Giver to stop a little the Emanation, to close
> the Hand, even, till then, open to the Voice of the Horse-
> leach, crying *Give, Give;* as soon as the Streams of this Ocean
> Ebb'd from them, Native Spleen hardened them even to a
> Crust, to Rage, Envy, Hatred, Strife, and toward their
> Sovereign all Unmannerliness.[30]

Defoe's intemperate outburst is interesting in several ways as

an example of political rhetoric. For one, the libel of Nottingham as a "Horse-leach, crying Give, Give" employs a specific
Biblical allusion and a richly metaphorical, Old Testament-like
style to denounce Harley's enemies, thus raising it a cut above
the usual name-calling.[31] Further, it does so in a context that is
at once ideological and political: that is, where questions of civic
virtue and public policy are both present. Nottingham, Defoe
believed, had overstepped the limits to which he might pre-
sume to dispute the royal authority: the one-time counselor
had become an adversary. In fact, a pamphlet had recently
been published setting forth the main points of Nottingham's
opposition, though perhaps Defoe was mistaken in concluding
that Nottingham had written it. It was this pamphlet, entitled
Observations Upon the State of the Nation in January 1712/13, that
had prompted Defoe to describe Nottingham as a "Horse-
leach." Whether written by Nottingham or for him, the pamphlet clarifies the political differences between Harley, Defoe,
and Nottingham. According to the *Observations,* the first objective of the opposition platform was to prevent the signing of the
Peace of Utrecht by raising an alarm about the adequacy of the
Barrier against France in the Low Countries and the necessity
of conquering Spain and placing it in the hands of the Emperor. With Spain in Austrian hands, the pamphlet argued,
England could afford to have relations with France, but not if
France and Spain were united in the Bourbon family. Employing the doctrine of indefeasible right—a remarkable position for a friend of the Whigs to take—the author declared that
a renunciation by Louis XIV of his grandson's right to the
Spanish crown could not be valid, though the writer did not
draw the obvious conclusion that, by the same rule, the Pretender's claim was also valid, and thus Anne was a usurper. But
because he opposed renewed relations with France unless
Spain were in Austrian hands, the author also denounced the
proposed Treaty of Commerce between France and England,
arguing that France would have an advantage through its trade
with the Spanish West Indies. And finally, Nottingham's author
insisted on strict enforcement of the Oaths of Allegiance and
Abjuration by Scottish ministers, Episcopalian and Presbyterian
alike, in spite of a recent declaration by the General Assembly
of the Church of Scotland that the oaths merely duplicated
"their known Principles and Church Government," and were
therefore unnecessary.[32] He regarded their refusal of the oaths
as proof of their Jacobite sympathies, which he contrasted with

the willingness of the English Dissenters to accept the Act against Occasional Conformity for the good of the Hanover succession.

Defoe's eagerness to destroy the opposition standard raised by this "trifling Embryo of a Politician," coupled perhaps with some overconfidence in Harley's ability to protect him, was the source of the serious troubles that followed; it was not Defoe's quarrel with the Whigs that led him, like Robinson Crusoe, into currents of which he had no knowledge, but his passionate hatred of Nottingham. In the same number of the *Review* in which he first suggested that the Pretender should be brought over to purge England of its closet Jacobites, Defoe pleaded guilty to a pretended indictment of himself for having identified Nottingham as the author of the *Observations.* "I shall do as I did once to an Indictment drawn up by Order of the same Person," he said, referring to his prosecution at Nottingham's order in 1703, "acknowledge the Matter of Fact charged." But that his intent in identifying Nottingham had been malicious, he denied; in his best ironic manner, Defoe suggested that his intent had been to defend Nottingham against all the slanderous rumors caused by his defection to the Whigs. It was not true, Defoe protested, that Nottingham had abandoned the cause of the Pretender; not true that, once he had displaced Harley and erected a Tory Ministry of his own, he would have no further use for the Whigs; not true that his ultimate design was that "the High Church [should] have the Dissenters' Noses in a Cleft Stick, and may lead them as they please." After all, Defoe said, "The Learned are not agreed in the Case, (viz.) Whether my Ld. . . . . came over to the Whigs, or the Whigs went over to my Ld." The latter seems more likely than the former, Defoe argued, since the Whigs had brought two million Dissenters with them as a sacrifice. Thus Nottingham had not really gone over to the Whigs, but rather was "one, who, which side soever he turns his Coat, can keep his Pockets always standing the same way."[33]

But while Defoe was amusing the town with ironies at Nottingham's expense in the *Review,* he was also offering explicitly political answers to the opposition platform for which he believed Nottingham was responsible. In his pamphlet *Nottingham Politicks Examin'd,* Defoe argued that Nottingham's *Observations* contained no real observations at all, but was filled with "Apprehensions." There were no charges or statements of fact in it that could be proven or disproven, only "Suggestions

... designedly framed and wrought up to such Constituencies, as to amuse the People with terrible Views in the Dark, placing such Spectres and Apparitions in their Sight, which at proper Distances may duly magnifie to their sick Imaginations, and represent innumerable Monsters, an Abyss of Confusion, and every Thing that may create Horror and Amazement." Nottingham's prose was full of phrases such as "it is not therefore unlikely," which Defoe reminds the reader "in Rhetorick are always taken to signifie something uncertain, and to argue from which is therefore called begging the Question, as his Lordship very well knows." Nottingham's analysis of the balance of power in Europe was "Partial and Erroneous" because Nottingham overlooked the fact that the interests of France and Spain were different, whether their monarchs stemmed from the same family or not, and only a royalist like Nottingham could think that in these times a monarch was not constrained by national interest. As for the trouble in Scotland, Defoe reminds Nottingham that "it was once very much in his power" as one of the framers of the Toleration to have established the Episcopal and Presbyterian churches on an equal footing, which was not done. The Presbyterians had obtained some security by inserting into the Treaty of Union a clause "that no Oaths should be imposed on them contrary to their Principles," which Nottingham is threatening to overturn by insisting on the Oath of Abjuration. For a Scottish Presbyterian to take the oath is to swear that he will not obey a Presbyterian king, on which the Anglican Church has no right to insist. There is a danger from Scotland, Defoe admits, but not only from the Presbyterians: "it must be from the Growth and Increase of the Pretender's Interest there among a People many Ways disaffected to the English Nation," a disaffection nurtured by the efforts of the Church of England absolutely to subject the church establishment of Scotland to itself.[34] For Nottingham's remarks about the Treaty of Commerce, Defoe had no immediate reply, but it may well be that Defoe's commitment a few months later to defend the treaty was based in part on Nottingham's opposition to it.

3. Defoe Is Swept Out to Sea

The antagonism Defoe felt toward Nottingham—and toward those Whigs and Hanover Tories who allied themselves with

Nottingham in an effort to overturn the Harley ministry—must be seen as the immediate cause of the incident that followed. On 21 February 1713 Defoe published the first of the three books that have come to be known as the "Succession pamphlets," which were the basis for a prosecution against him in April of that year. The pamphlets have been discussed at some length, but always as a way of explaining the prosecution, and usually with the assumption that they were wholly ironic in intent.[35] No historians of the incident have been able to go much beyond the explanation Defoe himself offered for the prosecution in a letter to Harley dated 12 April 1713, the day after his arrest. Defoe named his prosecutors to be William Benson, Thomas Burnet, and Goerge Ridpath, all three of whom were themselves under prosecution by the government for "scandalous" pamphlets. Defoe assumed that their motive was to see that the author of the *Review* received some of the treatment they had been subjected to, but he also suggested some political motives: all of these men being Whigs, they would demonstrate their zeal for Hanover to their superiors in the party by discovering the author of the book that had suggested it was not in the interest of Hanover to come over to England upon the death of Anne; further, since the ministry refused to discover and prosecute that author, they would embarrass the ministry by delivering the miscreant up to justice, thereby forcing the ministry to betray its Jacobite leanings and its connection to Defoe by quashing the prosecution.[36] To accept this explanation of the prosecution, one must believe either that the Whigs did not understand that Defoe's writings were ironic—which is not likely—or that they deliberately disregarded the irony and pretended that Defoe had actually written against the succession. On the other hand, comparatively little attention has been paid to the ideological content of these pamphlets. When they are set in the context of Defoe's feud with Nottingham, it is clear that the real issue was not whether the pamphlets were ironic, but rather the fact that Defoe exposed in them the failure of the Whigs and Hanover Tories to secure the succession and suggested that it was due to their obstructionism that the succession was in danger.

The first of these three pamphlets, *Reasons Against the Succession of the House of Hanover*, grew directly out of Defoe's animadversions on party strife in the *Review*. The struggles of those men out of office to overthrow the ministry have so weakened the nation that "we are not in a Condition to stand by the Succession now." The Elector "does not pretend to come . . . in his own Strength," that is, as an armed invader; if he cannot be assured of a peaceful accession, he will not and should not be expected to come. Any attempt by a minority faction to impose a successor by military force "will make you all like Monmouth's Men in the West, and you will find yourselves lifted up to Halters and Gibbets, not to Places and Preferments." To invite George to accept the crown in the midst of unreconciled strife is to invite his ruin, "and this I think is a very good Reason against the Succession of the House of Hanover."[37] Defoe constructed his argument in such a way that he could plead an ironic meaning if he were challenged; he could claim, with justice, that his real intent had been to suggest that the succession be protected, rather than relinquished. But the irony here does not depend on a reverse statement of the author's true meaning, as irony usually does; in fact, it was not much more than a literal statement of what the Whigs themselves were to allege to be true in April of 1714, when they opposed the Court resolution in Parliament that the succession was not in danger under the queen's administration. The Whigs and Hanover Tories who claimed that the succession was in danger would have been all too ready to agree with the literal meaning of Defoe's pamphlet until they discovered that agreement with it was a confession of factionalism and partisanship, the very elements that, according to this book, most endangered the succession.

The elaboration of this point does very little to reassure the reader that the writer intends nothing more than an ironic joke. On the contrary, Defoe confronted the Whigs with their own worst fears by summoning up some historical analogies that seemed to prove the literal truth of his point. A case of recent memory was that of Augustus II of Poland, who had been forced to yield his crown in 1706 to the pretender, Stanislaus I, because factionalism had weakened his support. A far more discomforting analogy, however, was to be found in England's own history. In 1553, the dying king, Edward VI, had settled the Protestant succession on the Lady Jane Grey in an effort to prevent the crown from passing to the Catholic pretender, Mary Queen of Scots. High and Low Protestants fell out against one another, and, "by Reason of their own Strife and Divisions, not being able to maintain Her in the Possession of that Crown, which at their Request She had taken, She fell into her Enemies Hand, was made a Sacrifice to their Fury, and brought to the Block."[38] According to this analogy, then, the Whigs and Hanover Tories were exposing the Elector of Hanover to the same fate that had come to the fifteen-year-old girl who had ruled for nine days before being beheaded by the Catholic pretender.

It must be admitted that Defoe's analogy is not a particularly good one. George was not a fifteen-year-old girl, but a general with a proven record of success in battle. His title to the crown rested on an act that had received the consent of both Houses of Parliament twelve years ago, before the beginning of the present reign. The Protestant church in England was a good deal more secure and able to defend itself against Rome than it had been in 1553. For these reasons, the Whigs had a right to be outraged by Defoe's ahistorical analogy. Nevertheless, it was their political sensibilities, rather than their historical imagination, that Defoe offended. His analogy suggested that the Whigs were failing to confront the implications of the succession, and in so doing were neglecting both the Protestant faith and the succession itself. The divisions between the Protestants in 1553 had arisen because Mary, as the eldest daughter of Henry VIII, had had the clearest hereditary right to the crown, and for that reason many Protestants "let the Protestant Religion and the Hopes of its Establishment go to the D——l, rather than not have the Right line of their Princes kept up." In the alliance that the Whigs had made with High Church royalists such as Nottingham and Anglesey at the expense of the staunchest enemies of *jure divino,* the Dissenters, Defoe saw the same pattern of concern for hereditary right taking precedence over the security of the Protestant faith. "It is evident," remarked Defoe, "that the Divine Hereditary Right of our Crown is the Main Great Article now in Debate." Most Whigs, though calling themselves true Protestants, were willing to concede that James had the clearer hereditary right. "Let any true Protestant tell me, how we can pretend to be for the Hanover Succession?" exclaimed Defoe, meaning that there was only one way: by repudiating the notion of hereditary right.[39] Yet the Whigs refused to make any such repudiation, preferring instead to ignore the contradiction posed by their alliance with High Church Tories. Convinced that Harley was firm in the Hanoverian interest but aware that there were other members of the ministry who were not, Defoe saw the failure of the Whigs to support Harley as the greatest danger to the succession, and resented as hypocritical and opportunistic their presentation of themselves as the champions of the succession.

Defoe took a similar line through the other two pamphlets that were involved in the prosecution. The first of these, published under the title *And What if the Pretender Should Come?*, directly extended the attack on the alliance between the Whigs and the High Church Tories that Defoe had begun in the *Review* and in *Reasons Against the Succession of the House of Hanover*. Pretending to be written from a Jacobite viewpoint, the pamphlet attacks the author of the *Review* as "that Scandalous Scribbler" who would alarm us about the "strange and terrible Things [that] shall befal the Nation in case of [the Pretender's] coming in."[40] On the contrary, many advantages would accrue to England by a Stuart succession: no expensive and corrupt elections; no meetings of Parliament to take country gentlemen away from their wives and harvests; no need to pay back the debts of the nation (owed mostly to Whigs); no need to attempt to maintain the troublesome Union with Scotland (by which the Presbyterian church had been established, to which Nottingham objected); no need to make noise over liberty, which would be abolished; no need to pillory pamphleteers, who would be hanged instead; no need to quarrel over church matters, which would be replaced by Popish doctrines; and best of all, England would have a standing army to protect it from itself, so that there would be no more mobs, no militia or trained bands, no street crime, and no need for guards to protect the Bank of England's cash, which would all be conveyed to the Tower for the use of James III.

Had the satire stopped there, the Whigs could have had no objection to it. But like its predecessor, the real target of the pamphlet was not the Pretender, but the weakness in the ideological position of those who claimed to support the interest of Hanover. Referring again to the author of the *Review* as "one of the most Furious Opposers of the Name and Interest of the Pretender," the supposed Jacobite author of the pamphlet notes that the author of the *Review* "openly grants [the Pretender's] Legitimacy, and pretends to argue against his Admission from Principles and Foundations of his own forming"— apparently a subtle reference to the position taken by the Whig prosecutor, Thomas Wharton, in the opening stages of the Sac-

heverell trial.[41] The Whigs admitted James to be the son of the
Dowager, which made him the legitimate successor no matter
who his father might be, if at the same time the notion of
hereditary right is also maintained. Since "the Doctrine of Hereditary Right being Indefeasible, is a Church of England Doctrine ever received by the Church," then a true Church of
England man must necessarily be against the House of
Hanover. The supposed Jacobite has the Whigs on the horns of
a dilemma: they cannot be both Hanoverians and Church of
England Protestants. To hold true to the High Church doctrine
of hereditary right is to accept the "advantages" of the Pretender's coming that the Jacobite has set forth. The unspoken, yet
very evident conclusion is that by their alliance with Nottingham, the Whigs have either turned their faces away from
Hanover, or at the very least have corrupted the ideological
basis on which they would defend the succession.

The last of the three offending pamphlets contained no satires or ironies of any sort, and it might have escaped official
notice but for the title, which Chief Justice Parker, the Whig
who tried Defoe, regarded as "sawcy."[42] Though titled *An Answer to a Question that No Body Thinks of, Viz. But what if the Queen
should die?*, the pamphlet does not really provide an answer, but
merely repeats the question at the end of each of a series of
paragraphs having to do with the rights Englishmen presently
enjoy to property, constitutional law, religious toleration, preservation of public credit, and security against external threat.
Though the author's intent is "rather to put the Question into
your Thought, than to put an Answer into your Mouths," the
reader is told that the "several answers which may be given"
may "not be proper for a publick Print," and "some may not be
fit so much as to be spoken." In a manner not a little remi-
niscent of the "apprehensions" over the peace, which he had
criticized Nottingham for raising, Defoe suggests that each of
these rights depends on "the Nice and tender Thread of Royal
Mortality . . . we are happy while these last, and these may last
while Her Majesty shall live. But What if the Queen Should
Die?"[43] The answer that was settled by law, of course, was that
the government would pass into the hands of a regency until
such time as the successor could be crowned. But as everyone
knew, if the transfer of power became the occasion for factional
struggle, the Pretender could seize the opportunity to make his
claim to the throne. Thus the thrust of *An Answer to a Question*

that No Body Thinks of is, once again, that factional strife at home
is the worst danger to the succession, without which the Pretender has no chance of making his claim. The implication of the
pamphlet is that those who are truly interested in the succession
will cease their factionalism, while those who do not cease are
not true to Hanover; and since the Harley ministry was established by the queen, the only way to end factionalism is to
support Harley. Defoe could hardly have expected the Whigs
to be affected by this line, but it may have had some effect on
the Hanover Tories, who had rebelled against their party to
consort with the Whigs. The fact that it was included as the
third of the pamphlets for which Defoe was prosecuted suggests that it was perceived by his enemies as an attempt to drive
a wedge between the Whigs and their Tory allies.[44]

Exactly who Defoe's enemies were has never been proven.
The motives of Benson, Burnet, and Ridpath may have been
much as Defoe described them, but it is unlikely that these
three understrappers dared to beard Her Majesty's government solely on their own initiative, without the protection and
encouragement of men in higher places than they. That Defoe
did not think that his three prosecutors were acting on their
own is very evident from his letters to Harley; he informed the
treasurer that "Their Design is Aim'd at your Ldpp and Her
Majties Interest, to let the Nation See how formidable Their
Faction is," and later pleaded that he not be made "a Sacrifize to
a Party who would Sacrifiz your Ldpp and The queen also, if it
Lay in Their Power."[45] There is also Defoe's later assertion in
his *Appeal to Honour and Justice* that he had "disobliged" some
"no inconsiderable People," a description he would not have
applied to his three known prosecutors.[46] Literary historians
have generally believed that the leaders of the Modern Whigs
were behind his troubles; yet Defoe seems to have been genuinely surprised that men ideologically committed to the defense
of the Hanoverian succession could act so contrary to principle
as to punish him for writing in defense of it. Perhaps he had
never understood the deep embarrassment he caused the
Whigs by his exposure of their opportunistic alliance with Nottingham; or perhaps we have been too narrow in our interpretation of the phrase "no inconsiderable People." Certainly the
Jacobites, the High Church Tories, and the Hanover Tories
included some "no inconsiderable People," among them Defoe's old nemesis, Nottingham, and these people had been even

more "disobliged" by Defoe than the Whigs. Whoever his
prosecutors were, the incident was for Defoe proof of two important facts: that ideologies were not principles, but fictions
imposed on the world for particular ends; and that even the
currents that one knew best could sometimes sweep one out to
sea.

4. Defoe Returns to the Offensive

In his letters to Harley and in those numbers of the *Review*
that immediately followed his arrest, Defoe maintained an opti-
mistic and aggressive attitude—so much so that his raillery
against the "Injury and Oppression" he had met with led the
lord chief justice to believe himself personally libeled, for which
Defoe spent more than a week in the Queen's Bench prison.[47]
If he was able to maintain the offensive through his personal
troubles, however, the defeat of the Treaty of Commerce in
June of 1713 alerted him to the danger the ministry faced from
the combined strength of the Whigs and the Hanover Tories,
together with the independent or "Whimsical" members. In an
effort to return more moderate members in the fall elections,
Defoe published a new variant in the "Faults on both Sides"
tradition, which indeed found no faults in the Harley ministry,
but rather demonstrated that Whigs and Hanover Tories both
acted on principles that each party condemned in the other.
The purpose of *Whigs Turned Tories, And Hanoverian-Tories,
From their Avowed Principles, proved Whigs: Or, Each Side in the
Other Mistaken* was not to attack either party, but to suggest that
they had a common enemy in the Jacobites, who were able to
make great gains from the struggle of the parties against each
other and against the ministry. As he had done during a key
moment in the debate over the Treaty of Commerce, Defoe
relied on the metaphor of blindness to explain how the parties
could be so ignorant of their own true interests. In this case,
however, it was a blindness introduced by "the Misapplication
of some popular or hateful Terms," among which Defoe included "Church, Passive Obedience and Non-Resistance, Heresy, Schism, Government, State, Rebellion, Faction, Sedition,
Tory and High Church, Whig and Low Church." These terms
are "often used by the Vulgar, tho' not one in ten of either Side,
understand the true and proper meaning of any of these

Words." The misuse of these terms played directly into the hands of "the Papists, the Non-jurors, or their confederates, but our more dangerous Enemies, the SWEARING conforming JACOBITES," whose purpose it was to exaggerate the antagonism between the interests of High Church and other Protestant sects. Thus Defoe made it his business in this book to attempt a redefinition of the common terms of political discourse in such a way as to emphasize the community of interests that existed between Low Church, Dissenters, Hanover Tories, and the ministry—a strategy that he predicted would be attacked as "Latitudinarian" by "Fiery Men, of all Sides."[48]

What sets *Whigs Turned Tories* apart from the usual propaganda of the times is the careful wording of the definitions that Defoe uses as a basis for his ideological categories. The Church of England is defined as including "all those Persons who do believe all our Thirty-Nine Articles, by Law established, and do sincerely endeavour to conform themselves to the practical Doctrines by Law and Gospel enjoined, and to those Modes and Ceremonies of Worship, which the Legislature hath ordered to be observed." The reference in this conventional definition to the thirty-nine articles and the need for doctrinal conformity clearly exempt the Dissenters from Church membership, though the exhortation that one should "sincerely endeavour" to conform seems to promise a loophole. But the reader finds that this definition of the church is not to be the basis for membership in the political state that Defoe contemplates. Rather, Defoe defines "A True Son of the truly Catholick Church"—that is, universal, as opposed to Roman—as "one who believes all Things necessary for, and nothing inconsistent with Salvation, and conforms himself, in all Sincerity, to the practical Duties now incumbent upon him, from both Law and Gospel, and hath Charity towards, and can joyn in Worship with all those, whom he believes to hold all the Terms essential to Salvation, and nothing inconsistent with it, and require no Terms of Communion, but what he thinks may be lawfully complied with." This very different definition of the church stresses liberty of conscience through the use of phrases such as "he believes" and "he thinks," and admonishes the believer to accept only what is necessary for salvation, and nothing inconsistent with it—a rejection of doctrine and ritual not immediately related to belief. Defoe's definition preserves the admonition to conform oneself to practical duties of worship ordained by law and gospel, but omits mention of modes and ceremonies of worship, and in fact mandates charity for all those who believe similarly regardless of ceremonies observed. The Schismatic, on the other hand, is one who, "tho' true in his Credendas, believing all Things necessary to be believed, yet for some unjustifiable *Cause,* refuseth to communicate with that Church, whom he believes to hold all things necessary to Salvation, and to believe nothing inconsistent with it, nor requires any Terms of Communion, but what are both lawful and proper to be observed." Thus the Non-juror, who refuses to abjure the Pretender and swear allegiance to the Protestant successor, by Defoe's definition stands outside the church, while the Dissenter stands within it. As it is with religious orthodoxy, so it is in secular matters—and one of the remarkable features of *Whigs Turned Tories* is its perception of the similarity of religious and secular ideological institutions. "By the Government, or State of England," Defoe explains, "I mean, that Political Mode of Government, by our Laws established, whereby the Prerogatives of the Crown, are ascertained, limited and preserved against any Invasions or reflections from the Subject, and settled in the Protestant line: and the Rights, Liberties, and Properties of the Subject (both Clergy and Laity) defended, both against any Arbitrary Power of the Sovereign, and the Frauds and Violences of the People." Defoe's definition of the political state carefully balances the Tory and Whig interests by emphasizing that the laws preserve the prerogatives of the crown while at the same time they protect the subject against arbitrary authority. The rule of law is further stressed in his definition of loyalty: "that Duty which the Subject owes to the Sovereign; and that Duty (in this Kingdom) is owing from the Subject, which the Laws (and not the Arbitrary Will of the Prince) command to be paid to the Prince." The loyalty of the subject is not voluntary, nor is he to be praised for giving it; yet it is not commanded by his sovereign either, but by the law, which is supreme over all.[49]

This political definition of the ideology underlying and connecting church and state was sufficient in itself, were it to be accepted by the voters, to contribute to a moderate majority in the next Parliament. But it had another purpose as well, which followed directly from the definitions that had been made. If law were supreme over all, and law commanded the obedience of a subject to his sovereign, then treason and sedition are the creation of "illegal and tumultuous Dissentions in the Multitude against what is legally transacting, or Done." Likewise, faction is "the driving on a Design, between several Persons, by illegal Practices, to the destroying, or opposing of what is legally established." Under this definition, then, ministers of state who expose subversive plots against what is legally established cannot be accused of factionalism; on the contrary, there is "no Crime greater" than the corruption of "former Reigns" in which ministers who had opposed arbitrary and illegal designs were convicted of treason. Though the extension is not made explicit, Defoe evidently saw the need to begin preparing the ground for a defense of Harley and his ministry should the coming election go the wrong way, or should the queen's death bring in the Whigs with the new king. In making the peace and proposing the Treaty of Commerce, the Harley ministry was carrying out the wishes of the queen. For a succeeding administration to prosecute them for doing so reminded Defoe of the "ingenious Parson" who, when asked "which was the Orthodox Church?" replied, "That must always be the Orthodox Church, which hath Tyburn on its Side."[50]

5. Preparing for the End

The more aggressive defense of the Harley ministry on ideological grounds that began with *Whigs Turned Tories* rapidly became a consuming theme not only in Defoe's pamphlets, but also in his letters to Harley. On Christmas Day, 1713, he wrote Harley a pointed reminder that "These Men must alter Their Conduct to the Governmt or the Governmt must alter its Conduct to Them." With an unusual directness that suggests his irritation at Harley's complacency, Defoe remarked that "there is a Time when Clemency becomes Criminall," and suggested that Harley's government was being treated with contempt. Five days later, Defoe wrote again to repeat his advice, insisting to Harley that the time for moderation was now past: "This Spirit of Rage and Fury is gone too Far for the Clemency and Moderation of the Administration to have any Effect upon." On the contrary, moderation would have an opposite effect: "The Mercy of the Governmt to them, is but like a little water Cast on a great fire, which makes it Burn with the More Fury."[51] The paradox of water feeding a fire pleased Defoe so much that he made it the dominant metaphor in his next pamphlet attacking the Whig opposition. *A Letter to the Whigs,* published early in 1714, is remarkable for the literary power of its comparison between these "Hot Whigs" and a volcano, whatever one may think of its author's knowledge of geology:

> [Should there be] a prodigious quantity of Sulphurous Matter in the Body of the Earth, which, by natural Agitations, have been many Ages ago set on Fire, spreading to an extraordinary Extent of Ground, by its Force consuming the Earth, and that Earth again falling in as the Parts supporting it are Consumed, meets at length with some Subterraneous Waters, whose Current the Earth that prescribed it like Banks, being fallen away, turns, and at once pours it self into the horrible Gulph of Fire; where the Rarification being sudden and unspeakably violent, vents it self through the Cavities and Passages of the Mountains into the Air, casting up Streams of Liquid Fire, vast Stones, Clouds of Ashes and Smoak, to the Terrour of the World, as may be described by throwing Water hastily into the Mouth of a Furnace, when the Fire being Fierce it shall burst out in your Face, Ashes, Smoak, and Coals coming out together, with Ten times more violence than the Water went in with.[52]

Apologizing for this digression, Defoe represents himself as pouring water on the "enflamed Spirits" of the Whigs, and predicts a violent reaction. These Whigs are the same as those who made up the "Old" (i.e., Godolphin) ministry, and who, though out of office, did not disband, as had been the case with former governments, but stayed together to forge their resentment into a standing opposition. In a question that was probably more wishful than otherwise, Defoe suggests that there has been a split in the Whig opposition—"What is the Reason that your Friends have left you, and indeed are frighted from you?"—because the great body of Whigs "can neither in Honour or Conscience, join with you" in "Railing and Cursing bitterly." In context, it is clear that Defoe means to imply that the Dissenters are frightened to follow the Whigs in their opposition—a fear to which Defoe had endeavored to contribute with his recent *A Letter to the Dissenters.* In that pamphlet, as in this one, Defoe warned the Dissenters that the Whigs were like "a Man setting Fire to a Magazine of Powder, and not giving himself time to get out of the Blast."[53] As proof of the danger,

Defoe cites a recent "Seditious Sermon, which scandalized a Pulpit lately by asserting the Lawfulness of taking up Arms against a Tyrant." The danger is all the greater in that the preacher was a Dissenter—Thomas Bradbury, who was later to figure as one of Defoe's major targets—though, "to the Honour of the Dissenters . . . not a Man in a Hundred of them, approve that Flame-kindling Discourse, but Universally condemn it, and blame the Preacher of it, as a Rash unconsidering Young Man, who, to gratify a Party, has done a manifest Injury to his Friends the Dissenters." Taking Bradbury's own example of the resistance of David towards Saul, Defoe denied that David had been justified, on the grounds of his "personal oppression," in taking up arms against a king who "was yet no Tyrant to his People." Relying on the rule of law that he had elucidated in *Whigs Turned Tories,* Defoe strictly circumscribed the right of resistance to the state to those instances of "Oppression or Arbitrary Power put in practice" in which laws had been broken. No such instances had occurred under Queen Anne since Harley came to the head of the government; if violations of the law had occurred, "Let all you can say be brought to the Test of the Law, and let the Ministry be fairly Accused, or fairly Vindicated."[54] Thus Defoe at once dared the Whigs to impeach the ministry and warned the Dissenters to stay out of the way of what he promised would be a volcanic reaction.

The aggressive line of attack that had distinguished Defoe's *Letter to the Whigs* continued in a pamphlet that appeared on 16 April 1714, the day after the Commons had debated the Court motion that the Protestant succession was not in danger under the queen's administration. Entitled *Reasons for Im[peaching] the L[or]d H[igh] T[reasure]r,* the pamphlet was another of those practical jokes through which Defoe drew unsuspecting enemies of the ministry into purchasing a book that presented the ministry's case. The original owner of the copy now in the William Andrews Clark Memorial Library erroneously filled in the blanks in the title as "Reasons for Imprisoning," and then wrote underneath it, "By rights it shd. have been Hanging Them!" The owner might well have agreed with the author's intitial observation that there ought to be some more effective method of redressing grievances "than merely bewailing them to one another, and crying out against those we think are the Causes of them." Why then, the author asks, are we standing still? "Either these Dangers are real, or they are imaginary;

either these Men are guilty, or they are innocent; why stand we thus gazing at one another?" Every man, the author reasonably argues, has a right to bring "a true Charge, and to try the Validity of that Charge," though perhaps not to "raise Scandals, evil Surmises, and Suggestions of Guilt without Ground."[55] But the question is complicated by the fact that the charge raised by the Whigs is directed at the ministers only, and not at the queen. This point of view had been presented quite clearly in a Whig pamphlet entitled *Dunkirk or Dover,* which in turn was a response to Defoe's *Reasons Concerning the Immediate Demolishing of Dunkirk.* The author of *Dunkirk or Dover* had charged that "all our Calamities proceed from the weakness or viciousness of our Ministers," rather than from "the errours or deviations of the Prince." The ministers are "the eyes by which the Monarch sees, the ears by which he hears, the heart by which he advises, and the hands by which he executes," and consequently his behavior is dependent upon "the representation made of those matters by his proper officers." Should the prince insist on a wrong course in spite of advice to the contrary by his ministers, they are chargeable if they continue in his service in order to hold their places.[56] Pretending to agree with this point, the author of *Reasons for Impeaching* asks why the motion currently before the House refers to the danger of the succession under the queen's administration. "We know that the Queen does all things by her Ministry, and they are accountable to the Laws for all Male-Administration, even tho' it were by her Majesty's Command, and may lawfully be impeached, if any thing can be fairly laid to their Charge." No such charges, however, have been brought, no doubt because of the difficulty of separating the "administration" from the government itself. Despite the admission on both sides that the ministry formed a separate branch of government, such a distinction was not consistent with the "Three Estates" theory of the Constitution that was commonly held. Thus, to impeach the ministry was, necessarily, to impeach the queen's administration of her government, "which no good Subject can entertain a Thought of without some Horror."[57] So while the author of the *Reasons for Impeaching* called for a thorough and impartial investigation of the charges before the House of Lords—which had already voted on April 5 that the Protestant succession was secure—he knew that the Tories would not join in the clamor for an impeachment that would be regarded as an attack on the

queen herself; and his confidence was vindicated by the fact
that no more than 208 of the 467 members of the Commons
could be persuaded to vote against the resolution that the succession was not in danger.[58] To what degree Defoe's pamphlet
was responsible for this result is impossible to say, but many
"Hot Whigs" who had bought it to fuel their fervor for an
impeachment must have found their tempers cooled by the
water Defoe's pamphlet cast on them.

Through the summer of 1714, Defoe's pen was primarily
occupied with the hopeless struggle to salvage the Treaty of
Commerce by means of the thrice-weekly *Mercator,* and with
the vain effort to prevent the passage of the Schism Act, a bill
outlawing Dissenting academies as a threat to the hegemony of
the church. The Schism Act was a joint project of Bolingbroke,
the Lord Chancellor Sir Simon Harcourt, and Francis Atterbury, bishop of Rochester, who had come to inherit the leadership of the High Church wing of the Tory party.[59] As a result
of their emergence and the passage of the Schism Act on June
25, Defoe gradually retreated from his political offensive
against the Whigs, and Harley began vainly courting support
from the Junto. The first pamphlet that reflects this new orien-
tation is Defoe's *Advice to the People of Great Britain,* published
after the death of Queen Anne on August 1, but before the
coronation of George I. Though its title offers to advise its
readers on the points of conduct that they owe the new king,
the real message is very brief and very familiar: "that we cease
that foolish strife of parties . . . joining together under a disinterested Principle, to cultivate our own Advantages."[59] But the
moderate political message that Defoe had once used to
strengthen Harley's hand against the extremes of both parties
is now intended to ward off the almost certain prosecution of
Anne's leading ministers under the new regime. All that has
been fought for has been won: a Protestant king, the church
preserved, toleration for Dissenters in practice if not in law,
Parliamentary authority protected, and "nothing remains for
us but for every Man to Study to be quiet, and to do their own
Business." Even the Jacobites are no longer a threat, says Defoe, if only they are allowed to live "quietly and inoffensively
under his Majesty." The spirit of retribution "will make the
King's Reign, which we hope to see Mild and Merciful, turned
into a general Judicature."[60] More interesting than Defoe's predictable call for moderation on the part of the incoming gov-

ernment, however, is his effort to reconstruct the history of the Harley ministry in such a way as to spread out the blame for those events that could be regarded as evidences of treason. The "Breach at Court" that came with the dissolution of the Whig ministry under Godolphin in 1710 was the beginning of the political divisions that wracked the country through the last four years of Queen Anne; not until then did a ministry ever continue to operate as a party once it had left office. Refusing to accept the names "Whig" and "Tory" as legitimate ways of describing a government, Defoe distinguished the Godolphin and Harley ministries as "The People Displaced" and "The People in Place," and as the "Old Ministry" and the "New Ministry." The people displaced, instead of joining the New Ministry or retiring to private life, took the unprecedented step of banding together in an effort to force their sovereign to take them in again. The people in place, to justify their offices, accused the people displaced of prolonging the war for their own advantage, thus committing themselves to a peace; and, in order to retain their places, were forced to accept the aid of persons now suspected of Jacobitism. The breach between the old and new ministries gave encouragement to a "secret Party" that aimed at "no less than the Prime Ministry" and was "secretly inclined to propagate the Interest of the Pretender."[61] This secret party was responsible for the Schism Act, which was one of the strokes by which they forced Harley out of office, hoping thereby to get the White Staff into their own hands. Sketchy as this history of the Harley ministry is, it brings together the major ideological themes that Defoe had developed in the course of defending Harley's administration over the last four years. Harley was the victim of Whig partisanship, Jacobite intrigue, and his own fidelity to the queen's interest, which had prevented him from engaging in the corruption and scheming through which his enemies had brought him down. The practical politics of defending the Peace of Utrecht, the Treaty of Commerce, the succession, and the moderate or nonpartisan approach to government now gave way to the ideological concretions that precipitated out of those practical struggles. Harley himself probably did not want the history of his own ministry written, knowing that whatever was said would resemble self-justification, and his correspondence with Defoe ceased soon after Defoe announced his intention to write it.[62] But Harley's collaboration was not required; Defoe believed he understood Harley's affairs at least as well as Harley had, and he was not, after all, writing history. He was writing a dramatic poem in prose about a faithful servant who had been ensnared by the designs of his enemies and the ambitions of his false friends. If his readers insisted upon finding modern parallels of his tale of the White Staff, then that was entirely their own affair.

6. The Tragedy of the White Staff: A Historical Fiction

Perhaps no books in Defoe's canon have suffered as much from the liberties Defoe took with historical fact as the three parts of the *Secret History of the White Staff*. From the contemporary Whig reactions, which represented the books as a ploy by Harley to escape the punishment he deserved,[63] to the admirable recent biography of the bishop of Rochester by G. V. Bennett, Defoe's *White Staff* has been regarded as an "amazing tissue of lies."[64] The reason is that the *White Staff* is almost always read as a primary source for information about Robert Harley, Queen Anne, Francis Atterbury or another historical figure, and never as a work of fiction. As a historical document, the *White Staff* does contain more than its share of lies—or at least of allegations and scenes that appear to have been composed out of the author's imagination. To cite only one example, the author of the *White Staff* suggests that it was Harley who, in the critical hours before Anne's death, convinced the queen to pass the symbol of the treasurer's office to the duke of Shrewsbury, rather than to Bolingbroke. This appointment, which is represented as having guaranteed the Hanoverian succession, was only one of many steps "the late Staff, for so we must now speak of him, had made to overthrow the Measures of these People."[65] But the details of these steps, which are said to have been concerted between the queen and her most faithful minister in private, have gone with Anne to the grave. Subsequently, competing claims for the honor of the stroke of political management in which the queen was advised to rely on Shrewsbury were made on behalf of the duke of Argyll, Sir Simon Harcourt, and even Bolingbroke himself.[66] At the very least, the author of the *White Staff* would appear to be taking advantage of the death of the queen in order to state as a fact an assertion that cannot be proven or disproven.

But the orderly transfer of the White Staff from Harley's hands to those of the queen, and from hers to Shrewsbury's, plays a dramatic and ideological function in the book that far outweighs the historical concerns that Defoe might have had. It had been a main theme of Defoe's defense of the Harley administration, and (as he claimed) a main reason for this attachment to Harley, that the queen's minister was her servant, though he might know best how to serve her. Harley's gracious surrender of power—which was truer of him in 1708 than it was in 1714—represents the submission of a dismissed servant to the will of Providence and his sovereign, the want of which in the Whig Junto had led to all of Anne's troubles in the last four years of her life. On the other hand, Harley's resourcefulness is demonstrated in the revelation that he had convinced Anne to give the staff to Shrewsbury so that she might give it back to him at a later time, which would be nearly impossible if it fell to Bolingbroke. While it is clear that Defoe regards this mixture of submission and subterfuge as a favorable reflection on Harley personally, it is equally evident that Defoe is here constructing a portrait of an ideal minister that has been inspired by, but is not limited to, what happened historically to Robert Harley. If the *Secret History of the White Staff* were written only to exculpate Harley personally, then it was indeed a "tissue of lies"; but if it were written as an interpretation of faithful service and the tragedy of good designs thwarted by fate and bad men, then it was Defoe's first major—and probably still one of his most important—works of fiction.

The interpretation of *The Secret History of the White Staff* as a fiction rests not so much on its formal characteristics as on its intention. Formally speaking, the resemblance of the *White Staff* to fiction is slight. It was written as a narrative, but in the third person, while most of Defoe's major works now recognized as fictions were written in the first person. It contains little reflection on the states of mind of the actors, no doubt because Defoe almost never explored the subjective dimension of experience except when writing from the first person. Its power depends not so much on the use of authenticating detail, which is cited all too often as the hallmark of Defoe's fiction, but rather on the appeal of its characters as actors in a real-life tragedy. Harley may not have been a hero for Defoe, but he was certainly a protagonist, and the effectiveness of the *White Staff* depends upon our willingness to accept him in that role. Like classical tragedy, the story of Harley's fall at the hands of absolutist conspirators affects us even if we are no longer personally touched by the circumstances; one modern biographer of Queen Anne betrayed the affective power of the *White Staff* by describing it as "fascinating, if in parts sickening."[67] It is the intended effect of the *White Staff* to sicken us, shock us, and alarm us into an appreciation of Harley's service in the queen's interest and into the necessity of his politics of moderation as the best response to absolutism from both sides. Historical fact, no matter how cogently presented, could never had had this same effect. History rarely conforms itself to effective dramatic structures, and the actors of history are seldom unmixed ideological types. Despite its title, the *Secret History of the White Staff* was not written to be history, but to portray one tragedy and to ward off the tragedy that Defoe clearly saw was to come.

As a work of fiction, then, the *White Staff* idealizes Harley while it sinks his enemies to a contemptible level. In keeping with the direction that Defoe had taken in the *Review* and in such pamphlets as *Whigs Turned Tories*, he did not make the Whigs into Harley's enemies, but merely blamed them for not helping Harley in his struggle against the Jacobites. The description of Harley's enemies is reserved to the end of the first part of the *White Staff*, when, at "a private Assembly of all their Confederates," the Jacobites hear of the successful transfer of the Treasury to Shrewsbury. Their reaction was to stand "looking one upon another speechless and confounded for some Hours." Finally, one of them, whose possession of the Purse marks him as Sir Simon Harcourt, gives vent to his despair in a damning speech:

> The Blast of Hell and the Rage of a Million of Devils be on this Cursed *Staff, said He, flinging the Purse, &c. on the Ground,* IT IS HE that has ruined us, and broken all our Measures: Did I not warn you from breaking with him? *(said he)* I told you always it was impossible to supplant him with the Queen. That she could never hear him speak, such as the Magick of his Tongue, without being enchanted with his Words; and that if he got but the Liberty for Five Words, he would undo us all.

Harcourt's outrage at having been duped is answered by Bishop Atterbury, who, in swearing by Lucifer, taking God's name in vain, and referring to James as the "lawful heir" commits three forms of blasphemy and treason in one breath:

> *Give away the Staff!* said the Bis. . . . By Lucifer I could not have believed she durst have done it! What can we do without it, we have but one way left, *France* and the Lawful Heir; it must, and shall be done, By G—d.[68]

The use of a swearing magistrate or bishop to represent the corruption of moral authority was one of Defoe's favorite tricks, and one of his oldest.[69] But in the *White Staff* pamphlets there is a sustained effort to make the behavior of these conspirators credible by inquiring into their characters so that, as Defoe puts it, "the Judicious" may know "whether what has been said . . . is fit to be believed or not." Thus the first among the conspirators, Lady Abigail Masham, who had been raised from a low station by the duchess of Marlborough and had then supplanted the duchess in the queen's affections, is described as having "insinuated herself into Favour, more by the want of Merit in those that went before her, than by any real Significancy in her self." She made it her daily study to detect the weaknesses of the duchess and report them to the queen, a method that "failed not to gain to this She-Artist the same Ground in the Persons Favour which the other had lost." This story, of course, was well known and generally received as true, which tended to support Defoe's further assertion: that when she "improved it to oppose the Staff," she produced a struggle in the breast of her Majesty between "her Justice and her Affection," which was the immediate cause of "that Black which now the Nation wears" for Anne.[70] But Defoe's purpose is not merely to make Lady Masham responsible for Anne's death; it is to gain credit for the theory that a palace revolution was underway, with an absolutist government as its object.

The characters of the other conspirators also support the theory of an absolutist plot. Atterbury is "unsufferably haughty, supererogant and enterprizing, restless and indefatigable in pursuing his Design, and ambitious beyond Measure." He is one of those whom Harley was forced to employ by the failure of the Whigs to come into his government, though Harley suspected him and "kept him at Bay as to Secrets." On the surface he appeared to be a true Christian, but beneath his Ecclesiastical cape there was "all sorts of Tyranny in every Step of his Conduct."[71] His "abhorrence of a mild Government, and aversion to the Liberty of the Subjects," would have been all too believable to readers who had heard of the bishop's troubles as dean of Christ Church in 1712, where Atterbury's arbitrary administration had ended in chaos.[72] Atterbury's tool was the lord chancellor, Harcourt, whose "Moral or Personal Infirmities in Times past" the author of the *White Staff* will not give himself the liberty of discussing; Harcourt was taken into the plot for "his Power, not his Capacity," and as "rather an Agent than an Employer" of other conspirators. The prize that was held out to him to betray his old friend Harley was the hope "of being Prime Minister in an Arbitrary Despotick Administration," for which he was prepared to hazard the queen, the Constitution, and the sucession.[73]

That it was Defoe's intention in writing the *Secret History of the White Staff* to delineate this absolutist conspiracy is clearly indicated in a letter to Harley written while the first part of the *White Staff* was still in manuscript. It is "absolutely Necessary," says Defoe, to show "the Distinction between your Ldpps administration and That which would have followed."[74] It was not Defoe's intention to prove that the conspirators were in the Pretender's interest; in fact, he went to extraordinary lengths in the second part to describe Bolingbroke as firm for Hanover. As he had almost dared to suggest seriously in his three pamphlets on the succession, it would not matter who sat on the throne if the English did not have a commitment to constitutional government. Harley and the moderate, nonpartisan form of government he represented to Defoe was not an alternative to either Hanover or the Pretender, but to absolutism and one-party control, whether that party be High Church, landed interest, City merchants, or moneyed men. In this respect, then, the *White Staff* pamphlets are concerned not so much with exonerating Harley's few "false steps" while in office as they are with setting forth and justifying the "Old Whig" philosophy of government as Harley's administration had attempted to apply it. According to Defoe, Harley had acted in accord with the "Revolution principle" that "a just Goverment seeks the Love of the People, rather than a forcible Subjection from them."[75] This principle is dramatically and ideologically counterpoised with the specter of an absolutist administration, which Defoe specifies was not to be the assumption of a personal authority by the individual schemers, but the permanent altering of the

Constitution in a reactionary direction. The laws that declared and protected the rights of the people were to be repealed under the slogan of delivering the crown from the tyranny of the subjects; the practice of investing Parliament with the right to determine the appropriation of money was to be discontinued as a way of preventing Parliament from becoming "an awe upon the Government," and so forth; the ultimate design was "to take away the Necessity of the frequency of Parliaments" altogether.[76]

In retrospect, the threat of a conspiracy headed by Harcourt, Atterbury, and Mrs. Masham appears exaggerated, even if it had the support of the entire High Church party. That they were conspirators in an effort to overturn Harley is a fact accepted by modern historians, but the danger they posed to the English Constitution was no more than symbolic—that is, they symbolized the danger of reaction and absolutism that *was* present, though not to the degree that the *White Staff* pamphlets would suggest.[77] Yet it is Defoe's exploitation of this symbolic meaning which proves that he was writing in a genre that can only be described as fiction.[78] Quite apart from the use of emblematic labels such as "White Staff," "Mitre," "Purse," and "John Bull" for Bolingbroke, which might have been done for legal as well as for artistic reasons, Defoe is very evidently more concerned with the ideological meanings of persons and events than with their historical meanings. The White Staff emerges at the end of these books as the true representative of Revolution principles; a major part of Harley's tragedy is the fact that he is nearly alone in defending them. Those others (i.e., the Whigs) who profess to believe that the Hanoverian succession is necessary to the preservation of the Revolution are nowhere to be seen, still withholding their support from the Staff for their own party interests. Though martyred by his enemies and false friends, the Staff so manages the queen's affairs that the succession is secured and the conspirators thwarted. Despite his personal disgrace, his administration passes into history as the emblem of an ideal of government that will remain valid as a model for ministers in more stable times to follow. Though the story as thus related has little historical value, it is ideologically very powerful. It presents Harley as the alternative to a system of government that the Whigs were pledged to oppose, making it difficult for them to desire his complete disgrace, while it presents his High Church enemies as corrupt courtiers for the

enlightenment of Country Tories. Its strategy is not to reproduce historical circumstances, but to transform them into
ideological types, which are then presented *as* history. If
neither Defoe nor his audience were comfortable with the
blend, he had nevertheless found the formula out of which he
was to make his major fictions.

Notes

1. Maximillian Novak, *Defoe and the Nature of Man* (London: Oxford University Press,
1963), p. 137. See also John Robert Moore, *Daniel Defoe, Citizen of the Modern World*
(Chicago: University of Chicago Press, 1958), p. 144.

2. Daniel Defoe, *Some Account of the Life, and Most Remarkable Actions, of George Henry
Baron de Goertz* (London, 1719), pp. 36–40.

3. Geoffrey Holmes, *British Politics in the Age of Anne* (New York: St. Martin's Press,
1967), pp. 400–403; Angus McInnes, *Robert Harley, Puritan Politician* (London: Victor
Gollancz, 1970), pp. 161 ff.; Alan Downie, *Robert Harley and the Press* (Cambridge: At
the University Press, 1979), pp. 117–30.

4. McInnes, *Robert Harley*, p. 107.

5. Defoe, *An Essay Upon Publick Credit* (London, 1710), p. 21.

6. For a discussion of Simon Clement, see Downie, *Robert Harley and the Press*, p. 121;
for Davenant, see Isaac Kramnick, *Bolingbroke and His Circle* (Cambridge, Mass.: Harvard University Press, 1968), pp. 241–43.

7. Simon Clement, *Faults on Both Sides* (London, 1710), reprinted in *Somers Tracts*, ed.
Walter Scott (London, 1809–15), 12:701.

8. Defoe, *Rogues on Both Sides* (London, 1711), pp. 3–4.

9. Defoe, *Rogues on Both Sides*, pp. 10, 15. For another discussion by Defoe along the
same lines, see *The Conduct of Parties in England* (London, 1712).

10. G. H. Healey, ed., *The Letters of Daniel Defoe* (Oxford: Clarendon Press, 1955),
p. 31.

11. Defoe, *Review*, ed. A. W. Secord (New York: Columbia University Press, 1938), I
(IX), # 50.

12. Ibid., # 19, 20, 21.

13. Ibid., # 15, 16.

14. Ibid., # 9.

15. Henry St. John, Viscount Bolingbroke, "The Idea of a Patriot King," in *The
Works of Lord Bolingbroke* (1844; reprinted London: Bohn, 1967), 2:378–81.

16. Defoe, *Review* I (IX), # 23, 26.

17. Ibid., # 20.

18. Ibid., # 18.

19. Ibid., # 22, 23.

20. Ibid., # 61.

21. Healey, *Letters*, pp. 5, 8.

22. For complete discussions of this affair, see Moore, *Daniel Defoe*, pp. 104–49, and
James Sutherland, *Defoe* (Philadelphia, Pa.: Lippincott, 1938), pp. 86–97.

23. W. A. Aitken, ed., *The Conduct of the Earl of Nottingham* (unpub.) (New Haven,
Conn.: Yale University Press, 1941), p. 2.

24. Ibid., pp. 138–39, 144.

25. NRO, Finch-Hatton MSS 281, Nottingham to his wife, 16 December 1711, quoted in Henry Horwitz, *Revolution Politicks: The Career of Daniel Finch, Second Earl of Nottingham* (Cambridge: At the University Press, 1968), p. 229.

26. Ibid., pp. 232–33.

27. *A Vindication of the Earl of Nottingham from the Vile Imputations, and Malicious Slanders, which have been cast upon Him in some late Pamphlets* (London, 1714), p. 44. Alan Downie has attributed this pamphlet and *Observations Upon the State of the Nation in January 1712/13* to William Wotton. See Downie, "Anthony Hammond Miscellanea," *Notes and Queries* N.S. 24 (1977): 219–21.

28. Healey, *Letters*, p. 363.

29. Defoe, *Review* I (IX) #12, #37.

30. Defoe, *Not[tingh]am Politicks Examin'd* (London, 1713), pp. 4–5

31. Proverbs 30:15; Harley used the same reference in "Plaine English." Alan Downie to author, 26 July 1981.

32. [Wotton?], *Observations Upon the State of the Nation in January 1712/13* (London, 1713), pp. 2, 14, 28–29.

33. Defoe, *Review* I (IX), #61, #62, #63, #64.

34. Defoe, *Not[tingh]am Politicks Examin'd*, pp. 6, 7, 12–13, 25–29.

35. Sutherland, *Defoe*, pp. 195ff; Harley *Letters*, p. 406n; Downie, *Robert Healey and the Press*, pp. 172–73. Downie, however, does not regard the pamphlets as ironic.

36. Healey, *Letters*, pp. 405–6, 409–10.

37. Defoe, *Reasons Against the Succession of the House of Hanover* (London, 1713), pp. 5–6.

38. Ibid., pp. 9–10.

39. Ibid., p. 11.

40. Defoe, *And What if the Pretender Should Come?* (London, 1713), pp. 8–9.

41. J. P. Kenyon, *The Stuarts: A Study in English Kingship* (New York: Macmillan, 1959), pp. 219–20.

42. Healey, *Letters*, Parker to Bolingbroke, 15 April 1713, p. 410n.

43. Defoe, *An Answer to a Question that No Body Thinks of, Viz. But what if the Queen should die?* (London, 1713), pp. 43–44, 21.

44. An anonymous pamphlet published in the previous year, *No Punishment No Government* (London, 1712), ostensibly written by a High Churchman, may have given Defoe the idea for *And What if the Queen Should Die?*. *No Punishment No Government* is framed around the question of what would happen "if [Anne] were translated to the Fellowship of Saints," and accuses the Whigs of a "plot" to "deprive Her of all Her Principal Officers."

45. Healey, *Letters,* pp. 409, 415.

46. Defoe, *An Appeal to Honour and Justice* (1715) in *The Shortest Way with the Dissenters and other pamphlets* (Oxford: The Shakespeare Head Edition, 1927), p. 215.

47. For accounts of this incident, see *Review* I (IX), #84 and 85; Sutherland, *Defoe* p. 198; and Moore, *Daniel Defoe*, p. 353.

48. Defoe, *Whigs Turned Tories, and Hanoverian-Tories, From their Avowed Principles, proved Whigs: Or, Each Side in the Other Mistaken* (London, 1713), pp. 1, 4, 10.

49. Ibid., pp. 2, 10, 3, 20.

50. Ibid., pp. 16, 5, 9–10.

51. Healey, *Letters*, pp. 427–29.

52. Defoe, *A Letter to the Whigs* (London, 1714), pp. 5–7.

53. Ibid., pp. 3, 13–14, 26.

54. Ibid., pp. 22, 19, 23. The sermon by Thomas Bradbury to which Defoe refers was preached on 5 November 1713 and published as *The Lawfulness of resisting Tyrants, argued from the History of David, and in Defense of the Revolution* (London, 1714).

55. Defoe, *Reasons for Im[peaching] the L[or]d H[igh] T[reasure]r* (London, 1714), pp. 8, 34.

56. *Dunkirk or Dover* (London, 1713), pp. 6–7.

57. Defoe, *Reasons for Im[peaching]*, pp. 10, 14.

58. Holmes, *British Politics*, pp. 282, 423. See also J. H. and Margaret Shennan, "The Protestant Succession in English Politics, April 1713–September 1715," in *William III and Louis XIV*, ed. Ragnhild Hatton and J. S. Bromley (Toronto: University of Toronto Press, 1968), pp. 260–61, and Eveline G. Cruickshanks, "The Tories and the Succession to the Crown in the 1714 Parliament," *Bulletin of the Institute of Historical Research* 46 (1973); 176–85.

59. G. V. Bennett, *The Tory Crisis in Church and State, 1688–1730* (Oxford: Clarendon Press, 1975), pp. 177–79.

60. Defoe, *Advice to the People of Great Britain,* (London, 1714) pp. 14–15, 24.

61. Ibid., pp. 5–6, 8–9.

62. Healey, *Letters*, pp. 445.

63. Downie, *Robert Harley and the Press*, p. 187.

64. Bennett, *Tory Crisis*, p. 190.

65. Defoe, *The Secret History of the White Staff* (London, 1714), p. 64.

66. Shennan, "Protestant Succession," p. 263; Bennett, *Tory Crisis*, p. 181.

67. David Green, *Queen Anne* (New York. Scribner's, 1970), p. 318.

68. Defoe, *Secret History of the White Staff*, p. 71.

69. For an early example, see Defoe, *The Poor Man's Plea* (London, 1698), p. 15.

70. Defoe, *The Secret History of the White Staff, Part II* (London, 1714), pp. 38–39.

71. Ibid., pp. 40–41.

72. Bennett, *Tory Crisis*, pp. 156–59.

73. Defoe, *The Secret History of the White Staff, Part II*, pp. 43–44. The "infirmities" of Harcourt on which Defoe does not elaborate may include Harcourt's role as prosecutor in Defoe's trial in 1703. See Moore, *Daniel Defoe*, pp. 129–31.

74. Healey, *Letters*, p. 445.

75. Defoe, *The Secret History of the White Staff, Part III* (London, 1715), p. 65.

76. Ibid., pp. 62–64.

77. The idea of a conspiracy is endorsed by Bennett, *Tory Crisis*, pp. 179–82.

78. For the suggestion that *emblematic* and *symbolic* are equivalent terms where Defoe is concerned, see J. Paul Hunter, *The Reluctant Pilgrim* (Baltimore, Md.: Johns Hopkins Press, 1966), p. 101.

4

Fiction and the '15: Defoe in the Service of the Whigs

The dismissal of Harley on 27 July 1714, followed five days later by the death of Anne, left Defoe without the protection of his only two benefactors. Though Defoe welcomed the accession of George I as much as anyone, he knew that it would also bring into power the coalition of Modern Whigs and Hanover Tories that he had charged with failing to help secure the Protestant succession. The transfer of power seemed certain to end his career as a writer for the government, if not to signal the beginning of a campaign of retribution against many of those who had served the old ministry. In ill health at age fifty-five, in disfavor with the new government, Defoe apparently believed that his writing career was over, and perhaps his life as well. His apology for his life and work, *An Appeal to Honour and Justice*, put a period to his career with its retrospective tone, and numerous references to his own death in the work suggest that he was preparing to resign from the mortal toils of political strife and submit his case to the superior Judge. The tone of the *Appeal* is so convincing that Defoe's early biographers would not believe that Defoe wrote any more political works after 1715.[1]

It is possible that, early in 1715, Defoe genuinely intended to devote the rest of his energy to writing such works as *The Family Instructor,* which, if not entirely without political significance, were at least far removed from the turmoil at Westminster. It is also possible that the *Appeal* was a mere subterfuge, a way of going underground in order to continue to pursue his old career for a new set of masters. Defoe had never been slow to trim his sails to new political winds, but in this case he may have had little choice. On August 28 of the previous year, Defoe had been arrested for printing in Hurt's *Flying Post*, which he edited, a letter that described the earl of Anglesey as a member of "the new modelled Juncto of the last Ministry" and alleged that Anglesey had planned to weaken the defense of the Protestant interest in Ireland by removing army officers who had demonstrated their commitment to Hanover.[2] Defoe's use (if, as accused, he was the author of the letter) of the phrase "new modelled Juncto" recalls Part II of *The Secret History of the White Staff,* which he was composing about the same time, in which he referred to "This Juncto of the New Party" while describing the characters of Mrs. Masham, Bishop Atterbury, and Sir Simon Harcourt; the allegation that Anglesey was part of this "Juncto" suggests that he was guilty of conspiring to subvert the Constitution and bring over the Pretender.[3] Perhaps Defoe's inclusion of Anglesey in this "new modelled Juncto" reflected a lingering resentment on Defoe's part over the role Anglesey had played in the defeat of the Treaty of Commerce more than a year earlier, or, more generally, proceeded from his bitterness at the whole Anglesey-Nottingham-High Church wing of the Tory party that had failed to come to Harley's aid. Whatever the reason for his attack on Anglesey, it plunged Defoe back into circumstances similar to those that had put him at Harley's disposal more than a decade before.

Since Anglesey was a regent as well as a peer, his complaint against Defoe could not be dismissed without prosecution, nor would the Whigs have wished to let Defoe off so easily. They were well aware of the usefulness of a writer of Defoe's talents, particularly after the lessons Harley had given them on the value of controlling public opinion through the press.[4] Defoe's vendetta against the Hanover Tories conveniently dovetailed with their plans to consolidate their control over the ministry by driving out all the Tories.[5] The solution to the problem was to convict Defoe of libel but to suspend his sentence, thereby keeping him in a sort of purgatorial state in which he was neither entirely damned nor entirely redeemed. The renunciatory tone of the *Appeal to Honour and Justice,* published six months after Anglesey had made his charges and four months before judgment was passed, was part of a deliberate effort on Defoe's part to demonstrate his penitence and to lay to rest a public persona that the Whigs found objectionable. Having made the equivalent of a public confession, which nevertheless yeilded no ground on ideological points important to him, Defoe found himself ready to come to terms with the Whigs. Apparently at Defoe's suggestion, the lord chief justice proposed to Charles Townshend, the secretary of state, that Defoe be taken into the king's service late in 1715, which was accordingly done.[6] The experience was recalled and expressed in Defoe's subsequent writings in terms of a Providential deliverance, in which an angelic voice gives him the words he writes to the judge.[7] Nevertheless, for all the formal apparatus of a religious conversion, it was less a conversion than a negotiated settlement by which the Whigs obtained a writer and Defoe was allowed to "come in from the cold" of the Harley administration.

1. The Transition from Stuart to Hanover

Most commentators on Defoe's career have seen his change of loyalties from Harley's party to that of the Whigs as at least ideologically inconsistent, if not cynical and opportunistic. Other writers in Harley's camp who were neither forced nor invited to join the Whigs, such as Jonathan Swift, have been accorded a measure of glory for their subsequent opposition to the Whig ascendancy, while Defoe's reputation has suffered from his compliance. Ideology and party politics, however, are not necessarily the same thing; the inconsistency of Defoe's politics does not by itself prove that he reneged on his ideological commitments. Rather, the record of the years after Harley's fall suggests that Defoe's decision to serve the new king through his Whig ministers might have been motivated in part by the belief that he could bring the party back to its own ideological roots in the Revolution, or at least blunt some of that party's most dangerous tendencies. Only in terms of such a "hidden agenda" can a reader understand how Defoe could publish pamphlets vindicating Harley and raising him to martyrdom, while also writing on behalf of the chairman of the Secret Committee charged with Harley's prosecution, Robert Walpole. It appears to have been Defoe's intent to play each side against the other in order to achieve his own ideological ends. The definition of these ends, as well as the proof that he had these intentions, requires a close, but interpretive, reading of the political "fictions" he imposed on the world.

One such "fiction" that is generally believed to have been

written by Defoe reflects in its title the mood of transition, transformation, and accommodation to a new political tune that Defoe—and all other politically active men—were learning to hum. Assuming that the pamphlet is Defoe's, *The Fears of the Pretender Turned into the Fears of Debauchery* reveals his efforts to find equivalents in the new world for the fixed ideological points he had steered by in Harley's time; whether it is his or not, it is useful in suggesting the transformations in political rhetoric that were taking place at the time of the new king's coronation and the public Thanksgiving of 20 January 1715, which, according to the pamphlet, "is but in View, even between the Writing and Publishing of these Observations."[8] The central idea of the pamphlet is that the fear of the Pretender, which has been the cry of politicians and pamphleteers before the accession of George, has been replaced by the fear that the Church is in danger from the debauchery of the new reign. Though the writer does not identify the political sources of these cries, the reader has little trouble recalling that the fears of the Pretender were raised primarily by the Whigs and Hanover Tories in an effort to dislodge Harley, and that the fears for the church are now raised by the High Church Tories and Jacobites. If Defoe were the writer of the pamphlet, it is ironic that he cites as instances of the raising of the fear of the Pretender two pieces written by Defoe himself: he complains in particular of the "lively manner" in which some persons have represented the scheme to erect a "Tyrannical Administration" that is said to have been afoot in the final days of the last ministry. According to this account—which is evidently Part II of Defoe's *Secret History of the White Staff*—the Jacobites planned to rule with "a Rod of Iron" and that "an absolute Subjection should have been demanded of the People." He further complains that these same writers assured us that "Orders were issuing, to be sent to Ireland, to dispose both the Civil and Military Government into such Hands, as should be sufficiently modelled for the Design"—the same charge Defoe had made in the *Flying Post* that the "new modelled Juncto" planned to replace loyal Irish officers with Jacobites. The writer suggests that these fears were raised primarily for their political effect, though he will not say ("'tis of no signification to enquire whether the Facts are real or not, while they are believed to be so") that they were groundless.[9]

Perhaps Defoe's references to his own work were a private

joke, or perhaps they were his way of proving that he had been a Whig beneath the skin all along. There could be no better proof of his fidelity to Hanover than for his work to be attacked by an anonymous pamphleteer as having raised an alarm about the Pretender. The writer's real target, however, was not Defoe, but the bishop of Rochester, Francis Atterbury, whose *English Advice to the Freeholders of Great Britain* is cited as the source of the current fears that the Church is in danger. These fears are based on the fact that the king is a Lutheran, though now a communicant of the Church of England, and that his accession is not justified by a direct hereditary right. The writer of *Fears of the Pretender,* who appears to be a devout churchman himself, cites addresses from Dissenters and Church of England congregations alike that emphasize the providential nature of the deliverance from the threat of the Pretender that George I represents (though the writer fears that in some of these addresses "God has been egregiously mocked many Ways at once.")[10] Even more to the point, he cites incontestable evidence that George's election to the crown was providential, such as the fact that the wind "held contrary" all the time that George was delayed by his affairs in Holland, but turned around and "blew the fairest, and gentlest Gale that had been known for many Months" as soon as His Majesty was prepared to come across the Channel, whereupon "the same Night the Wind changed, and came fair to carry the Dutch Squadron of Men of War, who were his Majesty's Convoy, Home again to their own Country." The "Hand of Heaven" was so apparent in these "happy Circumstances" that "nothing but a hardened Atheist" could fail to take them as signs of the king's divine right.[11] This proof of the Providential nature of the succession, which is at the same time a proof of the concealed atheism of the bishop, is all the more devastating in that it comes from the pen of a loyal churchman, and not one of the "few officious *Fanaticks* and *flattering Presbyterians,* whose Brains were turned with the Surprize of having got the Queen into her Grave, and her late Ministry out of Power."[12] Though himself a Tory and a High Churchman, the author of *Fears of the Pretender* sees the clergy of his own church as the primary source of trouble for the new king, and as the equivalent of the disloyal opposition that the Whigs had mounted in the reign of the late queen.

The moderate country Tory perspective and the anticlericism of *Fears of the Pretender,* then, were ideological weapons that Defoe brought with him from one reign to the next. But another commitment that he wished to maintain was his sympathy for the original aims of the Societies for Reformation that had grown up in King William's time. These societies, which were identified with Whiggism, were much more deeply resented by the common people for their efforts to suppress popular pastimes than was the moral authority of the Church.[13] The problem Defoe encountered in *Fears of the Pretender* was how to dispel the fears that the church was in danger without dismissing at the same time the grounds for the work of the Societies for Reformation. The answer he devised is a telling one in what it reveals about the secular nature of Whig political thinking. Reformation, according to the writer of *Fears of the Pretender*, is not promoted by the church, nor are the clergy sincerely concerned to preserve moral order; on the contrary, the clergy encourage disorder for the political advantage they can make of it, while the nobility and gentry, lulled into a false sense of security by George's arrival, inadvertently abet the work of the clergy by turning their "Excess of Joy" into "an Excess of Riot, Gayety, Balls, Plays, Masks, Revels, Drunkenness and Debauchery; building New Theatres, enticing the People to be as Wicked as possible, and giving them all the Encouragement that the Examples, of those who ought to Refrain and Punish them, is capable of giving."[14] Foremost among these is the author of the *Spectator*, Sir Richard Steele, whose mere mention of a play is enough to fill the house. The lewdness of the plays is such that the houses have become "the Receptacles of the Scandalous, the Nests of Rakes, Bullies, &c. that Fightings, Whorings, Murthers, are the common Practice of these Places," and that "the Youth of the Kingdom receive there a general Tincture of Debauchery, and Wickedness."[15] In context, it is plain that Defoe's animus is not against the theater as such, but rather the political advantage that such disorders give to the Church, even though the Church is partly responsible for them. If it were not so, then the supposed writer of the pamphlet, moderate Tory churchman that he is, might suggest that the church should be strengthened as a voice of moral authority. Instead, he suggests the contrary—that the king, "when his Majesty shall be rightly and fully informed of these Things," will use his authority as head of state to accomplish the Reformation by political and legal means, much as William attempted to do. The king, this writer expects, will "let the Nation

know, that it is their Reformation, not their universal Destruction that is the Thing desired by him; and that he can by no
means gratify them in a Liberty so fatal to themselves as this will
be." If the nation continues in its vices, "God may make the
King a Scourge in his Hand, to execute his Anger . . . our Hope
is in the King, that his Majesty, when he sees the Fruit, will be
justly provoked to pluck up the whole Plantation by the Roots,
as a Plant which his Heavenly Father hath not planted."[16] If the
king's ministers should not prove to be the men for such work,
then he must obtain some who are. Thus the *Fears of the Pretender,* which had begun by dismissing the reality of the fears both
of the Pretender and the danger to the church, becomes by its
conclusion a blueprint for the extension of the authority of the
state into the suppression of popular amusements and disorders on the grounds of the fear of debauchery.

2. The Rebellion Begins

Through the early months of 1715, as the "debauchery" in
numerous English towns shaded into open rebellion, the emphasis of Defoe's writing began to shift from the defense of
Harley toward an offensive against the Jacobites. Defoe settled
on James Butler, duke of Ormonde, as his target, a choice
largely made for him by Ormonde himself and by the rioters.
Ormonde had allowed himself to become figurehead of the
rebellion by his flight to the Pretender in July and his acceptance of a post at the head of the Pretender's forces, for which
his titles and estates were confiscated by an act of attainder.[17]
As early as 31 May, Defoe had addressed an admonishing pamphlet to Ormonde as "one of the High Ones, whose Head is
exalted above the People," an echo of Defoe's earlier warning
that the attempt to impose a successor by force will raise those
who should try "up to Halters and Gibbets, not to Places and
Preferments."[18] Writing in the guise of a Quaker, Defoe warns
Ormonde about his weakness for flattery and vanities; Nature
had furnished her most humble creatures with the means to
avoid the snares that are laid for them, but in this "thou has
come infinitely short." Defoe probably wished to avoid accusing
Ormonde of Jacobtism by design, since to do so might implicate
Harley in the prosecutions that were yet to come for Ormonde's refusal in 1712 to engage the French troops while
negotiations for the Peace were under way; but he felt free to

rebuke Ormonde for acting in a manner "monstrously naked, and unguarded; neither hast thou been Careful to keep thy Foot out of the Snare."[19] Though not yet attainted, Ormonde has disgraced himself by becoming "no other than Captain of the filthy Ones, who turned their Faces against the King, and who shouted for Idols." The Quaker warns Ormonde that the king will not suffer these demonstrations long, but "with a strong Hand will he chastise them, and with Power will he go forth against them, letting them know that his Wrath is as the roaring of a Lion." Again harking back to his earlier succession pamphlets, Defoe likens Ormonde to the foolish young Lady Jane Grey, who was beheaded after being "seduced by Evil Counsellors" into seeking "to place herself upon the Throne, to which she was not called by the Laws of the Land."[20] The Quaker's admonition, of course, was directed not only to Ormonde, but to all those who were leaning toward the Pretender's interest.

After the attainder, Defoe published at least one, perhaps two more attacks on Ormonde. A vindication of Ormonde's conduct, first published in 1712, had been reprinted in the summer of 1715;[21] Defoe responded to it briefly in his vindication of Harley, published on 9 July.[22] Shortly thereafter, an "examination" of the pamphlet defending Ormonde appeared under the supposed authorship of an officer who had campaigned with Ormonde, but very possibly written by Defoe. It repeats the widespread accusation that Ormonde had acted in concert and upon orders from the French general Villars, which, however damaging to Ormonde and to Anne, who had ordered him not to engage the French troops, tended to excuse Harley from any involvement. It further explains that the notorious "generosity" of Ormonde to his troops in returning to them the money that had been withheld from their bread contracts was a ruse, contrived by stating the sum in Dutch money rather than in English; nevertheless, through this mistaken impression of generosity, Ormonde "has acquired, we see, such Reputation among the MOB, as that they have now openly proclaimed him their Champion and Leader, and advanced him into the Place which Sacheverel held in their Favour."[23] Finally, the author promises that Ormonde's character will soon be set "quickly in its true Light . . . when it is stript of that fallacious Disguise"—an apparent reference to a forthcoming character study of Ormonde.

Such a study, which has been definitely attributed to Defoe, did appear within a month after the outbreak of the rebellion in September 1715. The character of Ormonde is consistent with what Defoe has said of him before: Ormonde is a man of distinguished birth, but that kind of honor is now "pretty much out of Fashion with Wise Men," who value personal merit more than birth. Ormonde's character is drawn in a way that suggests that his birth, and the show he has been able to make by his generosity, have opened every door for him without any effort on his part, with the result that Ormonde, though "exceedingly beloved by the Army," is a vain, foolish, ignorant man.[24] All the more shocking, therefore, is the news that the students of Oxford are presently engaged in rioting in the streets, breaking windows, pulling down meetinghouses, and crying, "Ormonde, Ormonde, No George." Since the cry of "Ormonde, Ormonde, No George" is not a "rational" one, because Ormonde himself makes no claim to the crown, then by Ormonde the students must mean the Pretender, which they cannot cry out "openly and avowedly," for fear they might "open the Peoples Eyes too soon." Likewise, George and the church cannot be set in opposition unless the church is taken to mean "Popery, right line, indefeasible, hereditary Right." Thus the writer construes the ideological meaning of the students' cries for Ormonde as covert Jacobitism. Even more important, their support of armed rebellion implied in the cries for Ormonde contrasts strangely with the doctrine of nonresistance to the monarch that the church had maintained as long as a Stuart was on the throne. Though Ormonde's character in itself is nothing more than that of a vain and foolish man, its emblematic and ideological significance is much greater. To the students, as well as much of the church and the landed interest, Ormonde was, in the words of a modern historian, "the last representative of the old Cavalier tradition."[25] To Defoe, the Dissenters, the Low Church and the moneyed interest, Ormonde was a symbol of the unprincipled opportunism and abuse of privilege that Jacobitism represented, and which a Stuart restoration would bring back. Ormonde's flight to the Pretender and his appearance at the head of the Jacobite forces removed the last barrier between Defoe and the Whigs, whose common purpose became the countering of the Jacobite threat.

Defoe's attack on the clergy and the Jacobites peaked in November 1715, approximately the same time as his agreement with Chief Justice Parker and Lord Townshend, as well as the month in which the rebels suffered the decisive defeat at Preston. None of the pro-Hanoverian pamphlets that Defoe had written to that date reflect as much of what one historian has called the "transparently anti-libertarian" attitude of the new ministry[26] as does Defoe's *Bold Advice: Or, Proposals for the entire Rooting out of Jacobitism In Great Britain.* The "Adviser," as the author calls himself, addresses his book to "many whose Hands were deep in the very first Measures of [the last] Ministry," but who yet "possess great Posts in the Present." These same persons "are warmest and forwardest in pushing on the People in Resentments, and for calling the People to account under the present government for what was done in the past."[27] This extremely selective definition of the audience would exclude such Whigs as Sunderland, Townshend, and Walpole, who had stood out from the last ministry, as well as all of Harley's followers, who possessed no power in the present; it would seem to leave out such Hanover Tories as Sir Thomas Hanmer and William Bromley, who held seats in the Commons but had no places in the ministry.[28] By elimination, then, Defoe would seem to have in mind such whimsical Tories as the earl of Anglesey and the earl of Nottingham, who held the office of lord president of the council, together with Nottingham's relatives who held offices and his followers in the House of Lords. It would be stretching a point to imply that Nottingham's hands were deep in the measures of the last ministry, but it was true that Nottingham and his relative, the earl of Aylesford, were among the most vigorous supporters in the present ministry of the prosecution of those in the former.[29] No doubt the "Measures of [the last] Ministry" to which the Adviser refers are not those sponsored by Harley, but rather those of Bolingbroke, Atterbury, and those High Church Tories whom Defoe had represented as a Jacobite conspiracy in the White Staff pamphlets. Thus Nottingham and his friends stand accused of covert Jacobitism, from which suspicion they may clear themselves by coming into the Adviser's proposed measures for rooting out traitors in positions of trust; failure to do so, of course, would seem to confirm the implicit charge. It would appear, therefore, that *Bold Advice* was a strategem conceived by or for the benefit of those Whigs such as Townshend and Walpole who deeply resented Nottingham's place on the council, and who were willing to use the specious charge of Jacobitism in an attempt to drive him out.[30]

To condition his readers for the extreme nature of the proposals he is about to make, the Adviser commences by evoking a state of emergency. Defoe, of course, had previously used the fear of secret Jacobite agents as a reason why the Whigs should support the Harley ministry; he was now even more skilled in evoking the sense of an emergency, and though his rhetorical skill had never moved Walpole to support Harley, Walpole was no doubt sensible of its effect on others. Jacobitism, according to the Adviser, is "an Evil harboured in the Bosom of the Nation, which like a running sore, exhausts the Vitals, and will, in Time, if not healed, taint the Blood, and turn to an incurable Plague." If not suppressed, it "will subject us all to the Yokes, which we were not able to bear, and which in the happy Revolution under King William, was cast off from our Necks."[31] The Adviser cites the famous Doway letter, which John Robert Moore believed was one of Defoe's own forgeries, as proof that the Pretender's friends are relying on internal subversion, rather than military force, to set the Pretender on the throne.[32] The presence in Scotland of the Pretender's forces only increases the need for measures to suppress internal subversion. The list of these measures, which resembles the manner of Defoe's books of projects for improving social and economic conditions in England, includes the absolute acceptance of George as the only Protestant successor; the swearing of an oath of abjuration of the Pretender by everyone, which if refused is proof of treason; the imposition of "due restraints" on the "Jacobite missionaries, who strowl about the Nation"; and the prosecution for treason of all who recognize James as king, whereas now an overt act of treason must be committed. These measures may be enforced by making it criminal for any clergyman to "meddle" with affairs of state from the pulpit, particularly to allege that the church is in danger from the Dissenters and from George; by rejecting the dogma that the line of descent of the crown, which is granted to be hereditary, must be "direct," rather than subject to parliamentary settlement; and by creating an adequate professional army to match the Pretender's "standing Army" of 20,000 troops. Of particular importance is the settling in law of the quarrel over passive obedience and nonresistance; the rights of a prince and a subject must be specifically set forth, so that "thereby, as the Prince may know how far his Power of Commanding may extend, so the Subject may know where his Obedience may legally Stop."[33] In the abstract, many of the proposals of *Bold Advice*, such as the legal definition of the rights of a subject and the separation of the powers of church and state, were very desirable; in the context of the rebellion, however, they were anticlerical arguments intended to strip the church of its political power by taking advantage of the fear of Jacobitism.

Of course, there may have been good reason for blaming the emergency on the inferior clergy. The emergency itself was real enough, though Defoe's estimate of the Pretender's army was more than twice its actual size, and it was hardly the professional force that the phrase "standing army" implies.[34] Modern historians are inclined to agree that the inferior clergy were largely responsible for raising the Sacheverellite mobs of 1710, and therefore it may have been reasonable for Defoe to assume that the mobs of 1715 were raised by the same methods. There is, however, no direct evidence of clergymen inciting any riots in 1715, nor even that Jacobite agents in general were influential in promoting unrest.[35] The rebellion against Hanover has recently been shown to be an expression of popular resentment against George himself, against the Whigs, and against the Dissenters, as a result of the unemployment, the war policy, and the campaign for the reformation of manners with which this new hegemony was associated.[36] Nowhere in *Bold Advice* or any of the other Hanoverian pamphlets attributed to Defoe are these grievances discussed as possible sources for the rebellion, though it is inconceivable that a writer of Defoe's perspicacity could be unaware of the popular unrest caused by war, unemployment, and the repression of popular pastimes. Therefore, the attack on the clergy in *Bold Advice* and the related pamphlets must be seen not as the product of dispassionate observation, but as the result of the writer's ideological attachment to the establishment of the Protestant succession in the Hanoverian line, together with the complementary objective of whittling away at the political power of the church.

3. Defoe's "True Account" of the Rebellion

The "antilibertarian" tendencies of the new administration have been epitomized for most historians by the passage of the Septennial Act in April of 1716.[37] It must have been something of a nasty surprise for Defoe to see the earl of Sunderland and

James Stanhope introduce a bill that did precisely what the
bishop of Atterbury had predicted the Whigs would do. Atterbury had predicted in his *English Advice to the Freeholders of Great
Britain* that the Whigs would move quickly to consolidate their
power by a number of measures that contradicted their claim to
be the inheritors of the Revolution principles. These measures
included a new war, with new taxes; a comprehension of all
Protestant sects into a new church, without prayer book or
bishops; a repeal of the Triennial Act, which mandated parliamentary elections at least every three years; the admission of
foreigners into places at court, and therefore into authority
over Englishmen; the creation of a standing army; the repeal of
the limitations on the crown that had been part of the Act of
Settlement; the imposing of restraints on the press and the
pulpit; the encouragement of the people to abuse the memory
of the queen, through impeachments and prosecutions; and
eventually, a thorough revolution against constitutional government. Defoe had delivered two direct, and many indirect,
rebuttals to Atterbury's predictions, though there is in his rebuttals an underlying message to the Whigs that they must
prove Atterbury wrong through their actions for his defense to
have any meaning. Now the tide was plainly running in the
direction Atterbury had indicated it would. Defoe himself had
argued, on the grounds of the civil emergency, for restraints on
the liberty of the pulpit and for strengthening the army. The
impeachment of Harley for treason, which Defoe had long opposed, was not being dropped by the government, and Harley's
confinement in the Tower seemed to represent an indictment
of the last four years of Anne. Foreigners were still not permitted to hold titles, but everyone knew that the way to preferment at court was through the two German barons who were
the king's advisors, Bothmer and Bernstorff.[38] Though Sunderland and Stanhope's bill did not repeal the Triennial Act,
but only suspended it for four years, the difference was seen to
originate not in their respect for the liberties of the subject, but
in their desire to avoid appearing to undo a law that had dated
almost from the Revolution itself and on which the Whigs'
political identity was founded. The bill was a sharp reminder of
the difference between the Old Whigs and the Modern Whigs,
and though Defoe undertook to defend it, the bill might well be
taken as the point at which he began to separate himself from
the new ministry.

The argument made for the Septennial bill, both by Defoe and by the Whig leadership in Parliament, was based on the necessity for a stable administration during the civil emergency, though by mid-1716 the rebellion had been crushed and the participants in it executed, transported, or escaped into the highlands of Scotland. The fear of the Pretender and his Jacobite agents in the pulpit had been invoked so many times that virtually all of Defoe's narrative and descriptive skills were needed to animate it one more time. The rebellion was the "Hellish Design" of "a wicked Set of Men among us" who, despite their Oaths of Abjuration of the Pretender, spread "the Poison of Disaffection among the common People of this Nation." The rebellion is "still in Being," even though the rebels have been "every where defeated, beaten and dispersed"; the country is not yet secure because "the obstinate Remains of them having their Hopes in the Refuge of inaccessible Mountains, keep together in Arms, rather because they have no reason to expect Mercy and Pardon from a Prince, in so gross a Manner offended, than from any Expectation of Success."[39] Because of their desperation, the "Spirit of Rebellion" is "rather increased than abated," so that the danger now is greater than before. The next manifestation of the rebellion will not be an invasion, but an attempt upon the court's majority in Parliament. The opportunity "must be taken from them, or they must some way or other be disabled from making an Advantage of it: For, doubtless, while the Prospect remains, of the Jacobite Party having a Majority in the next Parliament, they have an Argument that can never be refuted, to keep up the Spirit of Faction and Fury among the People."[40] Upon this admission of expedience disguised as necessity rested the entire claim of the bill to legitimacy; no defense of the bill on constitutional grounds was attempted. The constitutional objections of the bill's opponents were dismissed in two pages with the observation that it was the suspension, not the repeal, of the law that was proposed.[41] The Whig-dominated House of Commons is described as "the Dread of Jacobitism; their very Breath strikes Rebellion with Convulsions and Death." One could loyally describe no power greater than George except Providence, and even he is "made more Terrible by the Accession of such a House of Commons."[42] The tone of the conclusion of Defoe's pamphlet on the Septennial Act is so imperious and aggressive, so confident in the power of the Commons to make foreign and domestic enemies retreat before it, that it reads like a prophetic announcement of a new age in British politics.

Yet Defoe had felt, along the way to the conclusion, the need for a still more dramatic approach. He painted in some detail the compelling picture of the thousands of miserable Britons who had been drawn into the Jacobite snare and then been abandoned by their deceivers. He promised, "tho' it be a Digression here," to show "with what Bluster, what haughty Behaviour, what insolent Boasts, the late Rebellion was undertaken," and then "with what abject Baseness they deserted their own Cause." If the cowardice and incompetence of the leadership of the Jacobite army were "duly reflected upon," Defoe mused, "it would assist to expose the Party, and to undeceive the unhappy People" to whom the Jacobites now looked for assistance.[43]

The world did not have to wait long for the fulfillment of Defoe's promise. According to a manuscript note in the British Library copy, *A True Account of the Proceedings at Perth* was published in May 1716, just one month after the passage of the Septennial Act.[44] Long thought to have been written, as its title page indicates, by one of the Scots rebels, the *True Account* is a narrative of the final days of the rebellion, in which the Pretender arrives at Perth, discovers the weakness of the army there, and returns to France with his officers, abandoning his forces to the duke of Argyle. Like the *Memoirs of Count Tariff &c.* and the *Secret History of the White Staff,* it relies heavily on the generic conventions of the "secret history," but adds to these conventions an ideological perspective that buttresses the cause in which Defoe was currently engaged. It is superior to both of these forerunners as a fiction, however, because its characters are not mere ideological types, but rather persons whose lives have ideological meaning. No doubt part of the improvement is due to the change from a third- to a first-person narrator, who is necessarily limited by the confines of his own knowledge—a factor especially pertinent to this book, which contains the discovery of the secret of the failure of the rebellion. But another improvement is the subordination of the ideological message to the narrative, in which the reader, if not the writer, is primarily interested. This adjustment in the due proportions of ideology and narrative heightens, rather than diminishes, the credibility of the ideological perspective that the narrative advances.

The reason for Defoe's choice of a first-person narrator for his fictions is a crucial issue in Defoe criticism. The prevailing tendency to read Defoe's fictions as spiritual autobiographies has resulted, according to Paul Alkon, in a "general agreement among critics that Defoe's concern with questions of repentance and providential patterns led him to favor narratives told in the first person from a retrospective viewpoint."[45] If Defoe were primarily concerned with repentance and providential patterns, then he was interested in the quality of life only insofar as it is prepatory to repentance, and as a barrier or a highway to what Alkon has called the "future outside time," or eternity. But the narrator of *A True Account of the Proceedings at Perth* is not a penitent; in the retrospective opening pages of his narrative, he regrets only "the ill Conduct of those on whose Councils all Things at that Time depended."[46] He observes repeatedly that, except for the want of resolution and concerted action on the part of the Jacobite leaders, the rebellion in the North would have succeeded. At the conclusion of the book, he and his fellow rebels have retreated into the Highlands, where they intend to preserve themselves from Argyle's army and wait for another day, which the Pretender has promised them. Nor is there any suggestion in the book that Providence brought about the defeat of the Pretender's attempt as a favor to Hanover; aside from two casual references to "Fate," the whole burden of responsibility for the disaster is placed on the shoulders of the earl of Mar and his officers, "whose Abilities for the Field were no way equal to what they had undertaken."[47] The focus of *A True Account* is entirely on this world, not on the next; the narrator does not even offer a religious motive for his being in arms for the Pretender, leaving the reader to conclude either that he is a professional solider or that he is fighting for the temporal kingdom of Scotland. *A True Account* proves that the motive for Defoe's recourse to fiction is broadly ideological, not merely theological, and that Defoe was at least as interested in influencing events in this world through his fiction as he was in preparing souls for the next. It is true, as G.A. Starr and others have pointed out, that Defoe's fiction makes use of elements of spiritual autobiography, but it uses them, as it uses the political biography and the "secret history," to serve temporal and ideological ends.

The ends that Defoe's fiction served directly determined his practice of it. Alkon has shown how Defoe's choice of the retrospective first-person viewpoint was brilliantly adapted "to stress the importance of looking backward during conversion."[48] The role of memory in Defoe's spiritual autobiographies is to review scenes that had occurred earlier in life with a new awareness of their moral significance, now that the journey is almost completed. The narrator of *A True Account* is also in a retrospective position with regard to the rebellion, which he calls "that most remarkable Time, in which all the Hopes we of that Party had, were defeated." But he is not at all on the road to conversion; rather, his tone is one of disappointment verging on despair. It may be true that, as in the later story of Crusoe, the arrival at despair is the first stage of conversion, but this narrator never despairs completely, no doubt because for him to do so would remove the symbolic threat of Jacobitism that his determination represents. His memory ranges back over the whole history of the rebellion, which he promises to write at another time; his purpose in this memoir, however, is to account for the failure of the rebellion in the light of knowledge that was concealed from him and the other Scots at the time of the events that he recounts. Just as the lives of Crusoe, Moll, and Colonel Jack are radically altered in their own perceptions when they reexamine their lives in the light of secrets unfolded to them in old age, so the narrator now understands the hidden significance of events that had seemed unaccountable before. His discovery of this hidden significance of things provides a basis for the ideological content of the narrative.

The secret that he has discovered is hinted in the very first pages of the book and referred to frequently thereafter, but is not fully revealed to the reader until the fiftieth page. As Alkon has shown that the seduction of Moll Flanders is no less suspenseful because we are told the outcome at the start, but do not know how it came about, so here the narrator's early acknowledgment that the rebellion was lost due to cowardice and betrayal only increases our curiosity to know the secret of its failure.[49] We eventually discover that on the advice of the Jacobites in England, the earl of Mar and his officers, long before conducting their sham councils of war with the Scots rebels, decided to call off the rebellion and escape by sea to France until the political situation in England became more favorable—meaning, in particular, the election of a new parliament. Knowledge of this secret makes comprehensible events that had been inexplicable before, such as the refusal of Mar to defend the town of Perth, though the Scots had proven to him that Argyle's army could not take the town by seige in the winter and were too few to take it by storm. But it also puts into a new moral light actions that the Scot soldiers had taken in the belief that a defense was intended, such as their destruction of all the nearby villages, together with the food and forage, so that none of it would fall into the hands of Argyle's army. This "Severity," the narrator recounts, was not "to be blamed in us, if our Resolution to defend our selves had held," but in fact the leaders did not intend to make a stand against Argyle, and so the Scottish villagers were undone for nothing.[50] Similarly, knowledge of the secret explains why the Jacobite officers decided upon a retreat after being presented, in the sham war councils, with the plainest proofs of the readiness of their troops to fight and the likely success of a defense of Perth. Finally, it explains the failure of the Pretender to inspire his troops, though they had eagerly anticipated his coming: the reason for his dispirited look is his discovery that he has been betrayed, a discovery which the common soldiers share only after the Pretender has fled back to France. Thus the device of the secret, besides being an effective way of sustaining the narrative tension, contains a warning about the treachery that lurks beneath the surface of political events, and is meant to put second thoughts into the minds of all passionate but inexperienced persons who would commit themselves to causes that have no chance of success.

But there is another fictional device in the *True Account* that is instrumental to the narrative's development of an ideological meaning. The story is told from the viewpoint of the rebel forces, to which the narrator is attached. Because he is never converted to the Hanoverian cause, all of the terms in which he views the failure of the rebellion must be reversed by the reader in order for the "true" ideological meanings to emerge. For example, the reader learns early in the narrative that he must convert the narrator's references to the *Chevalier* into the politically opposite term, the *Pretender*, in order to arrive at a reading that is correct for a loyal Englishman. This process of reversal takes place at a nearly subconcious level, since the reader accepts the term *Chevalier* as appropriate for the narrator, if not for his own political world. In using terms appropriate to a rebel viewpoint, then, Defoe is not merely applying a gloss of "realism" to a faked history, but is establishing a pattern in which signs are accepted on one level and reversed on another.

From these elementary reversals, the narrative proceeds to much more complicated ones: the narrator's desperation is a cue not for the reader's sympathy, but for his thankfulness, and redoubled vigilance against Jacobitism; the Pretender's flight is the occasion not for the bitter reflections that fill the narrator's mind, but for rejoicing, with the tempering realization that the threat still exists. By the time the narrator has fully revealed the reasons for the Jacobites' decision to abandon the Pretender's cause, the reader has learned to view these reasons as the keys to preventing another outbreak of the rebellion in the future. These reasons are, first, that "a certain powerful Prince" upon whom the Jacobites depend has asked them to desist and retreat until he has succeeded in embroiling the Emperor Charles VI of Austria in a war with the Turks, at which time he would "talk another Language, and would more openly and powerfully assist them."[51] Who this prince might be is deliberately left ambiguous, perhaps so that the reader may fill in the name of Philip V of Spain, Charles XII of Sweden, or whatever other monarch he suspects of ties with the Jacobites.[52] The second reason is the government's discovery of the Jacobite conspiracy in England, by which means "the Assistance which they depended upon from that side was at present rendered impracticable"; and the third was "the Vigour and Unanimity of that cursed Assembly of Whigs, as they called it, now in being." The Jacobites, knowing that this Whig House of Commons "could not sit above a certain limited Time," and believing that the people of England were well disposed toward them, resolved "to quit the present Design, and depend upon a bloodness, yet as effectual a Victory in the next Elections of the British Parliament."[53] By the process of reversal that has been established in the reader's mind, these reasons for the postponement of the rebellion become reasons for condoning the measures that the government had already taken: greater vigilance against foreign intervention in British affairs; suppression and vigorous prosecution of domestic Jacobites; and resignation to the necessity of a septennial parliament. But these conclusions are drawn by the reader, who discovers them buried in the narrator's remarks, much as the narrator discovered the secrets of cowardice and betrayal in the sham councils of war and the Pretender's expression. By this means, the ideological purpose of the narrative is served while the sense of a true account is maintained.

4. The *True Account* and the Sources of Fiction

The genesis of *A True Account of the Proceedings at Perth* offers a revealing glimpse at the manner in which Defoe constructed his fictions, as well as the end that fiction served. John Robert Moore has recounted the steps through which the Jacobites who escaped to France arranged for the writing of a pretended journal of an officer on Mar's general staff, which was intended not only to clear Mar's reputation as a military commander, but also to preserve some shreds of support for the Jacobite organization in England and Europe by portraying the Chevalier as a brave and compassionate man displaced by a crowd of "Foreigners."[54] Written by Robert Leslie with Mar's corrections and printed in English at Avignon in May 1716, the supposed journal was sent in packets to Jacobite agents in England for distribution and was soon in the hands of the government. Instead of suppressing it, however, the government authorized the printing of a new edition with a fourteen-page introduction that is generally believed to be Defoe's. Openly sold in the shop of John Baker on Pater Noster Row at least by July 7, when a surprised Jacobite agent sent a copy of the government's edition to Mar, the pamphlet became a source of considerable embarrassment to the Jacobites because of its susceptibility to a reverse reading, particularly when prefaced by an introduction in which all the adverse implications are drawn out. Thus, for example, Leslie's version of the journal admitted that "a Month before the Chevalier landed, the Resolution was taken of abandoning Perth, as soon as the Enemy should march against it" because the rebel army had "neither a sufficient Number of Men, Ammunition, nor Arms" to defend it.[55] The intent of this admission had been to dramatize the need for foreign assistance, which had been expected to arrive with the Pretender. In Defoe's introduction, however, this passage consitutes proof "that they enter upon such an Undertaking in the most rash, unconcerted Manner, and have drawn their Friends into Destruction upon the absurdest Foundation" that men have ever acted upon; that not until the publication of this journal has it been known to what degree they were "Fools, or Idiots, disconcerted, thoughtless, unfore-seeing, and uncapable"; and that the journal is "a Testimony to the World, that they begun a Rebellion without any Measures taken, or Friends engaged, for Support."[56] On top of this organizational incompetence, Defoe draws out the arrogant carelessness of the Jacobite officers, who would commit their men to a campaign without first possessing the means to win it. Though he did not mention it in his introduction, Defoe apparently took notice of the original journal's prideful mention that "tho' this Resolution [to abandon Perth rather than defend it] was known to a good Number in our Army, yet the Secret was so well kept, that it never came to the Public," and he made the discovery of this secret the major narrative hook in *A True Account of the Proceedings at Perth.*

If Defoe found evidence in the original journal of the incompetence of the Jacobites, he also found evidence of the strength of the Hanoverian regime, again by a process of reversing the intent of the original. In Leslie's repeated complaints that the Jacobites had received no foreign assistance, Defoe found proof that all the princes of Europe stood in awe of the new king and his parliament, though he emphasized that the failure of "some of our Neighbors" to come to the aid of the Pretender was due "more to their Prudence than their Integrity," thereby preserving the grounds for continued vigilance. In Leslie's excuse that the coming of the Pretender was delayed on the advice of his friends in England, and then further delayed by the discovery and arrest of many of the most prominent English Jacobites, Defoe found proof of "the Truth of a Plot, or general Insurrection in England, upon the Foot of which so many Gentlemen have been apprehended, and continue still in custody."[57] And finally, in the tone of the original journal, which is that of an unrepentant, unreconstructed rebel "making his last Speech and Confession, tho' not at the Place of Execution, yet at the great Exit of the Rebellion . . . only with this Difference, that he is so far from Repentance, that he tells us all plainly, he resolves to be a Rebel again if ever he has an Opportunity," Defoe found the point of view from which he was to write *A True Account of the Proceedings at Perth.*[58]

In his *Checklist of the Writings of Daniel Defoe,* Moore placed *A Journal of the Earl of Marr's Proceedings* after *A True Account of the Proceedings at Perth,* although he was not able to determine an exact publication date for either book.[59] But he has shown that the Avignon edition of the Jacobite journal was in print early in May of 1716, and that Defoe, as "chief writer for a government which had the best secret service of the day," probably knew the contents of the Jacobite parcels even before the Jacobite agents in England received them.[60] Thus it is entirely possible that

Defoe had the Avignon edition at hand early in May, when Moore believes *A True Account* was written. Though Defoe delayed publishing the government's edition of the journal, complete with the introduction that reversed its signs and implications, until July 1716, he appears to have rushed his fictional account of the end of the rebellion into print very soon after reading the Jacobite journal. Several intriguing though entirely speculative reasons may be advanced for this timing: the greater creative challenge offered by the idea of a first-person narrative may have appealed to him more than the task of revising and introducing another writer's work, or it may have taken some time to get Townshend's approval to republish the Jacobite journal in the form that Defoe proposed. Or it may have been that Defoe mistrusted the propagandistic effect of a pamphlet that could be read two ways, even with an introduction, without first preparing the way with a fictional account that used the same information as the journal but was less ambiguous in the conclusions that it allowed the reader to draw. In any case, it is clear that the retrospective point of view, the unrepentant narrator, the discovery of the secret plans to abandon the rebellion, and the crippling effect on the rebellion of the government's repression of the Jacobites at home and its discouragement of foreign intervention, which formed the major fictional and ideological elements of *A True Account,* were drawn from the Jacobite journal that Defoe was preparing for the press.

In the broadest perspective, however, *A True Account of the Proceedings at Perth* derived not only from Leslie's *apologia,* but from the swift ideological current Defoe had been riding ever since the succession. The distaste for the Modern Whigs that he had often voiced while in the service of Robert Harley had been quite genuine, though he did have a working relationship with individual Whigs such as Lord Sunderland and seems to have had some respect for the vigor with which Townshend pursued his duties as secretary of state.[61] He was obliged to overcome his conviction that the Modern Whigs were not the inheritors of the Revolution principles by two circumstances: the prosecution initiated by Anglesey, which put him at the service of the Whigs whether he would or no, and the dependence of the Dissenters upon the Protestant succession in the Hanoverian line. The threat to the succession came primarily from the Church, and secondarily from the landed interest which supported it; Defoe's attacks on Bishop Atterbury, the earl of Nottingham, and the duke of Ormonde were not personal vendettas so much as offensives against the interests of which they were emblems. From the relatively moderate ideological goal of limiting the rights of the clergy to "meddle" in state affairs, Defoe was led by the escalation of the rebellion into measures for suppressing the influence of the university, extending the Parliament for four more years, and strengthening the army, none of which was consistent with Revolution principles. These measures were, however, important to the formation of a strong central parliamentary government, which Defoe saw as essential to the preservation of the succession and the discouragement of foreign intervention, and so he accepted them. Not only did he accept them, but he campaigned for them with his pamphlets written from pretended or reversed points of view, employing such narrative devices as secrets, dire emergencies, threats and fears, and desperate but unrepentant narrators. His recourse to fiction in *A True Account of the Proceedings at Perth,* then, was not the result of an inspiration brought on by reading Robert Leslie's Jacobite journal, though that book may have furnished him with the immediate materials, but rather the product of nearly two years of thinking up new ways to put before the public a vision of the peril of the succession and the necessity of defeating the interests that were ranged against it. As in his defenses of the Treaty of Commerce and of Robert Harley, it was the struggle of interests and ideas that was the source of his fiction.

Notes

1. John Robert Moore, *Daniel Defoe, Citizen of the Modern World* (Chicago: University of Chicago Press, 1958), p. 209; William Lee, *Daniel Defoe: His Life and Recently Discovered Writings* (1869; reprint ed., Georg Olms Verlagsbuchhandlung, 1968), 1: 261–62.

2. For the full text of the letter to the *Flying Post,* see Lee, *Daniel Defoe,* 1: 233–34. See also Moore, *Daniel Defoe,* pp. 206–11, and James Sutherland, *Defoe* (Philadelphia: Lippincott, 1938), pp. 213–18.

3. Defoe, *The Secret History of the White Staff, Part II* (London, 1714), p. 44.

4. Henry Horwitz, *Revolution Politicks: The Career of Daniel Finch, Second Earl of Nottingham* (Cambridge: At the University Press, 1968), pp. 249–50. See also Ragnhild Hatton, *George I, Elector and King* (Cambridge, Mass.: Harvard University Press, 1978), p. 127.

5. J. A. Downie, *Robert Harley and the Press* (Cambridge: At the University Press, 1979), pp. 193–95.

6. G. H. Healey, ed., *The Letters of Daniel Defoe* (Oxford: Clarendon Press, 1955), p. 450n, and Lee, *Daniel Defoe*, 1: 258.

7. The passage is appended to the *Serious Reflections of Robinson Crusoe* under the title "A Vision of the Angelick World," and discussed in Moore, *Daniel Defoe*, pp. 208–9.

8. Defoe, *The Fears of the Pretender Turned into the Fears of Debauchery* (London, 1715), p.8.

9. Ibid., pp. 9–10.

10. Ibid., pp. 12–14.

11. Ibid., pp. 11–12.

12. Ibid., p. 15.

13. The origins and political implications of the Societies for Reformation are discussed in T. C. Curtis and W. A. Speck, "The Societies for the Reformation of Manners: A Case Study in the Theory and Practice of Moral Reform," *Literature and History* 3 (1976): 45–64.

14. Defoe, *Fears of the Pretender,* p. 29.

15. Ibid., pp. 24–25.

16. Ibid., pp. 25–28.

17. See G V. Bennett, *The Tory Crisis in Church and State* (Oxford: Clarendon Press, 1975), pp. 195–96, and W. A. Speck, *Stability and Strife* (Cambridge, Mass.: Harvard University Press, 1977), p. 178.

18. Defoe, *A Seasonable Expostulation with, and Friendly Reproof unto James Butler* (London; 1715), p. 6; *Reasons Against the Succession of the House of Hanover* (London; 1713), pp. 5–6.

19. Defoe, *A Seasonable Expostulation,* p. 20.

20. Ibid., pp. 24, 26, 13.

21. *The Conduct of His Grace the Duke of Ormonde, in the Campaigne of 1712* (London; 1715).

22. Defoe, *An Account of the Conduct of Robert Earl of Oxford* (London; 1715), pp.2–3.

23. (Defoe?) *An Examination of a Book Intitled, The Conduct of the Duke of Ormond, Anno 1712* (London; 1715), pp. 37–38.

24. Defoe, *An Account of the Great and Generous Actions of James Butler* (London; 1715). The character of Ormonde occupies pages 28–48; the attack on the university is in the form of a pretended dedication, pp. 3–27.

25. Bennett, *Tory Crisis,* p. 195.

26. Nicholas Rogers, "Popular Protest in Early Hanoverian London," *Past and Present* 79 (1978): 98.

27. Defoe, *Bold Advice: Or, Proposals for the entire Rooting out of Jacobitism in Great Britain* (London; 1715), pp. 6–7.

28. Romney Sedgwick, *The House of Commons, 1715–1754* (London: History of Parliament Trust, 1970) 1: 25.

29. Horwitz, *Revolution Politicks,* p. 249.

30. Hatton, *George I,* pp. 127, 175.

31. Defoe, *Bold Advice,* pp. 14–15.

32. Defoe, *Bold Advice,* p. 16; see John Robert Moore, *Checklist of the Writings of Daniel Defoe,* 2d ed. (Hamden, Conn.: Shoe String Press, 1971), items 189 and 328.

33. Defoe, *Bold Advice,* p. 32.

34. David Daiches, *The Last Stuart: The Life and Times of Bonnie Prince Charlie* (New

York: G. P. Putnam's Sons, 1973), pp. 62–67; John Baynes, *The Jacobite Rising of 1715* (London: Cassell, 1970).

35. Geoffrey Holmes, "The Sacheverell Riots: The Crowd and the Church in Early Eighteenth-Century London," *Past and Present* 72 (1976), pp. 55–85; Rogers, "Popular Protest in Early Hanoverian London," p. 9l.

36. Rogers, "Popular Protest," pp. 91–92.

37. For the Septennial Act and Atterbury's pamphlet, see Bennett, *Tory Crisis*, pp. 193, 198–99, as well as Atterbury's *English Advice to the Freeholders of Great Britain* (London; 1715), and Defoe's response to it in *His Majesty's Obligations to the Whigs Plainly Proved* (London; 1715) and *A Reply to a Traiterous Libel* (London; 1715).

38. John M. Beattie, *The English Court in the Reign of George I* (Cambridge: At the University Press, 1967), pp. 220–21.

39. Defoe, *Some Considerations on a Law for Triennial Parliaments* (London; 1716), pp. 17–21.

40. Ibid., pp. 23–24.

41. Ibid., pp. 34–35.

42. Ibid., p. 39.

43. Ibid., pp. 29–30.

44. Moore, *Checklist*, item 348.

45. Paul Alkon, *Defoe and Fictional Time* (Athens: University of Georgia Press, 1979), p. 86.

46. Defoe, *A True Account of the Proceedings at Perth* (London; 1716), p. 2.

47. Ibid., p. 9.

48. Alkon, *Defoe and Fictional Time*, p. 53.

49. Ibid., pp. 117–19.

50. Defoe, *A True Account*, p. 23. For other accounts of the burning of the villages, see Peter Rae, *The History of the Rebellion* (London; 1746; first published in 1718 as *The History of the Late Rebellion*), pp. 360, 364–65, in which Rae closely follows Defoe's pretended eyewitness account; Christopher Sinclair-Stevenson, *Inglorious Rebellion* (London: Hamish Hamilton, 1971), pp. 128–29; and Baynes, *The Jacobite Rising*, pp. 168–70, both of which rely in part on *A True Account*.

51. Defoe, *A True Account*, pp. 53–54.

52. For the relations of Charles XII and Philip V with the Jacobites, see Hatton, *George I*, pp. 174–75, 226; Bennett, *Tory Crisis*, pp. 207–9, 284–85; George Lockhart, *The Lockhart Papers* (London: W. Anderson, 1817), 2: 7–8.

53. Defoe, *A True Account*, pp. 54, 56–57.

54. John Robert Moore, "Defoe's Hand in *A Journal of the Earl of Marr's Proceedings* (1716)," *Huntington Library Quarterly* 18 (1954): 209–8.

55. *A Journal of the Earl of Marr's Proceedings* (London; 1716), pp. 2–3, 15–16, 21.

56. Defoe's introduction to *A Journal of the Earl of Marr's Proceedings*, pp. iii–iv.

57. *A Journal of the Earl of Marr's Proceedings*, p. 27; Introduction, pp. xii–xiii. For the arrest of the Jacobites in England, see Sinclair-Stevenson, *Inglorious Rebellion*, pp. 78–79.

58. Introduction to *A Journal of the Earl of Marr's Proceedings*, p. xii.

59. Moore, *Checklist*, item 348.

60. Moore, "Defoe's Hand in *A Journal of the Earl of Marr's Proceedings*," p. 223.

61. Healey, *Letters of Daniel Defoe*, p. 256n, 450–51.

5

A Novelist in Progress: Defoe and the Whig Split of 1717

Defoe's works from the period shortly before he wrote his masterpieces of fiction receive very little attention, primarily because he is generally believed to have spent those years producing hackwork for the Whig ministry, somehow reserving the best of himself for the writing of his novels when that work tapered off. It is true that Defoe's taste in literary and political pursuits ran to the covert: he enjoyed appearing to write in behalf of causes that he did not support and vitiating those causes by revealing their internal contradictions; he enjoyed rewriting history in the light of "secret" facts that changed the face of events that the world thought it knew; and he enjoyed composing the memoirs of persons whose "crimes" he exaggerated or exonerated according to what he believed were the best interests of the Hanoverian regime. These covert fictions may be found in many of his pamphlets and books, but they are especially evident after 1716, when the loss of Harley's patronage and the absence of another patron in the Whig ministry who could maintain both his post and his fidelity to Revolution principles forced Defoe into a more or less independent stance. Neither Charles Townshend, Robert Walpole, nor the earl of Sunderland could claim Defoe's complete confidence; all of them were Modern Whigs who lacked the Old Whig commitment to the Country interest that Defoe believed Harley to have had. Defoe had frequent occasion in this period to exercise the techniques that were the basis for his fictions—not for any literary purpose, but in support of his efforts to manipulate these men in what he believed was their own—and the country's—best interest. To this extent, he was

121

neither spy nor propagandist, but a novelist-in-progress who made other men make his fictions into realities.

1. The Weaknesses of the Whig Ministry

It would have been very reasonable for Defoe, and for all those others who had waited so long for the fruits of the Glorious Revolution, to assume that their time had finally come in the spring of 1716. The defeat of the rebels at Preston and the breaking-up of the Jacobite army in March removed the immediate threat to the Hanoverian succession. The execution of a limited number of the rebels, the transportation of hundreds of others, and the promise of a pardon for the rest demonstrated, at least to Hanover's supporters, that the king was prepared not only to use his authority, but also to moderate it in an effort to win over those Tories who were not Jacobites. Negotiations were underway for a treaty of alliance with France, which, while not opening commercial relations between the two nations, would guarantee and perfect the terms of the Peace of Utrecht. The king's firm reliance on Whig ministers promised to end the party strife and factionalism that had disrupted the affairs of his predecessor. A petition from the Dissenting interest to take off the Occasional Conformity and Schism Acts had been favorably received, though the rebellion had prevented the king from acting upon it.[1] Defoe himself was living in relative retirement in his suburban home in Stoke Newington, where he tended his garden and kept his distance, both physically and ideologically, from the affairs at court.

Beneath this placid surface, however, the weaknesses of the Whig ministry were beginning to appear. The execution of the rebel leaders, which began with the beheading of Lords Derwentwater and Kenmuir on 24 February 1716, brought on a recurrence of the popular unrest and tumults that had signalled the beginning of the rebellion, with the difference that these disturbances were, in the words of a modern historian, expressions of "helplessness and despair" by an alienated class of laboring poor who were "unable to come to terms with the prospect of a long-standing Whig supremacy."[2] The suppression of the riots by means of more executions did nothing to remove the underlying resentment against Hanover or the suspicion that the court planned to extend its authority at the expense of liberties that even poor Englishmen regarded as theirs by constitutional right. Moreover, the removal of the emergency conditions that had united the Whig party during the rebellion and the riots revealed a deep division among the king's ministers, who gradually formed into two camps: one led by the duke of Marlborough and the earl of Sunderland, the other by the duke of Argyle, who had recently been replaced as commander of the army for what was thought to be a reluctance to pursue his countrymen, the Scots rebels.[3] A quarrel between the king and the Prince of Wales over the latter's powers as regent during the king's planned sojourn to Hanover caused the prince to ally himself with Argyle. Meanwhile, anxieties among members of Parliament over the power of the king's German advisors blew up into the fear that the king intended to use the British fleet to secure the provinces of Bremen and Verden, risking in the process a war with Sweden. The French alliance, which would have freed English ships for Baltic service, was seen as an element of this strategy, and Townshend's reservations about the alliance, which fell within his province as secretary of state, were interpreted as opposition to Hanover's plans in the Baltic. Townshend's inability to handle the alliance to the king's satisfaction, his suggestion that the king should make peace with Sweden even though he should be "obliged to make some sacrifice" to obtain it, and his opposition to the awarding of an English title to the king's mistress, Madame Schulenberg, were all regarded as signs of his disaffection and his inclusion in Argyle's faction. Equally important, no doubt, were the misrepresentations of Townshend's loyalty that were made to the king by Sunderland and the German advisors, which the departure of the king for Hanover prevented Townshend from counteracting. The upshot of these intrigues and misunderstandings was Townshend's demotion to lord lieutenant of Ireland in December of 1716.[4]

Defoe was not as unaffected by these changes at court and in the national sentiment as he appeared to be. At the time of Townshend's demotion, Defoe had been employed for more than six months by the secretary of state to keep his hand in among the Tory journalists and to moderate their most offensive productions.[5] As Defoe later explained in a letter to Charles De la Faye, Sunderland's under-secretary, one of the projects that he and Townshend had begun was a monthly news magazine called *Mercurius Politicus,* which was intended to appeal to the Tories by expressing moderate Country sentiments while ultimately serving the ministry's interests.[6] In the issue for July 1716, for example, the author of the *Mercurius Politicus* apologized for not having printed earlier the arguments against the Septennial Act. Hinting that he dared not do so for fear of government reprisal, he nevertheless admitted an obligation "to give Posterity a true Account who appeared for their Liberties and who against them, and what was said as well on one side as the other."[7] Tory readers might be pleased to take this ambiguous phrase to mean that the Septennial Act had been a stroke at their liberties, though it is impossible in the context to prove that that is what the author intended; in any case, the main point had been gained in that the arguments against the act were not circulated in this Tory journal until the bill was safely passed.

Yet, to a degree that has not previously been appreciated, the *Mercurius Politicus* occasionally presented anti-Whig sentiments that far exceeded the limited objective of passing as a Tory paper. Particularly in his accounts of the prosecution of persons in the lower classes for crimes with obvious political implications, Defoe seems to have been sensitive to the popular resentment against the Whig and Hanoverian government, and to the necessity for soothing this resentment by moderate measures. For example, when popular unrest over the execution of the rebels boiled over into the attack on Read's mug-house off Fleet Street in July 1716, for which five Tory demonstrators were hanged while the Whiggish owner of the mug-house was acquitted of the shooting of one of the demonstrators, Defoe noted several circumstances unfavorable to the government's case. He pointed out that the mug-houses were themselves provocations, being places where the health of miscellaneous members of the court were drunk far into the night; that the riot started as the result of aggressive behavior on the part of a constable and a watchman toward the mob; that the act against rioting that was the grounds of the prosecution was a recent one, with which the rioters were probably unfamiliar; and, finally, that the rioters were "young, inconsiderate, poor and mean Fellows" who had "no Design in what they did, and were far from being concerned in any Party-measures to raise and form these Disorders."[8] Though Defoe was still convinced of the necessity to support the Protestant succession in the Hanover line with the force of law, he was clearly troubled by the one-sided application of Whig justice.

Nor did Defoe stop at expressing doubts about the quality of

Whig justice in this one case. In the issue for September 1716, Defoe reported on a robbery that was alleged to have occurred on the road to Clifton, near York, for which Thomas Barron, a solider, and Edward Bourn, a sailor, were hanged. They were accused of taking three half-pence from "one Mr. King and one Jackson a Printer," though in their defense the "Poor Men insisted that they begged it, and also that they had it not neither, but the merciless Prosecutor insisted and swore positively that it was demanded, and the two poor Creatures were both hanged for it." Describing the prosecution as "an Example of Justice, unmixed with Mercy . . . as the like has not happened in our Memory, or scarce in History," Defoe noted that "they were greatly lamented by the Country" because their "simplicity and downright way of expressing themselves" caused people universally "to think they were not Guilty of the Fact." He concluded that "Three Half-pence is a very small Sum to be hanged for, and he must be a very hard-mouthed Fellow that swore it a Robbery."[9] Defoe's mention of the occupations of the defendants and of one of the prosecutors suggests that the prosecution and the verdict were based on social and political differences, rather than on legal issues. Certainly the judges in the case drew this inference from the passage, since they arrested the printer of the *Mercurius Politicus* and sought to discover the author. Addressing himself through De la Faye to Sunderland, who had in the meantime replaced Townshend as Defoe's employer, Defoe denied responsibility for the passage, admitted that he had plagiarized part of it from another source, described it as a thing "but Triffling in it Self," and protested that it had occurred when he was under Townshend's protection, and so immune from prosecution. At the same time, Defoe drew for Sunderland a compelling picture of the dangers to which he exposed himself among Jacobite agents and publishers for the sake of serving the ministry's interests, and apparently Sunderland was satisfied with this account. Defoe's biographers also have generally accepted his version of his activities, differing only over whether Defoe's deception of the Country interest in favor of the Court was "patriotic" or "not cricket."[10]

Such moral judgments, however, simply are not adequate to cover the complex motives for Defoe's activities under the Sunderland ministry. Instead, the multiple nature of his services and the consequent appearance of duplicity must be understood as the result of two related developments. One of these is the emergence of new conditions of literary employment, caused by the breakdown of the system of individual patronage and its replacement by a system of payment for "immediate productivity," without the moral obligation for continued loyalty on either side that had been an implicit part of the patronage system.[11] The other is Defoe's growing—and, to a large extent, forced—independence from either Whig or Tory party loyalties or the interest of any particular politician. Though he worked at various times for Townshend, Sunderland, Walpole, and the publisher Nathaniel Mist—in fact, worked at roughly the same time for all of them—he never again belonged to any party or interest as thoroughly as he had to Harley. Usually regarded as the most venial and opportunistic phase of Defoe's career, this period may instead be seen as a transitional stage in which Defoe came out from the intellectual shadows of a "great man" and developed a capacity for independent thought and action that made his success as a novelist possible. Equally important, it was in this period that he broadened his notion of civic virtue by probing, in a series of political fictions, the moral implications not only of Robert Harley's career, but also those of Townshend, Walpole, the French negotiator Mesnager, and the Duke of Shrewsbury. Though his purpose throughout this period remained the defense of Harley, the need to establish an ideological basis for that defense led him not only into a Machiavellian position with regard to the men whom he served, but also into a definition of liberal humanism that was to provide the basis for his first great work of fiction, *Robinson Crusoe*.

2. The Quarrel of the Ministers

The growth of Defoe's independence both as writer and as ideologist was assisted by the split that developed in the Whig party during the summer of 1716, and had widened to such an extent by March 1717 that Townshend, Walpole, and a number of their followers went into apparent opposition to the court. Though their defection is now generally regarded as little more than an opportunistic ploy to force the king to take them back on their own terms, at the time it may have seemed to Defoe to hold out the promise of a new centrist party to replace the moderate interest that had evaporated with the imprisonment of Robert Harley.[12] Like Walpole himself, Defoe was careful not to burn his bridges behind him, and so continued in his old employments for the Whigs when Townshend left the government in December of 1716. But in his role as pamphleteer, he secretly supported the defection of the Walpolean ministers against the Sunderland faction, for all the world as if his real convictions lay with the Country interest. Since it would have been safer, easier, and probably more profitable for him to have allied himself exclusively with one side or the other, his purpose in pursuing this duplicitous course must be sought by weighing, one against the other, the "fictions" he composed in this period on the theme of a courtier's duty to his king, his party, and himself.

Defoe's first publications on the split in the Whig party took a neutral position as to the blame, while calling on the king to return from Hanover and reconcile the quarreling ministers. The spat became the occasion for one of his boldest satires, which he reviewed in the *Mercurius Politicus* as "one of the merriest pieces of drollery . . . that has been met with in this age."[13] Titled *The Quarrel of the School Boys at Athens*, the satire casts George I in the role of a Greek scholar who becomes famous for his excellent teaching, and so is invited to set up a school in a neighboring community. After quelling several disturbances in the school, which is divided into upper and lower classes, he returns to his former country for a visit, leaving his son in his place as usher. Immediately some of the older boys become rowdy, and "fell all together by the Ears, and made a meer Bedlam of the School, putting it all into the extremest Confusion." The leaders among the boys are said to include one whose "peculiar Study was in those Parts of the Mathematicks, which relate to the Art of War," that is to say, Marlborough, and "a Youth of Northern Extract, of an ancient Gothick Race," a man of "a fiery Disposition, and a most impetuous Courage . . . but who wanted Temper to manage that Spirit, which would have otherwise been an Ornament to him," by which the reader recognizes Argyle. This boy had "long envied the Captain of the Mathematick Class, and aspired to be Captain General of all the School," and by his ambition had alienated everyone, including the schoolmaster, who had him expelled. A third leader among the boys was "one hot Youth who was entrusted with the School Cash," and who also had "the Power to enquire into, and expose the Conduct of those, who had opposed his Interest before his Coming." This boy—easily identified as Walpole—had been treated barbarously before the arrival of the new schoolmaster and forced to sit in the "Dunce's Hole," for which he now pursued his enemies "till, on Pretence of Justice and Revenge, he had frighted all the Boys that were not of his Party away from the School." This hot youth had a brother-in-law who was one of the chief clerks, and who did his business so well that he aroused the envy of some of the other boys, especially the captain general, who schemed to have him expelled. When the expulsion ocurred, most of the boys in the school ran to the captain general, "clapt him on the Back, and cry'd G—d a mercy John: and so took care to be thought his Friends, if the worst came to the worst." Other boys murmured privately that it was strange how those who had declaimed most loudly against forming into parties and factions in the school's public exercises were among the first to choose sides. Some claimed that the captain general was justified in his efforts to prevent the cash-keeper's party from pursuing its enemies to the point of ruining the school; some, that "now was the Time they had so long struggled for," in which "all wicked, debauched, refractory, and rebellious Boys" should be expelled for the safety of the school and its master. The conclusion of the book, which was written while George was still at Hanover, projects an image of the schoolmaster returning in anger, entering the door of the school, and looking around sternly and silently with his rod in his hand. The boys "no sooner saw the Master and his Rod, but they all sat down as quiet and as still, as if nothing had happened at all; not a Word was spoken, not the least Noise heard, all was perfectly calm and quiet in a Moment; the Master went peaceably up to his Chair of Instruction, and laid down his Rod; the Scholars fell very lovingly to their Books, and have been very good Boys ever since."

The Quarrel of the School-Boys at Athens is, of course, closer to satire than to fiction, if literary distinctions of genre are to be rigidly observed. But even as a satire, it puts the quarrel of the ministers in an ideological perspective. The fable not only ridicules the Whigs as rowdy schoolboys, but also warns that factionalism within the party is a threat to Whig hegemony and the Protestant succession. It puts equal blame on both factions—to do otherwise would be merely to assist one faction and increase the division—while reasserting the virtue of submission to the sovereign. It tends to exculpate Townshend as the only minister who had sought to maintain a moderate posture and to do his sovereign's business, while suggesting that Walpole's implacable pursuit of Harley's ministers was a major cause for the quarrel.

Had Defoe stopped with *The Quarrel of the School-Boys at Athens*, it might be said that he never committed himself to either side in the struggle between those ministers who stayed in and those who went out. His next book but one, however, was an "impartial enquiry" into the conduct of Townshend, in which he justified that minister's handling of the Barrier Treaty in 1709 and the severity of the steps he took to suppress the rebellion in 1715.[14] Townshend had had "no Hand in the Cause, nor any Share in the Management" of the unfortunate quarrel in the ministry, which has revived the hopes of the Jacobite party. In a long apostrophe to the "foolish Courtiers," Defoe accused all the ministers except Townshend of having no concern for the interests of either king or country, and therefore not even for their own. The effect of Defoe's "enquiry," then, was to transfer the responsibility for the factionalism from the shoulders of the one minister whom the king had demoted to those who were left in place, while elevating that minister to the status of an admirable, if not ideal, courtier.

3. Defoe's Polemic with the Modern Whigs

From the outlines of Defoe's defense of Townshend, it might appear that Defoe admired Townshend for his vigorous pursuit of the Jacobites and his efficient prosecution of suspected agents such as William Paul and John Hall, who were executed in July 1716.[15] But the ideological roots of his attachment to Townshend were deeper than mere anti-Jacobitism. Despite the emphasis in Defoe's "impartial enquiry" on the need for continued vigilance, Jacobitism was thoroughly suppressed in the early months of 1717, as the king's extended sojourn to Hanover suggested. Had Defoe's attachment to Townshend rested on nothing more than Townshend's severity towards the rebels, it would have been no great matter for him to transfer his loyalties entirely to Sunderland, who was to become his new employer in the ministry. Defoe had, after all, worked with Sunderland during the Whig ministry of 1708–10, and had singled him out for praise in the *Review* when that ministry fell.[16] But as the new Whig ministry began to show signs of breaking up early in 1717, Defoe had little reason to believe that Sunderland was ideologically committed to the preservation of Revolution principles. In the first place, Sunderland had been among the inner circle of Junto leadership that had decided not to join Harley's ministry in 1711, but rather had stood out in the hope of bringing Harley down, thereby forcing Harley to rely on conservative Tory support—a strategy for which Defoe had bitterly rebuked the Junto in numerous pamphlets and articles. More recently, Sunderland had emerged as one of the architects of the aggressive program of political reforms through which the Whigs planned to secure their oligarchy. Defoe had defended most of these reforms, notably the Septennial Act, against the attacks of Bishop Atterbury; but his defenses had always been premised on the assumption that the reforms were motivated only by the emergency of the rebellion, and thus did not constitute a disavowal of the Revolution. Now that the rebellion was suppressed and the emergency was past, however, only Townshend showed any signs of opposing the Whig-Hanoverian oligarchy in what appeared to be its encroachments on the Constitution.

The main objectives of this Whig program had been spelled out in a pamphlet by John Toland entitled *The State Anatomy of Great Britain,* published in January 1717.[17] Toland, born an Irish Catholic but now known as a radical freethinker, was regarded as a threat by the entire Dissenting community, which had presented his *Christianity Not Mysterious* to the Middlesex Grand Jury for condemnation and burning. Defoe, who had crossed verbal swords with him as early as 1698 over the standing army, and again in 1701 over the limitations to the succession,[18] described him as "a Man, whose life has been to act in a Mask, to pretend true Religion, and yet profess Heresie; to talk as a Protestant, and yet Worship as a Socinian."[19] Defoe's dislike of Toland was so great that his discovery that the Marlborough-Sunderland wing of the ministry had employed Toland to write a major policy statement might itself have been nearly sufficient reason for him to join Townshend's camp. But Defoe claimed, in his response to the *State Anatomy,* that he had known long ago that the ministry was preparing to attempt to void one of the most jealously guarded limitations to the Act of Succession, which was the prohibition against admitting to the English peerage any persons of foreign birth, the king and the Prince of Wales excepted. Not only the king's mistresses, but

the German barons Bothmer and Bernstorff were known to
desire English titles, which would have allowed them to enter
both the House of Lords and the judicature. Defoe had been
preparing since late in 1716 a denunciation of this plan, to
which he appended a rebuttal to Toland's *State Anatomy* when it
appeared, and published the book in February 1717 under the
title *An Argument Proving that the Design of Employing and Enobling Foreigners, Is a Treasonable Conspiracy against the Constitution.*

According to Defoe's *Argument*, the *State Anatomy* was the
product of "a Set of selfish and designing men, who to engross
Power, amass Wealth, and gratifie the unbounded Avarice and
Ambition of a few Care not . . . to what reproaches they expose
the King and Royal Family." He suggested that the scheme of
the *State Anatomy* was "long hatching" and was "talked of many
Days before it came abroad; Pieces of it handed about, and
rehearsed among the People it is calculated to serve."[20] Defoe
saw himself as responding, therefore, not merely to his old
antagonist Toland, but to a faction in the ministry that was
conspiring to please the king by its attention to his interests and
to consolidate their own power at the same time. Though un-
willing to say so, Defoe clearly thought that the interests of the
king and the British nation were not synonymous in this case,
and that the Sunderland faction intended to exploit George's
affection for Hanover by offering schemes that put Hanoverian concerns ahead of British interests. The awarding of British
titles to Bothmer and Bernstorff, who Toland predicted would
"by a particular Act" be made "Peers of this Kingdom," was
only the first of these schemes. Toland also predicted that the
Occasional Conformity, Schism, and Test Acts would be repealed on the grounds that "a Religious Test is a Political Monopoly." Roman Catholics, however, were to be excluded from
the Toleration not "on account of any speculative or scholastick
points," but " 'tis *se defendendo* that we do it." Finally, Toland
argued that even in the absence of external military threats or
internal disturbances, "we ought nevertheless at all times to
maintain such a competant land and sea force, as will render us
considerable to our neighbors (for we desire not to be formidable) and to deprive others of all hopes to surprize us unpre-
pared." Toland exhorted the reader not to "entertain the least
thought, as if I were pleading here for a standing Army," yet
that is precisely what his proposal for military preparedness
amounted to. At the same time that he denied that a standing

army was intended, he revealed that he had lately seen plans for some new barracks drawn up "by Mr. DuBois, one of his Majesties Engineers" for housing these soldiers.[21]

These proposals by no means exhausted Toland's plans for restoring the anatomy of England to its former healthy state. There are also suggestions that the king will soon become his own lord treasurer, thus perhaps lessening the authority of Parliament in money appropriations and credit; that the king intends to make a royal visitation to the universities at Oxford and Cambridge, upon which, if he finds that "they should neglect their duty, or depart from their province, he'll correct and punish them in proportion to their demerits"; and that the king intends to prevent "the growing of his Ministers gray in his service," for which reason "it is not necessary that each of them should always continue in the same individual post, a gradual rise and rotation fitting men for different Posts successively." This last, a transparent allusion to the "rotation" of Townshend to the post of lord lieutenant of Ireland, confirms Defoe's belief that the *State Anatomy* obtained its direction from Townshend's enemies in the Marlborough-Sunderland wing of the ministry. But Defoe did not attempt to dispute the right of the king to appoint his ministers as he saw fit, nor did Defoe disagree with the need for a royal inspection of the universities, and he knew that George was too dependent on Walpole's financial skills to take the treasury entirely into his own hands. Instead he concentrated his reply to Toland on those concerns held in common by his Country Tory and Old Whig readers—the peerage, Toleration, and the standing army. Not coincidentally, these three concerns—the preservation of aristocratic predominance in a republic, the subordination of religion to politics, and the preference for a militia over a standing army—were all central tenets of Machiavellian humanism.

It is true that Defoe countered Toland's proposals on grounds that would appeal to the prejudices, rather than the ideological principles, of his audience. Responding to Toland's suggestion that the peerage be opened to the two German barons, he charged in an uncharacteristically nationalistic vein that granting titles to foreigners would expose "the Lives, Honours, and Estates of a free and glorious Nation to the Breath of a covetous Dutchman, a mercenary Frenchman, a haughty insolent Spaniard, or a lewd, assassinating Italian!"[22] When Toland rebuked Defoe for his xenophobia, pointing out that Defoe was once known for his satire on nationalism, the *True-Born Englishman*, Defoe responded that "since we are now arrived to an Excellence which we believe is not out-done by other Nations, either in Science or Religion, and moral Virtue, *we should keep where we are*, and mix no farther *if we can help it*, unless we are sure to improve." Claiming that his pretended fear of a threat to the purity of aristocratic bloodlines had been "a jest," Defoe conceded that "our business is not now so much about mixing of Blood, *tho' that is not insignificant*, but about mixing our Politicks." In other words, the real argument was not over the composition of the House of Lords, but over its ability to perform as a stabilizing force in the state, and in particular to prevent the undue influence of Hanoverian interests on British policy.[23]

About the proposed Toleration, however, there could be no jesting. Defoe himself had long sought the repeal of all three acts, though he disapproved of the practice of occasional conformity by Dissenters, and he had pushed for a repeal of those acts at the conclusion of the rebellion.[24] But a Toleration proposed by a man he regarded as a heretic, backed by a faction that had sold out the Dissenters to the earl of Nottingham in 1711, and which contained such clear contradictions as Toland's exclusion of Roman Catholics on grounds of "self-defense," suggested to Defoe that the "Toleration" being offered was nothing more than a manipulative scheme to draw the Dissenters into the factional struggle on the side of the court—the same tactic that had been employed by James II with disastrous results for the Dissenters.[25] At the same time, Defoe may have been for author of another book that supported the idea of repealing the Occasional Conformity and Schism Acts, but only if "they that are embarked in it, instead of managing at *sixes and sevens*, have a good Majority at their back.[26]

The last ideological point on which Defoe rebutted Toland was perhaps the most explosive—the question of the standing army. The matter was explosive politically because it was known that George I expressly desired to maintain the army at its present size—whether because, as Toland said, England had an obligation to be the "Umpire" of the balance of power in Europe, or because George desired to appear formidable to his adversaries in the Baltic. But it was made more dangerous by the publication in January 1717 of an English translation of letters said to have been sent between the Swedish ambassador to England, Count Gyllenborg, and Baron Goertz, minister of state to Charles XII of Sweden. The letters were prefaced with a note signed by James Stanhope, recently converted to the anti-Townshend faction by the earl of Sunderland.[27] Announcing the event in the *Mercurius Politicus,* Defoe drew for his readers the connection between the publication of the letters, which seemed to promise Swedish support for a Jacobite invasion of England, and the king's desire to maintain the army. "His Majesty," Defoe said cautiously, "expressly said that there was a design to support a Rebellion at Home by an Invasion from abroad . . . these Things having been spoken from the Throne, there remains no more room to suggest the Improbability of a Design, which before, indeed, many People thought too irrational to give any Credit to."[28] With these judicious words, Defoe signaled his largely Tory readership to cease their now-treasonable skepticism of the need for a standing army, while at the same time he encouraged their mental reservations, and thus their passive resistance to it. This same strategy appears in a pamphlet on the standing army that has been attributed to him, in which he admits that, *if* the Swedes intended to come, a standing army would indeed be necessary;[29] and it also appears in the conduct of Robert Walpole in the Commons, who, in Defoe's words, sat "cold and silent in the hottest part of the Debate" over the king's request for the money to keep the army in readiness, as a result of which the measure passed by the humiliating margin of only four votes.[30] Toland was quick to declare that there was a conspiracy between Gyllenborg, the Jacobites, Defoe, and the disaffected Whigs to reduce the size of the army so that the Swedish invasion would succeed. The resistance to the king's request for money was led by "a few Whigs," said Toland, whom "D. F. or the Lord of Oxford knows who besides, was insidiously distinguishing . . . by the Character of 'some honest and loyal Patriots, who yet remain in the Administration.'" Dredging up the old false charge that Defoe had written a treasonable pamphlet against the Hanover succession, "for which a pardon was procured to him before the first of August 1714, by those that set him to work," and implying that Defoe's *Argument Against Employing and Enobling Foreigners* had been commissioned by Gyllenborg to weaken George's authority, Toland suggested that it would be "well worth the pains to detect those party-men, who, the Count says in his letter of the 15th of January, are so well inclined for the Swedes."[31]

Defoe was prepared to give back as good as he got on the question of the standing army. Abandoning all caution, he attacked Toland's call for a "nursery" of experienced officers and troops. "Can any Man call himself a Whig, which, as that Word is now understood, is a Lover of Liberty; and yet talk of having Nurseries of Red Coats bred up in Foreign Pay, always ready at Command, to be called Home for any Drudgery that a King, *who knows not Joseph,* may have for them to do?" exclaimed Defoe, insisting that while George could be trusted, it was the principle that he was concerned about. Since the time of James II, opposition to a peacetime army had been a consistent principle in orthodox Whig ideology. It was "astonishing," Defoe said, to see a Whig writer "openly appear for that, which the Whigs have in all Ages, with so much Justice to their Country, and Zeal for its Interest, so vigorously and so unanimously opposed."[32]

Defoe's pretended resentment of Toland's ideological heresy on the question of a standing army presents a clear case of the mutability of Defoe's own convictions, since Defoe was widely known for a pamphlet first published in 1698, in which he had argued that a standing army was "not inconsistent" with liberty as long as it was under the control of Parliament.[33] But for Defoe, there was a world of difference between 1698 and 1717, which was expressed in the integrity of the men at the head of the government. Though perhaps hypocritical, Defoe's resentment of the proposal to maintain the army marks the degree to which he had become alienated from the ministry from which he had expected so much, and also the length to which he was willing to go in recruiting Country Tory and Old Whig support for the opposition element in the Whig party that was coalescing around Townshend. His alienation proceeded from his disgust at what was being done to Townshend, his dislike of the political style of Sunderland's Modern Whigs, and his anger at seeing Whig writers such as Toland embrace the same low methods of misrepresentation and malice with which they had disrupted Harley's ministry and (as Defoe claimed) driven him into the arms of the Jacobites. Added to this was Defoe's concern that there was indeed a conspiracy in the Sunderland wing of the ministry to extend the powers of the king beyond their constitutional limits—the most recent proof of which was the sermon preached by Bishop Hoadly on 31 March 1717, in which Hoadly provided a theological basis for Toland's proposed Toleration. While Defoe accepted the general outlines of Hoadly's thought, he believed that Hoadly was being used as a means of drawing the Dissenters into the plan, and also that Hoadly's radical formulations so undermined the authority of Church and State that they "might all fall down on our Heads."[34]

4. Defoe and Walpole: Old Whig and Modern Whig

It was in this mood of anxiety and alienation, then, that Defoe took up Walpole's defense. There is no evidence that Defoe and Walpole had a personal relationship, and Defoe's writings about Walpole show none of the usual feelings of a writer for his patron. In his inquiry into Walpole's conduct, published shortly after Walpole resigned from the treasury in April of 1717, Defoe made little effort to clarify the reasons for the resignation, laying stress instead upon the regrettable proclivity of courtiers to fight among themselves and put their own interest ahead of their country's. He did not exempt Walpole from this practice, though he did employ brief fictional scenes in which courtiers gossiped about the removal in a way that suggested that Walpole had been forced out, rather than resigning voluntarily. Instead, he emphasized Walpole's financial genius, his mastery of Parliament, and his indispensability to the success of the ministry. He particularly cited the justice of Walpole's Sinking Fund, which he said was regarded by "the Landed Men, and Gentlemen throughout the whole Island" as "a healing, advantagious Proposal," while "the Moneyed Men, and Stock-jobbers, chiefly in the city of London," opposed it. He referred to his own pamphlet in support of the fund, called *Fair Payment No Spunge,* noted that some people said "it was done by Daniel Defoe," and expressed the opinion that "it had some Things of weight in it" and must have been "written in concert with the Authors, or Directors of the Thing it self."[35] Quoting a long passage from *Fair Payment No Spunge,* which had been intended to demonstrate that Walpole's scheme was no more than a means of doing justice to creditors who had loaned money to the government at lower interest rates than were now legal, Defoe claimed for himself the credit of having stopped the objections that had been made to the Sinking Fund.

The other accomplishment since the Hanoverian succession that Defoe cited to Walpole's credit was his work as the chairman of the Secret Committee charged with gathering evidence for the prosecution of the supposed malefactors of the last ministry. He described Walpole as "unwearied in Application, and successful, even beyond his own Expectation" in the "Herculean" labors of the investigation. Defoe ascribed the authorship of the committee's *Report* to Walpole, and remarked that, during the initial presentation of the *Report* to the Commons, "great Opposition was made, but Mr. W——never gave it over till he had carryed all the Points which were aimed at by the Committee."[36] On the basis of the *Report*, the Tory ministers had been impeached, and Robert Harley had been imprisoned in the Tower. To the casual reader, Defoe's approval of Walpole's implacable pursuit of the Tories sounds like that of a true Whig zealot; to the reader apprised of Defoe's long commitment to Harley, his endorsement of Walpole's work seems contradictory and callous. But Defoe's praise for Walpole was considerably more devious than either of those readings would suggest. In the first place, Defoe took pains to reprint in his defense of Walpole a scandalous letter that had appeared two years earlier in the *Evening Post;* the letter had supposedly been sent from Walpole to Sunderland, describing their plans to advance themselves politically by Harley's impeachment. Defoe denounced the letter in the strongest terms as a forgery, yet the gratuitous reprinting of it was enough to plant the idea that Walpole's zeal was politically motivated. Further, Defoe used an inordinate amount of ink defending Walpole from the charges of peculation that had caused his imprisonment in the Tower during Harley's ministry and showing how Walpole had thereafter made the destruction of Harley his personal affair. In other words, Defoe's vindication of Walpole served the dual purpose of praising that patriot for his zeal while destroying utterly the credibility of his prosecution of Harley.

It must not be supposed that Defoe allowed this to happen by accident or as the result of incompetence. On the contrary, it seems clear that his defense of Townshend and Walpole, in addition to the motives already adduced, was a deliberate tactic in his long campaign to secure Harley's release from the Tower. While Defoe lamented the division in the ministry, as in his *Quarrel of the School Boys at Athens,* he also knew that the chances of a successful prosecution of Harley were greatly diminished as long as the former chairman of the Secret Committee continued in opposition. His defenses of Townshend and Walpole so widened the breach in the ministry that there was no hope of reconciliation, even for so important a matter as the Harley trial.[37] Harley himself realized this and petitioned for his trial to begin in May, one month after Defoe's defense of Walpole. By July the trial had ended in confusion, caused in part by Walpole's cavils over the meaning of the word *treason* and Townshend's vigorous efforts in the Lords to throw the proceedings off course.[38] On August 1, with Harley safe in Herefordshire, Defoe closed the breach up again with his pamphlet titled *Old Whig and Modern Whig Revived,* which rebuked the Whigs for having let Harley escape and called for a return to a united party.[39]

5. Harley's Defense and Mesnager's *Memoirs*

The grounds for supposing Defoe to be capable of so Machiavellian an act require that we go back two years, to May 1715, when a writer believed to be Defoe attempted to influence the Secret Committee with a pamphlet titled *A Remonstrance from Some Country Whigs to a Member of a Secret Committee.* The author of this pamphlet flatters the unnamed member with praise for his impartiality and his concern for the rights of the innocent as well as for the just punishment of the guilty, and expresses his belief that the committee will permit "no strained points of Law, no illegal Conjunction of Circumstances, [to] be heaped up to make, as was observed by the famous Earl of Strafford, *Accumulatio Treason.*" As was frequently Defoe's practice, the author appeals to historical precedent, citing the cases not only of the earl of Strafford, but also Mary Queen of Scots, the earl of Essex, Lord Russell and Algernon Sidney as instances of executions for political reasons rather than proven treason, the latter cases being intimately bound up with the reasons for the Old Whig party having come into existence. Not only is the Old Whig commitment to the rule of law at stake in the impeachment of Harley, the writer suggests, but also the political future of the Modern Whigs; he reminds them of the capture by the Philistines of Samson, to whom "Heaven, provoked at the injury, gave Strength to the oppressed Prisoner to pull the House upon their Heads, and to bury them in the Ruins of their Triumph." The elevation of Harley into the company of Samson and Mary Queen of Scots enabled the author to shift the focus of the impeachment from such mundane questions as the fishing rights off Newfoundland, which Harley was charged with ceding too cheaply, to the more disturbing implications of a trial in which the last of the Old or Country Whigs was to be persecuted by the Moderns.

Nor did Defoe let the matter rest there. Simultaneously with presentation of the articles of impeachment before the Commons on 7 July 1715, Defoe published his *Account of the Conduct of Robert Earl of Oxford,* which attempted to refute the charges that were made in the *Report* of the Secret Committee.[40] Harley, Defoe argued, had not sought to be a prime minister, but had restricted himself to the part of the treasurer; he had not limited access to the queen to himself, but permitted others to attend her, from which proceeded all the troubles of his administration. He had played no part in the peace negotiations except "to set to Rights the Mistakes made by others" in order that the French should not profit by English ineptness. He had resisted Bolingbroke's efforts to engage the ministry in support of the Treaty of Commerce, remaining "passive and unconcerned" in the debates, believing that "the Ministry should entirely leave the Merchants to act as they thought fit." The whole affair of the peace "was transacted in the Council; or by the Secretary of State; or by the Queen through them both."[41] The published *Report* of the Secret Committee revealed a rather different version of the negotiations, including evidence that Harley had been present at an unauthorized meeting at Matthew Prior's home in which preliminary agreements with the French negotiator Mesnager were arrived at; that Harley had corresponded with the Marquis de Torcy about the important provisions of the treaty; that he had corresponded with Prior during the negotiations; and that he had personally traveled to Utrecht to carry "the final instructions of the Queen to her Plenipotentiaries."[42] But though the Secret Committee's *Report* was based on sounder evidence, it was Defoe's narrative of a treasurer so thoroughly undermined by factionalism and intrigue that he was no longer responsible for the conduct of his fellow ministers that gained currency.

As the time of Harley's trial approached, Defoe took advan-

tage of a hint given by George I in a speech in April 1717 that
he was considering two measures to reduce the antagonism to
his reign. One was a reduction in the size of the army, the other
was a general pardon of persons involved in the rebellion. It
appears never to have been George's intent to include in the
pardon those persons accused of acting in the Pretender's interest in the last ministry,[43] but Defoe endeavored to explain in
a pamphlet entitled *A General Pardon Considered* why they
should not be excepted from the contemplated Act of Grace.
Adopting the language of liberal humanism, Defoe applauded
the idea of a pardon, which he said would give a "new Face of
Satisfaction" to the nation. Even those who have no need of a
pardon will "find yet a secret involuntary Pleasure, in seeing
other People forgiven." The pardon will give offenders "Room
for the Operation of just Convictions upon their Minds," and
give them an opportunity "to rectifie past Miscarriages and
Mistakes, by a future Change of Conduct." Using historical
examples drawn from the reign of Henry VI of France, Defoe
suggests that the most trustworthy counselors are those who
have rebelled, repented, and been forgiven, rather than those
who have never experienced the need for pardon.[44] Of course,
not everyone can participate in this process of human reconstruction; surely, crimes that "give a General Offense, and
make the Person detestable to Mankind," and persons "dangerous to the Publick Peace," who have fled from justice or taken
up arms against their sovereign, should be excepted from the
pardon. A much more fitting candidate is that "great Object
near Hand, whose Name has been much talked of," and whose
case will soon be "the subject of Debate in a higher Place." A full
account of his conduct is "being prepared for Publick View by
those who are not ignorant of the nicest Part of that Affair," by
which Defoe alludes to his own *Memoirs of Some Transactions
During the Late Ministry of Robert E. of Oxford,* a revised version of
his earlier *Account of the Conduct of Robert Earl of Oxford.*[45] Defoe's pleas for a pardon general enough to include Harley,
however, are not advanced soley for Harley's benefit; the value
of such a pardon is that it would allow Englishmen to "forgive
one another, cease the unchristian Strife, bury the Remem-
brance of former Heats, Animosities, and Differences, and join
again in a new Union of Parties." In other words, Harley's
pardon would be a token of forgiveness for the thousands of
Englishmen who had been less than firm in the Hanoverian

interest but had not openly opposed it, and might thereby reconcile the disaffected Country interest to George.

As in his earlier ideological campaigns in behalf of the Treaty
of Commerce, the Harley ministry, the Hanover succession and
the Septennial Act, however, Defoe did not rely exclusively on
logical persuasion to gain his point. On 17 July 1717, at the
height of the confusion in Parliament over what to do about
Harley, Defoe published a thick volume purporting to be a
translation of the memoirs of Monsieur Mesnager, the French
agent who had first established contact with members of the
Harley ministry in 1711 and negotiated the preliminary terms
of peace. It may be true, as is sometimes said, that Defoe wrote
this 326-page book for the purpose of inserting a single para-
gragh exculpating Harley from any part in the negotiations.
But if that is so, he surrounded that paragraph with an ingenious narrative of the subtle conversations of Mesnager and
members of the English court, through which Mesnager is supposed to have established what the English wanted from the
Peace and what they would be willing to accept. It is true that
Harley's appearances in the book are limited to a few brief
mentions, including Mesnager's lament that he found Harley to
be "less our Friend at Last, then I had found him to be at
First."[46] But if Defoe's intent had been merely to minimize
Harley's involvement in the negotiations, he need not have
gone into elaborate detail about Mesnager's perceptions of the
intentions of the English, and it is the narrative of his discoveries in the English court that make the book effective as a
fiction.

A passage from the *Minutes of the Negotiations of Monsr. Mesnager* will show how Defoe employed the consciousness of the
perspicacious Mesnager to discover secret intentions among his
English counterparts. According to Defoe's version, the initial
difficulty in the negotiations was that, while Mesnager arrived
with a commission empowering him to treat, the pressure of
the Whigs on the queen was such that she dared not empower
anyone to negotiate a treaty, especially without the participation of the Allies. In his first meeting with an unnamed lord,
who can be identified as Charles Talbot, duke of Shrewsbury,
Mesnager asks for proof that his English counterpart speaks as
an agent for the English crown, which Shrewsbury is not able to
give; instead, he arranged an interview for Mesnager with the
queen:

The next Morning he took me in his Coach to Kensington, where I believe the Queen went for the Occasion, for the Court was not there; and where I had the Honour to kiss her Majesty's Hand; after which, my Lord speaking privately to the Queen, her Majesty turned about to me, and said, *Sir, My Lord — here,* directing her self towards his Lordship, *has given me an Account of what Steps you have taken, you may let him hear what you have to say:* I bowed, and was going to say something, tho' I hardly knew what; but her Majesty turned too quick from me to my Lord again, so I stopped; my Lord spoke a good while to the Queen again, and when he had done, the Queen turned to me, and said, *'Tis a good Work, pray God succeed you in it; I am sure I long for Peace, I hate this dreadful Work of Blood;* at which, her Majesty shook her Head 2 or 3 times, saying some other Words that I could not hear, which I was very sorry for; and then the Queen retired, and we withdrew: The Work was now on the Anvil, and we had nothing to do, but to appoint our Meetings, and go on with it; nor were we long about it.[47]

Besides authenticating the narrative, the details here—the direct quotation from the queen, the shaking of her head, the mumbled words—convey a significant ideological message. The peace was not the private project of a faction, but was set on foot by the queen herself. She sought the peace primarily because of her repugnance for war, not because of her brother's interest in the succession (though the words that are spoken too softly to hear might have touched on that subject). The faction that opposed the peace hounded her so closely that she dared not converse directly with Mesnager, for fear of being charged with having been directly involved in the negotiations. Defoe's representation preserves the integrity of her denials that she had spoken with Mesnager, while suggesting that she had commanded the work to go forward. Though Walpole had argued in the Commons at the reading of the *Report* of the Secret Committee that no minister or general could plead the orders of his sovereign as a defense against treason,[48] obedience to a sovereign's explicit commands could not be regarded as treason except by the most Whiggish members of Parliament. If it were Anne's will that there should be negotiations, and since negotiations necessarily include compromises, it would be very difficult to prove that the ministry's compromises were treasonable.

The use of detail not only to authenticate the narrative, but also to provide it with ideological significance is only the first of many signs of Defoe's fictional maturity. As in his successful narrative, *A True Account of the Proceedings at Perth,* the viewpoint of the *Minutes* is first-person retrospective, so that the narrator may recall and reinterpret his experiences in the light of events that happened subsequently. Also as in *A True Account,* the events are narrated from a viewpoint opposite to that from which they are intended to be seen—that is, from the Frenchman's point of view rather than the Englishman's. The reader must constantly reverse the ideological meaning of the narrator's remarks, construing Mesnager's laments and regrets as positive signs for England, and his moments of triumph as signs of trouble. Thus Mesnager's complaints about the lord treasurer's dilatory way of doing business reinforce the feeling that Harley acted as a brake on the negotiations, for want of which the treaty might have been worse for England; and Mesnager's exultation upon hearing the news that the duke of Marlborough was to be dismissed to forestall the possibility of a military coup becomes in the reader's mind a bitter reflection on the misconduct of the Whigs during the negotiations. Through such reversals and revelations the reader discovers a secret or undisclosed meaning in events that may have seemed, on their face, to be treasonable. Foremost among these events, perhaps, is Shrewsbury's adroit handling of the matter of the Pretender. According to Defoe's version, Shrewsbury let Mesnager know that his price for coming to a preliminary agreement was France's recognition of the queen's title to the throne and the settlement of the succession in the Hanover line. Mesnager, who "could not but smile at this Proposal," assumes that Shrewsbury insists on the latter point for the sake of form only, and desires to make a verbal stipulation that "we made no doubt, she [Anne] would find out Ways and Methods to restore the rightful Heir of her Father to his just Dominions after her Decease." Shrewsbury declines to make any such stipulation, saying that the private sentiments of the queen were not his business. Even so, Mesnager reports that Shrewsbury spoke "with such an Air, as let me understand that he gave a secret Assent to what I had proposed; at least, that I had not spoken so disagreeable of that Part as he seemed to suggest." Thus the two men conclude that the agreement is to call for "the Succession of the Crown, according to the PRESENT Settlement," which each understands in his own way, and Mesnager believes they have left open a loophole through which Anne may be able to assist the Pretender.[49] Subsequent events, however— which are not related in the book, but which Defoe's readers were sure to remember—revealed that Shrewsbury was firm for Hanover at the critical moment of Anne's death, and therefore presumably also during his negotiations with Mesnager. In this matter, as in his handling of the problem of the French fort at Dunkirk and his steps to guarantee the interests of England's allies in the proposed treaty, Shrewsbury displayed an understanding of the art of negotiation that was not paralleled in fiction until Moll Flanders and her third husband settled in writing the terms of their marriage.

Defoe's reason for showing off Shrewsbury's skill as a negotiator was not merely aesthetic. Shrewsbury was one of Harley's closest associates; while Harley officially took no hand in the negotiations, it was implied that Shrewsbury had consulted with him.[50] If Shrewsbury had outsmarted his wily French counterpart, then there had been no treasonable intent, at least in the Harley-Shrewsbury wing of the ministry. Like the secret histories of the Treaty of Commerce, the last days of the Harley ministry, and the Rebellion of 1715, Defoe's secret history of the peace negotiations revealed—or rather, created—a world of personal intentions that lay behind public acts and invested them with new meanings. Through his efforts to defend Harley and the actions of his ministry, Defoe had learned the knack of describing human behavior not merely as a series of public acts, but as a complex of intentions which, when properly understood, went a long way toward redeeming the apparently criminal or treasonable nature of those actions.

It was in this emphasis on intent rather than act that Defoe turned the corner from history into fiction. Henceforth, he would be interested in describing persons as the products of their own intentions, and their "crimes" as the products of opposed or subsequent intentions. Virtue in politics, Defoe had learned, was, like established religion, a matter of which faction had Tyburn on its side; only a liberal forbearance toward men who had acted with good intentions in former reigns, and the avoidance of extremes in the present, could preserve the political state from degenerating into the quarrels of schoolboys. That, perhaps, was the best lesson ever to be drawn from the Whig split of 1717.

Notes

1. Ragnhild Hatton, *George I, Elector and King* (Cambridge, Mass.: Harvard University Press, 1978), pp. 179; 181–84; 199.

2. Nicholas Rogers, "Popular Protest in Early Hanoverian London," *Past and Present* 79 (1978): 97–98.

3. Historical Manuscripts Commission, 72 Laing II, pp. 188–89. Patrick Erskine to Professor Charles Mackie, July 3, 1716: "We expect more changes every day, particularly that Townshend, Walpole, and Sir Davy Dalrymple are to goe next with many more that I can't name. . . . This is all the doings of Marlborough and his friends the Squadroni, because Argile proposed the making the Prince sole Regent, which the others would have had commissioned to six, of which they expected the majority."

4. This summary of the changes at court is derived from a number of sources, esp. Hatton, *George I*, pp. 180–210; J. H. Plumb, *Sir Robert Walpole* (Boston: Houghton Mifflin, 1956), 1:224–42; J. M. Beattie, *The English Court in the Reign of George I* (Cambridge: At the University Press, 1967), pp. 224–33; W. A. Speck, *Stability and Strife* (Cambridge, Mass.: Harvard University Press, 1977), pp. 185–96; William Coxe, *Memoirs of the Life and Administration of Sir Robert Walpole* (London: Longman & Co., 1816), 1:146–96.

5. D. H. Stevens, *Party Politics and English Journalism, 1702–1742* (New York: Russell and Russell, 1916, 1967), pp. 107–8.

6. G. H. Healey, ed., *The Letters of Daniel Defoe* (Oxford: Clarendon Press, 1955), pp. 450–54. Defoe gave his new journal the name formerly used by Marchamont Nedham, English republican and neo-Machiavellian, for a newspaper published by Nedham from 1650 to 1652. See J. G. A. Pocock, *The Machiavellian Moment* (Princeton, N.J.: Princeton University Press, 1975), pp. 381–83.

7. *Mercurius Politicus,* July 1716, pp. 134–35.

8. Ibid., August 1716, p. 182; September 1716, pp. 269–71; October 1716, pp. 272–80, 314.

9. Ibid., September 1716, pp. 261–63.

10. William Lee, *Daniel Defoe, His Life and Recently Discovered Writings* (Hildesheim: Georg Olms Verlagsbuchhandlung, 1968) 1:272, and James Sutherland, *Defoe* (Philadelphia: Lippincott, 1938), pp. 214–18. See also Stevens, *Party Politics,* pp. 108–10, and John Robert Moore, *Daniel Defoe, Citizen of the Modern World* (Chicago: University of Chicago Press, 1958), pp. 210–13.

11. The changed conditions of literary employment are discussed in Stevens, *Party Politics,* p. 103.

12. J. H. Plumb, *The Origins of Political Stability* (Boston: Houghton Mifflin, 1967), pp. 176–79. See also Coxe, *Sir Robert Walpole,* 1:137.

13. *Mercurius Politicus,* January 1717, p. 40.

14. *An Impartial Enquiry into the Conduct of the Right Honourable Charles Lord Viscount T[ownshend]* (London, 1717), pp. 72, 74–75.

15. Defoe, *Remarks on the Speeches of William Paul Clerk, and John Hall* (London, 1716).

16. Defoe, *Review,* 17, 20, and 22 June, 1710.

17. Giancarlo Carabelli, *Tolandiana* (Firenze: La Nuova Italia Editrice, 1975), p. 198.

18. John Toland, Anglia Libera, or the Limitation to the Succession of the Crown of England (London, 1701); Defoe, *The Succession to the Crown of England, Considered* (London, 1701).

19. Defoe, *An Argument Proving that the Design of Employing and Enobling Foreigners, is a Treasonable Conspiracy* (London, 1717), p. 51.

20. Ibid., pp. 5–6, 8.

21. John Toland, *The State Anatomy of Great Britain* (London, 1717), pp. 57, 31–32, 58–59.

22. Defoe, *Argument,* p. 24.

23. Defoe, *A Farther Argument against Enobling Foreigners* (London, 1717), p. 35.

24. Defoe, *The Case of the Protestant Dissenters in England* (London, 1716).

25. Defoe, *Farther Argument,* pp. 72–80. If Defoe had looked into his own conscience, he would have found another example of such manipulation. The Schism Act had been passed in 1714 after he had advised the Dissenters not to oppose it in his *A Letter to the Dissenters.* See B. G. Ivanyi, "Defoe's Prelude to the Schism Bill," *Times Literary Supplement,* 7 April 1966, p. 312.

26. (Defoe?), *The Repeal of the Act against Occasional Conformity, Considered* (London, 1717), p. 3.

27. *Letters which Passed Between County Gyllenborg, the Barons Gortz, Sparre, and Others* (London, 1717). For discussion of these letters, see G. V. Bennett, *The Tory Crisis in Church and State, 1688–1730* (Oxford: Clarendon Press, 1975), pp. 208–11, and John J. Murray, *George I, The Baltic, and the Whig Split of 1717* (London: Routledge and Kegan Paul, 1969), pp. 337–46.

28. *Mercurius Politicus,* February 1717, p. 75.

29. Defoe, *What if the Swedes should Come?* (London, 1717), p. 4.

30. *Mercurius Politicus,* April 1717, pp. 236 ff.; Defoe, *History of the Reign of King George* (London, 1718), 2:94.

31. Toland, *The Second Part of the State Anatomy* (London, 1717), pp. 27, 33–34. For another attempt to link Defoe and Gyllenborg, see E. Leigh, *The Plot Discovered; or, some Observations upon a late Jesuitical Pamphlet, written and published by the desperate Agents and Understrappers of Count Gyllenborg, intitled, Fair Payment No Spunge* (London, 1717).

32. Defoe, *Argument,* pp. 67, 54–55.

33. Defoe, *An Argument Shewing, That a Standing Army, with Consent of Parliament, is not Inconsistent with a Free Government* (London, 1698). See Pocock's discussion, *Machiavellian Moment,* pp. 432–35.

34. Defoe, *An Expostulatory Letter to the B[ishop] of B[angor]* (London, 1717), p. 28.

35. Defoe, *The Conduct of Robert Walpole, Esq.* (London, 1717), pp. 49–52, 57, 59.

36. Defoe, *The Conduct of Robert Walpole, Esq.,* pp. 36–37.

37. That Defoe's pamphlets on the conduct of Townshend and Walpole had this effect on the controversy is alleged by one of the ministry's defenders (probably Matthew Tindal) in *An Account of a Manuscript, entitled Destruction the certain consequence of division* (London, 1718), p. 21: "Tho' tis notorious, the Paper War was begun by the Deserters, and that the *Two Conducts &c.* were the libels that made the Attack, yet he heavily complains. . . ."

38. Plumb, *Walpole,* 1:254–55; see also George Sewell, *The Resigners Vindicated* (London, 1718).

39. Defoe, *The Old Whig and Modern Whig Revived, in the Present Divisions at Court* (London, 1717).

40. John Robert Moore, *Checklist of the Writings of Daniel Defoe,* 2d ed. (Hamden, Conn.: Shoe String Press, 1971), item 323. Plumb, however, reports the date of the first reading of the *Report* as 9 June 1715 (*Walpole,* 1:215).

41. Defoe, *An Account of the Conduct of Robert Earl of Oxford* (London, 1715), pp. 56, 88–89, 82.

42. *A Report from the Committee of Secrecy* (London, 1715), pp. 10–15, 39–40.

43. When the Act of Grace passed the Parliament on 26 July, it specifically excepted Harley, Harcourt, Prior, Thomas Harley, Arthur Moore, and ten others from the pardon. Defoe, *History of the Reign of King George*, 2:138.

44. Defoe, *A General Pardon Considered* (London, 1717), p. 9; Defoe, *The Defection Farther Considered* (London, 1718), pp. 14–19.

45. Moore, *Checklist*, items 323 and 378. Defoe, *A General Pardon Considered*, pp. 28–29, 36–37, 13.

46. Defoe, *Minutes of the Negotiations of Monsr. Mesnager* (London, 1717), p. 184.

47. Ibid., pp. 133–34.

48. Plumb, *Walpole*, 1:217.

49. Defoe, *Minutes*, pp. 152–55.

50. Ibid., p. 170.

6

Ideology and the Island

In the more than twenty years that have passed since Ian Watt described *Robinson Crusoe* as the beginning of the tradition of the English novel, Defoe's masterpeice has been read as a hymn to economic individualism, as a description of man's adaptation of his reason to the laws of nature, and as an extended parable of sin, repentance, and redemption.[1] Each interpretation of the novel is grounded in a set of assumptions about the source of Crusoe's story and the purposes Defoe intended the book to serve. James Sutherland found the origin in Defoe's awareness of the rise of a new, lower-middle-class reading public that wanted adventuresome heroes rather than tragedies; John Robert Moore found it in the new war with Spain and the opportunities thus created for colonization in the South Seas.[2] Maximillian Novak has said that the book was "probably, in part, a response to some of the quarrels that shook the Church of England and the Dissenters between 1717 and 1719." Looking back from Defoe's later writings, such as his *Tour Through the Whole Island of Great Britain* and *The Compleat English Gentleman,* Novak added that Crusoe's story "embodied a new social myth" of exploration, voyaging, and opportunity.[3] Isaac Kramnick, who awards Defoe the title of "laureate" of the age of Walpole, implies that Defoe wrote *Robinson Crusoe* to gain the approval of the Whig government.[4] Paul Alkon sees in Defoe's vague and anachronistic uses of time a deliberate effort to invent "a central myth of modern civilization."[5] In perhaps the most metaphysical of all the readings of *Robinson Crusoe,* John Richetti sees in it the effort of the eighteenth-century self to rise above the competing ideologies of an emerging capitalist ethos and a conservative religious tradition.[6] But while all of these writers sense some relation between *Robinson Crusoe* and the

historical conditions that prevailed in England at the end of the
second decade of the century, none of them have elected to
look closely at Defoe's work in the years immediately preceding
1719 for the source and the intentions of the novel.

Common to most readings of the book is the perception that
Defoe cast his hero away on a deserted island in order to regen-
erate him as a human being—either as a new economic man,
whose values accord with the laws of reason and nature, or as a
redeemed sinner—before reintroducing him into society
through his relations with Friday and then with the world at
large. Also common is the assumption that, while the allegory is
not as pronounced as it was to be in *Gulliver's Travels*, Crusoe's
need for regeneration reflects a certain moral or political de-
generacy in the English culture of which he is a product. But
instead of looking for the moral and political ills that most
disturbed Defoe, and which he may have represented emblem-
atically in young Crusoe's willful and reckless defiance of his
father's authority, the best-known discussions of Crusoe's way-
wardness focus on his personal characteristics, which include
his station as the third son of a middle-class family and an
obsession with going to sea, or on the "sheer rebelliousness and
obstinacy" of youth generally.[7] While both of these interpretations may be justified by references to the text, neither sheds
much light on the historical conditions that may have prompted
the writing of the book: Crusoe's difficulties remain specific to
himself, or at best to middle-class youth. The way in which
England as a culture appeared to Defoe to be in need of regeneration remains to be explored.

1. Defoe in the Wilderness

As the preceding chapters have shown, Defoe's situation
under the Whig administration was highly ambiguous. It is
simply not true, as one writer has said, that "in 1715 he began
working for Walpole and never stopped."[8] The only clear instance in which he gave Walpole his undivided support before
1718 was his pamphlet *Fair Payment No Spunge,* a defense of the
Sinking Fund which had been designed by Walpole, but which
also had the approval of George I and the Stanhope/Sunder-
land wing of the Whig party.[9] His defenses of the Walpolean
resigners from the ministry were replies to what he regarded as

the overly aggressive campaign by the Sunderland Whigs to dominate the party at the expense of principles that gave the Whig party its identity. A large part of his energy was consumed in continuing the defense of Robert Harley, in whom he could have had no interest had he been working solely for Walpole; and since Harley's health and his political career were both ruined after two years in the Tower, Defoe's interest in Harley was probably not predicated on some future return to power by his former patron, but rather on influencing the direction of the Whig party in favor of the Country ideology with which Defoe associated Harley. All of these factors, together with a large measure of resentment and mistrust that Defoe had generated among the Whigs by his association with such Tories as Bolingbroke, Arthur Moore, and Nathaniel Mist, forced Defoe into a sort of political wilderness, in which he was obliged to develop his own independent outlook.

But if Defoe inhabited a political wilderness in 1717 and 1718, so too did the rest of the country. The factional struggle of the leading Whigs, which Defoe had once ridiculed as the quarrels of schoolboys, now threatened to drag down the government, and possibly—given the rumors of support for the Pretender from Sweden and Spain—the king as well. On 1 August 1717, two weeks after the end of the session of Parliament in which Harley had been allowed to "escape," Defoe published a stinging denunciation of the practice among ministers of putting private interests before public ones. Titled *Old Whig and Modern Whig Revived, in the Present Divisions at Court,* the pamphlet bears abundant marks of Defoe's authorship, including bitter recriminations against the earl of Nottingham, praise for the Treaty of Union between England and Scotland, approving allusions to Defoe's *Secret Memoirs of a Treasonable Conference at S[omerset] House,* and a long history of political parties in England that is consistent with Defoe's previous treatments of the subject. As he had so often in the *Review,* Defoe suggested that the greatest danger to England lay not in external threats, but in internal divisions that prevented economic progress, interfered with trade, and exposed the nation to its enemies. The present split in the party is no more than a reenactment, Defoe asserted, of the conflict between Harley and the Junto that had nearly ended in the ruin of them both. "Whig against Whig!" Defoe exclaimed, "The Division is monstrous; 'tis unnatural: Whig against Whig in the Nation, is worse than Father against Son in a Family: For these will certainly destroy the House, lay open the Fences of the Laws, and let in all Sorts of Destroyers" (p. 40). In a division between father and son, the duty of the son to subordinate himself to the father's rule is incontrovertible.[10] The division among the Whigs was worse because it was a division among equals that no principle of subordination could decide, unless it was a self-imposed willingness to subordinate oneself to the common good. But for the modern Whigs, the "common Good is but a common Whore, and serves every Purpose; every Party will to Day condemn, to Morrow acquit; to Day reproach, to Morrow embrace the same Person" (p. 47). The recent trial of the earl of Oxford has revealed the empty opportunism of the ideology of the Modern Whigs; in the name of the good of his country, "a worthy Patriot to Day impeaches with all the Virulence of an irritated Spleen, even to a kind of Publick-spirited Rage; making Orations . . . to exaggerate the Heinousness of the Offence, and exasperate the People" against the person charged; and tomorrow, the same orator drops "out of the Chair of the secret Committee, appearing cold and lifeless, and in a Word, voting with the Men that espouse the Person impeached, and assisting to his Escape" (p. 42). This portrait of Walpole, to which is joined equally damning representations of the duke of Argyle and Viscount Townshend, suggests that Defoe's resentment has been stirred at least as much by the hypocrisy of his new masters as by the escape from justice of his old patron. Patriotism, defined as "a disinterested Zeal for the Publick, and . . . a true Principle of Love to our Country," was once found in abundance "among those Whigs, who from the Beginning, and upon the Foundation of real Principles only, have opposed Tyranny and Oppression, have stood in the Gap against the Invasion of Liberty and Religion *in the worst of Times;* that have refused Profits and Pensions, have gone through the Disgrace and Loss of being dispossessed of Places and Preferments, and in a Word, suffered Persecution for the Cause of their Country in the highest Manner"; but patriotism is now nothing more than a sham employed by dishonest men for their own preferment (p. 30). Harley's trial has failed to prove him either guilty or innocent, but it has raised him through suffering to the company of Old Whigs who were "insulted, disgraced, imprisoned, expelled, and in the highest Degree the Power of their Enemies were able to shew it, trampled upon for their Country," while it has revealed the opportunism of his accusers. It is noteworthy that, while the Walpolean Whigs bear the brunt of

Defoe's indignation, his pamphlet is not slanted in favor of the Sunderland Whigs, nor the Tories; Defoe's bleak conclusion is that it is no longer possible to be both a courtier and an honest man.

The evenhandedness of Defoe's assault on modern courtiers in *Old Whig and Modern Whig*, together with its unusually passionate and emotional tone, make the book particularly significant as an index to Defoe's personal feelings about the political state of the nation. Though it is always risky to regard any of Defoe's writings as expressions of personal feeling, it is even more difficult to see how *Old Whig and Modern Whig* could have served any purpose except as an outlet for Defoe's long pent-up frustrations over the efforts of the Walpolean and Sunderland Whigs alike to drag the names of Harley and Queen Anne through the mud. With Harley in retirement, Parliament in recess, and the king enjoying a temporary truce with the Prince and Princess of Wales at Hampton Court, there was little to be gained from any special interest by stirring up trouble.[11] *Old Whig and Modern Whig* is not propaganda, as his defenses of Townshend and Walpole may be considered to be, but rather proceeds out of that reforming and projecting strain in Defoe that had brought him to suggest two years earlier, in *The Fears of the Pretender Turned into the Fears of Debauchery,* a direct connection between the stability of the state and the condition of its morals. Defoe had called in that pamphlet for the suppression of playhouses as a means of buttressing the political state, betraying in the process his belief that political stability depended on moral restraint, and that morality was best served by those who learned to hold their passions in check. In 1717 and 1718, however, the major threat was not the playhouses, but the passions and ambitions of the Whigs, and it was this kind of immorality that Defoe sought to condemn in *Old Whig and Modern Whig*. He was to pursue this strain for two years through various rhetorical modes, including the semifictional *Memoirs of . . . the Duke of Shrewsbury,* and the entirely fictional *Life and Strange Surprizing Adventures of Robinson Crusoe*.

2. Shrewsbury and the Pursuit of Virtue

The death of Charles Talbot, duke of Shrewsbury, early in 1718 gave Defoe an opportunity to contrast what he regarded

as the moral and political corruption of his times with the
character of a man who ranked second only to Harley as an
emblem of civic virtue.[12] In one respect, Shrewsbury exceeded
Harley as a model politician, since he seems to have had very
little ambition for his own interests. It was, Defoe suggests,
precisely because he was so reticent that Shrewsbury was
courted assiduously by all the parties and was retained as lord
chamberlain by James II, Anne, and George I. He was a close
associate of Harley through the last four years of Anne's reign,
which, together with his refusal to commit himself to the party
led by Walpole and Sunderland, caused the Whigs to pressure
George to dismiss him in 1715.[13] It was Shrewsbury to whom
Anne had entrusted the White Staff on her deathbed with the
approval of her privy councillors, no doubt because Shrewsbury was the only man among them with no commitments except to the Protestant succession. He was, according to
Geoffrey Holmes, one of those "Managers" peculiar to the period 1689–1714 for whom ideology was less important than the
reconciliation of opposing interests, a strategy that (as we have
seen) Defoe urged Harley to pursue up to 1714.[14] If Shrewsbury—and Harley—may be said to have had an ideology at all,
it was that subordination of the role of the courtier to the interests of the country that Defoe believed was so deficient in the
patriotism of a Walpole or a Sunderland.

Defoe's intent in writing Shrewsbury's *Memoirs,* as he tells us
in the preface, is not to give "a Compleat History" of the man's
life, but rather only to "communicate to the World several remarkable publick Transactions" in which Shrewsbury was prin-
cipally involved; it is for this reason that the book is "with a just
Propriety Entitled, Memoirs of his Life."[15] The author makes
no pretense at writing in the first person, or that he is editing a
manuscript written by Shrewsbury, or that he had a "Personal
Intimacy" with the man who is his subject; rather, the author
has had a "particular intimacy with the Business which
[Shrewsbury] has been employed in." The distinction between a
memoir and a history, together with the author's claim to be
able to judge the political significance of the events he is to
narrate, are important justifications of the selective perceptions
that the book makes of Shrewsbury's career. The narrator exercises this right, for example, midway through the *Memoirs* when
he declines to enter into the particulars of George I's reception
by the regents, "because he [Shrewsbury] acted in that Affair,
no otherwise than in Company with the rest of the Nobility

placed in that Commission" (p. 116). In other words, the writer of memoirs is interested in the extraordinary acts or circumstances that reveal the character of his subject. As Maximillian Novak has pointed out, this interest in "marvellous incidents" frequently makes memoirs worthless as history, especially when the subject is writing about himself.[16] But Defoe has specifically disavowed any historical intention in writing the book, and his admission that it was not written by Shrewsbury disqualifies it as a true "memoir"; in effect, Defoe stops just short of admitting that Shrewsbury's *Memoirs* are a fiction.

Yet, a form of fiction they indubitably are, and a very powerful one. The character of Shrewsbury is shown to have been developed by a series of childhood experiences that taught him the dangers of exposing oneself in causes, the first of which was the death of his father in a duel with the duke of Buckingham in 1667. In 1669, as the *Memoirs* tell us, the young earl of Shrewsbury converted from Catholicism to Protestantism upon the discovery of the Popish Plot; yet he "took care not to be so active in the other Extreme, as to mark himself out for the revenge of the Popish Party," should they return to power (p. 7). Though now a Protestant and a young Whig, he avoided becoming caught up either in Monmouth's Rebellion or the Rye-House Plot, and so came to the attention of James II, who sought to convert Shrewsbury to his interest. In a scene of remarkable subtlety, Defoe describes an incident in which "the King took him aside one Evening, and retiring with him into the Closet, made him several very kind Proposals of Service," among which, the author implies, was that of emissary to the Pope at Rome (p. 14). Shrewsbury declines these dangerous offers in so pleasing a way that the king made him lord chamberlain instead, and assumed that "he had thoroughly engaged him, and that he was now his own, and consequently, that any Drudgery might be imposed upon him" (p. 15). However, after surviving several more such trials, Shrewsbury informs the king that he plans to go on a voyage, and secretly conveys to William of Orange a list of eminent persons who have given their solemn engagements to assist him should he come over to England. This episode in the life of the young courtier is not merely a "strange surprising adventure" fit for a memoir; it is also a model of Old Whiggism, of playing the game of politics by effacing oneself and keeping always to the middle way until the moment arrives at which one can be of service to country and religion.

The successful conclusion of this venture established a pattern for Shrewsbury, according to which "he had the happiness to stand in the middle between two Parties" throughout the reigns of William and Anne (p. 109). His middle stance and his ability to conceal his own ends in negotiations made him acceptable to everyone except his sovereign's enemies, notably the French and the Junto Whigs. Defoe cites a letter from a French minister to a friend in the English court in which Shrewsbury is referred to as an "amphibious Creature," one who is "neither for us, or against us, but in short is good for nothing" (p. 95). Blithely ignoring Abel Boyer's charges in *The Political State of Great Britain* for June 1717 that Defoe's *Minutes of the Negotiations of Mons. Mesnager* was a forgery, Defoe inserted long passages from the *Minutes* into the *Memoirs* to provide further proof that the duke's "unshaken Resolution of entering into no Dangers, and of running no Hazards for any Party whatsoever . . . made him preserve the Distance between all Parties" and to be in the interest of none (pp. 94–95). Mesnager, for example, relates an incident in which the Abbot Gaultier requests Shrewsbury to propose to the queen that she should resign her crown to her brother while she still lived; the comment of the narrator of the *Memoirs* upon this tale of Mesnager's is that "the Duke was too penetrating, after all the cautions of the rest of his Life, to be drawn into such a Snare as that" (p. 80). The lesson learned in childhood and reinforced in youth thus becomes a guiding principle to the man, protecting him in his old age when he can call no one his friend. The tragedy of Shrewsbury's politics is that his self-denial and nonalignment, which have made him such a faithful servant to queen and country, have isolated him and left him exposed to his enemies upon the death of his sovereign—exactly as Defoe had represented the fall of Harley, and as he was to view the execution of Baron Goertz upon the death of Charles XII.[17]

Shrewsbury's tragedy was completed, and the political moral of his life was underscored, by the contrast between himself and his enemies. It was well for Shrewsbury, Defoe writes, that he had no ambition to hold on to the treasurer's staff for very long, because there was another "Gentleman . . . who no question designed to get it from the first hour of the Revolution, whoever he dispossessed of it" (p. 122). The identity of this gentleman is "Mr. Walpole, a Person he had no relish of" (p. 132). As in the history of Harley's fall, Walpole represents that spirit of party-interest and self-interest that infects the age;

Shrewsbury represents no interest or ideology, unless it is the country ideology of selfless patriotism. The difference between the two types is carried out in the manner in which the staff passed from Shrewsbury to Walpole: though Shrewsbury "had resolved and openly declared he would not load himself" with the burden of the treasury, and though he might have resigned the post with honor, knowing that Walpole was scheming to arrange his dismissal, the duke "said openly, *that tho' he resolved not to serve, yet he would not lay it down in any manner that should appear disrespectful to the King; no, tho' he were sure to have it taken from him in a manner disrespectful to himself*" (pp. 125–26). The contrast between Shrewsbury's dismissal and the manner in which Walpole had recently resigned the same office would have been very apparent to Defoe's readers; Defoe comments that Shrewsbury's conduct "was a piece of Self-denial, which I have seen few People practice" (p. 126).

The duplication of Harley's tragedy in Shrewsbury's seems to suggest that Defoe was not interested in praising these men merely as individuals, but rather in defining through them the Country ideology of selfless patriotism, and recommending that virtue as a remedy for factionalism and corruption. Shrewsbury's *Memoirs,* therefore, was an idealization of the man—an effort to make the man the emblem of an idea—and as such, owes more to fiction than to history. The consistency of Shrewsbury's behavior as a diplomat with the lessons of his youth; the secret conversations with kings and foreign agents; the use of letters and false documents to authenticate the story; the retrospective discoveries of concealed meanings and plots— all these are the devices of a novelist, even if the assembly of them does not make a novel.[18] It was not Defoe's intent in writing Shrewsbury's *Memoirs,* after all, to write a novel; he wanted to produce a document that would be acceptable as fact. But he also had a larger purpose in mind, which was to raise Shrewsbury to the company of saints and martyrs known as Old Whigs or Country politicians to which he had previously raised Harley, and in so doing to contrast them with the moral and political corruption of the modern age. The novelistic devices that Defoe used, besides considerably enhancing what other- wise would have been a rather dull tale, were indispensable to that goal. The unity of Shrewsbury's life, the tragic circum- stances of his fall, and the short but peaceful retirement in the country that he enjoyed before his death give Shrewsbury's story a pleasing and identifiable shape as they point the political moral that Defoe found in his life.

3. From Shrewsbury to Crusoe

The "darling Principle" of the duke of Shrewsbury's life was his "unaccountable aversion to engage too deep," which had the effect of "centring his Ambition in his present Station in the World" (pp. 118, 123). It is difficult to see why Defoe called Shrewsbury's "darling Principle" an "unaccountable" one, since Defoe had accounted for it so thoroughly in terms of youthful experience, unless he intended by that adjective to imply that Shrewsbury's aversion was a compulsion that exceeded his rational control. The duke's compulsive pursuit of his "Ease, and Safety" (p. 122) contrasts sharply with young Robinson Crusoe's compulsion to escape the middle station in life by going to sea; the duke, in fact, spends his whole life avoiding the kind of adventure to which Crusoe commits himself so heedlessly and recklessly. But it is a social, not a psychological contrast that Defoe intends by these mirror-image compulsions. As the eldest son of an earl, Shrewsbury's life-long study was only to preserve his virtue against the snares of the court; but the means of preserving one's present virtue was a lesson lost on readers who had not yet arrived at the station in life that, in an increasingly mobile society, they sensed was possible. If Defoe wished to dramatize the means by which a man could harness his passions and direct them towards right ends, he would have to do it through the life of one who had a compulsion, rather than an aversion, to "engage too deep."

Defoe's purpose in writing *Robinson Crusoe*, therefore, was to erect a new model of conduct and self-regulation, but his experiences of the past decade had brought him too far to allow him to write merely a glorified conduct manual. Defoe's fictional method, as we have seen, had matured in the course of writing the *Minutes of the Negotiations of Mons. Mesnager* and the *Memoirs of the Duke of Shrewsbury* to such an extent that it would have been a step backward for him *not* to write a novel at this point. His defense of the Harley ministry, as we have also seen, had led him to an interest not in the morality of specific acts, which is the domain of the writer of conduct manuals, but in the intentions behind those acts—the subjective domain of the

fiction writer. The defense of Harley had further brought
home to him the need for a liberal attitude toward offenses
committed in former times and the salutary effect of such an
attitude on those in need of reformation. The factionalism of
the Whigs, both in opposition to Harley and among themselves
when they came to power, seemed to call for a new model of
personal and political conduct with regard to one's sovereign
and the public good; and the idea of sovereignty, which could
no longer rest on the basis of divine right and which no longer
commanded the respect among the king's ministers that it once
had, itself needed reexamination. Defoe had treated all of these
issues separately in various pamphlets since Harley's fall; what
was needed now was a way of putting his ideas together into a
new moral system that would help to resolve the clash of men,
parties, creeds, and interests. To the degree, then, that *Robinson
Crusoe* was written to answer a specific reforming end, and to
arrive at this end by systematizing the ideas of nature, kingship,
providence, opportunity, and self-restraint into a coherent new
personality, the novel is a work of ideology as well as a work of
fiction.

This study is not the first, of course, to suggest that *Robinson
Crusoe* is a work of ideological significance, but it differs radically from some earlier studies in its conclusions about the nature of the ideological system that Defoe offered the world in
the novel. Manuel Schonhorn's recent essay, "Defoe: The Literature of Politics and the Politics of Some Fictions," for example,
presents the view that *Robinson Crusoe* is essentially "an examination of, even the necessity for, a unitary executive
sovereignty," that is, a monarchy.[19] Professor Schonhorn notes
that Defoe had an "uncomfortable relationship to the orthodox
Whiggish doctrines of his day," though he attributes this discomfort not to a disappointment in the failure of the Modern
Whigs to carry out the Revolution principles, but rather to
Defoe's "yet unarticulated rejection of the major premises and
arguments which were the standard ingredients of Revolution
rhetoric."[20] Finding in Defoe a "natural hostility to parliamentary government," based on his perception that a "society of
hastening complexity could never be regulated by the fragmented will of innumerable self-seeking individuals,"[21]
Schonhorn argues that Defoe's political growth was away from
the Lockean antimonarchicalism of his famous satire of 1706,
Jure Divino, and towards a readiness to accept the divine provi-

dence of royal authority. In Schonhorn's interpretation, Crusoe earns through military prowess the right to the title of monarch over his island, though both had been granted to him by Providence. His rescue of Friday, for example, recapitulates "that essential sequence in which the latent monarch actualizes the potential necessary for his role as communal leader."[22]

The preceding chapters of this study have demonstrated the accuracy of Professor Schonhorn's perception of discomfort— even hostility—between Defoe and the Whigs of the modern age, though they have suggested that it was the Whigs, rather than Defoe, who had given up on the Revolution principles. This study also concurs with Schonhorn's observation that *Robinson Crusoe* was occasioned by Defoe's alarm over the difficulty of regulating a society of self-seeking individuals in an increasingly complex culture. The difference between this study and Schonhorn's is over how Defoe proposed to accomplish this end: whether through a return to the monarchy as God's instrument for achieving ideological unity among men, or through the propagation of an ideology that stressed the virtues of moderation, reserve, self-restraint, and dependence on the counsel of knowledgeable advisors. Several proofs may be examined in turn in order to demonstrate that Defoe intended to replace the idea of absolute monarchy with a political state composed of moderate men. These proofs include the limited and precarious nature of the "sovereignty" that Crusoe possesses on his island; his ultimate dissatisfaction with that state, expressed in his desire to escape; his reliance on Friday, and later on the old Portuguese, as his "pilots" or counselors; and the gradual perfection of his moral knowledge until he knows—very late in life, as Shrewsbury had known very early— that a man's proper business was to venture only where both ease and safety were assured.

4. Crusoe's Voyage of Self-Discovery

Crusoe's first fifteen years on the island are spent in solitude. It is the absence of any human society, rather than his own military or political prowess, that makes him the absolute master of the island. He arrives at this mastery by degrees, which mark the stages of his spiritual growth. Time and necessity, he tells us, taught him to reacquire those arts and skills that had been fragmented, in the European culture out of which he came, into various crafts and classes. By observation, error, and experiment, he becomes a "compleat natural Mechanick" capable of making a shovel as well as using it, or designing supports for the roof of his cave so that it does not fall down on his head.[23] His mastery of his natural environment is an outward sign of his mastery of himself, which he acquires through the discovery of his human limitations. This discovery is often painful, as he attests in his account of the labor wasted on the boat that he is unable to bring to the water, or in his initial miscalculation of the size of the enclosure he should make to keep his goats; but the effect of these self-discoveries is to make him eligible to receive the "secret Intimations of Providence" that come in the form of "pressings of my Mind" (1:203). The accidental growth of the barley outside his dwelling is the first incident which suggests to him that Providence directs his salvation. His recovery from illness is another, but both of these incidents would be worthless without his reflection upon them and his discovery through them that he holds his absolute dominion on the island at the sufferance of God. His sovereignty is not given to him by divine right, but rather as a mark of God's mercy to him after he has reflected on his misspent life and repented of it. The station of relative ease and safety that he enters towards the end of these fifteen years allows him to consider himself "the Prince and Lord of the whole Island" (1:171), but the analogy between himself and a monarch is a false one, since his authority is neither absolute nor irrevocable.

There are several limitations to Crusoe's authority as a monarch. Crusoe encounters the first of these at the end of his first year on the island. Having established both a coastal and a country residence—thus reconciling in himself the clash of interests between the mercantile seaport towns and the landed country estates of that other island that looms behind Crusoe's story—he admits that he has arrived at a station in which "it was possible for me to be more happy . . . than it was probable I should ever have been in any other Particular State in the World" (1:131). Yet he cannot bring himself to thank God for it, since he knows he would leave the island if he could. This dissatisfaction with his state causes him to sail out in his small canoe in an effort to extend his dominions by visiting the other side of the island. Like a "rash and ignorant Pilot," he enters a current that sweeps him out to sea, by which he discovered "how easy it was for the Providence of God to make the most miserable Condition Mankind could be in *worse*" (1:160–61). Eventually a breeze from SSE, which Schonhorn has remarked is the same wind that brought William III to the shores of England,[24] returns Crusoe to his island; he comes, however, not in triumph, but rather more like one who has just learned the "darling Principle" that guided Shrewsbury's life—that is, that the pursuit of ease and safety, not new dominions, is man's proper business. When next he goes sailing, Crusoe avoids any hazardous voyages, "nor scarce ever above a Stone's Cast or two from the Shore" would he go, "I was so apprehensive of being hurryed out of my Knowledge again by the Currents, or Winds, or any other Accident" (1:171). Crusoe's acceptance of his limitations perfects his harmonious relations with nature and with God, allowing him to fancy himself a king over his dog, his cats, and his parrot; but his sovereignty is predicated on his acceptance of the station appointed for him by God. When he relapses into his former moral condition, as he repeatedly does, he discovers again how limited his sovereignty really is.

The necessity of moderating not only his desire for new dominions, but also for other forms of accumulation, is stressed repeatedly in the novel. It is this branch of his moral education that has led readers to see Crusoe as a new "economic man," but such a reading obscures the fact that the lessons Crusoe learns are not primarily economic. What Crusoe learns is that, just as he may not exceed the limits of his geographic knowledge without jeopardizing his ease and safety, so he should not accumulate food or wealth beyond what is wanted to satisfy immediate needs. There is no reason for surplus accumulation because there is no division of interests; Crusoe may, if he pleases, call himself "King, or Emperor over the whole Country which I had Possession of. There were no Rivals. I had no Competitor, none to dispute Sovereignty or Command with me" (1:148). Where divisions of interest do not exist, there is neither money nor striving after places; it is not money, but the clash of interests that is the root of social disruption and moral degeneration. Crusoe addresses the lesson to "those discontented People . . . who cannot enjoy comfortably what God has given them: All our Discontents about what we have, appeared to me, to spring from the Want of Thankfulness for what we have" (1:150). Defoe was not, of course, suggesting the abolition of money in the English economy, though that "Drug" symbolized for him the surplus accumulation of value; he was, rather, suggesting that some of the pleasures of sovereignty over oneself would fall to those who sought to accumulate value only for the satisfaction of real needs, and thus avoided contributing to the clash of interests. The point of Crusoe's discoveries in economics, therefore, is not to support a particular theory of value, but to present in a new way the virtue of moderation and self-restraint.

The precarious nature of Crusoe's political and economic sovereignty, and the threat posed to it by a competing interest, is brought home to him by his discovery of the footprint in the sand. The footprint is a contradiction to his sovereignty and thus to all the harmony he has enjoyed; by injecting the suggestion of another's interest in the island, it makes Crusoe's dominance questionable, and necessitates all the cultural formations that follow from a division of interests, including surplus accumulation, military fortifications, and private property (1:186–92). Crusoe's first thought, which is to reestablish his absolute authority on the island through an act of war, is rejected on the grounds that it does not proceed from the consideration of what is most likely to result in his own ease and safety, but rather from motives of fear and revenge; his second strategy, "to conceal my self from them, and not to leave the least Signal to them to guess by, that there were any living Creatures upon the Island," more nearly accords with Shrewsbury's darling principle (1:200). The fact that "Religion joined in with this Prudential" seems to be a pleasing, but not altogether essential, consideration.

Crusoe lives some eight years under the threat of external invasion, from his fifteenth year to his twenty-third on the island, before the discovery of a cannibalistic feast taking place on his side of the island determines him to change the condition of life in which he now lives (1:208–14). The duration of time in which Crusoe lives in dread of being invaded is roughly equivalent to the time in which England lay in anxiety over the threat posed by the Pretender, from the trial of Sacheverell to the writing of *Robinson Crusoe,* but Defoe's intent could probably be described more accurately as phenomenological rather than allegorical: that is, he wished to suggest a span of time long enough to erase utterly the sense of sovereignty and security Crusoe had enjoyed when he had thought that his

dominion on the island was absolute. This new discovery over-
comes the lesson he had learned as a result of his nearly disastrous venture in his small boat, which was to be satisfied with
the condition that had been given to him, and prompts him
once again to attempt an escape. Knowing that he cannot escape alone, he works up the courage to visit the ship that is
wrecked on the rocks to the south of his island, amidst those
same currents that had almost swept him out to sea. This
episode, which otherwise seems to intrude in the narrative of
his plans to escape, shows his determination to rescue a companion for his contemplated voyage, while it marks the degree
to which he has overcome his aversion to venturing into waters
of which he has no knowledge. Crusoe's expedition to the
wrecked ship is the sort of "incident" that critics have charged is
the mainstay of Defoe's fictional method, but in fact the expedition is central, rather than incidental, to the book's moral intention.[25]

Crusoe hovers for some hours on the verge of committing
himself to this adventure. On the one hand, there is the possibility of being swept out to sea and losing the island that has
been given to him by Providence for his deliverance; on the
other, there is the chance of rescuing from the wreck a companion whose Christian conversation would be a comfort and
whose assistance might allow Crusoe to escape from the island.
Aruging against making the attempt is the miserable fate of the
sailors of the ship before him and of his own ship before that,
of which "not one Life [had been] spared but mine"; his deliverance out of so many others teaches him that "it is very rare
that the Providence of God casts us into any Condition of Life
so low, or any Misery so great, but we may see others in worse
Circumstances than our own" (1:217). Yet his thankfulness is
balanced by the "secret moving Springs in the Affection" which
impress upon him the possibility that someone may be alive
aboard the wreck, and, concluding that "the Impression was so
strong upon my Mind, that it could not be resisted, that it must
come from some invisible Direction, and that I should be wanting to my self if I did not go," Crusoe resolves to make the
attempt (1:219). Defoe thus suggests an antithesis in Crusoe's
psychological composition between his religious thankfulness,
which exerts a conservative influence, and his imagination,
which causes such "violent eager embracings" of the imagined
object "that the Absence of it is insupportable" (1:218). Crusoe

is drawn by his imagination toward objects that have a mental, but not visible reality. This compulsion to obey the promptings of his imagination is both dangerous and apparently ir-religious, but it makes Crusoe a more complete psychological study than the unimaginative duke of Shrewsbury, and a more apt subject for the moral focus of the novel: that is, when one may hazard an adventure and when one may not. In Shrews-bury's *Memoirs,* the answer was automatic: only when ease and safety were assured. In *Robinson Crusoe,* however, as this episode suggests, Crusoe's compulsion to follow his imagina-tion balances his aversion to the consequences of engaging too deeply. The dilemma reaches a crisis as Crusoe paddles along the shore and arrives at the very end of the island, where he is "to launch out into the Ocean, and either to venture, or not to venture" (1:220). Rather than committing himself to either ex-treme, however, Crusoe beaches his boat and sits down on a low rise of ground, "very pensive and anxious, between Fear and Desire about my Voyage." In this state of suspended judgment, he observes that the currents are controlled by the tides, and so their movements are predictable. This knowledge allows him to make a safe and easy voyage out to the ship early the next morning. By such incidents, Crusoe learns—though only very gradually, painfully, and imperfectly—the value of the "darling Principle" that Shrewsbury adopted in the first years of his adult political life; but because the novel depicts the process through which this moral sensibility is learned, rather than merely reflecting the advantages of a life lived according to a principle known from youth, *Robinson Crusoe* is much more satisfying than the *Memoirs,* both dramatically and as a psycho-logical portrait.

This balance between prudence and perseverence also marks Crusoe's rescue of Friday, to which he is prompted not by the evangelizing motives that have been attributed to him,[26] nor by a desire to ratify his status as a sovereign by obtaining a sub-ject,[27] but rather by his hopes of escaping from the uncomfort-ably limited and anxiety-ridden state into which he has fallen. In the dream that precedes his rescue of Friday, Crusoe tells himself that, having saved one of the cannibals, "now I may certainly venture to the main Land; for this Fellow will serve me as a Pilot, and will tell me . . . what Places to venture into, and what to escape" (1:230). Upon awakening, he is dejected to find it no more than a dream; yet the dream has shown him that the "only Way to go about an Attempt for an Escape, was, if possible, to get a Savage into my Possession" (1:231). Crusoe's new prudence has taught him that he must have a pilot to secure his deliverance, but he continues to mistake what he is to be delivered *from*: it is not the island, but his own immoderate desires and ambitions that are the source of his troubles. Even after he has rescued Friday and taught him English, so that a miniature state of society exists between them, Crusoe's hope continues to be that "one Time or other, I might find an Opportunity to make my Escape from this Place; and that this poor Savage might be a Means to help me to do it" (1:250). Friday does pilot Crusoe to his deliverance, though not in the manner Crusoe expects; it is through Crusoe's instruction of Friday in the principles of religion and submission to authority that Crusoe himself becomes a master of these principles, thereby bringing him into a way of obtaining his deliverance in a manner that accords with the design of Providence. Friday's function in the book is thus to make Crusoe neither a priest or a king, but rather to make him master of himself.

Though Friday pilots Crusoe to a knowledge of the first principles of prudence and moderation, he cannot help him perfect that knowledge. That perfection is the major subject of the sequel to the *Strange Surprizing Adventures,* entitled *The Farther Adventures of Robinson Crusoe.* The process begins with a Roman Catholic—yet strangely ecumenical—priest who helps Crusoe establish his colony upon a footing of morality and law. Concealing his specific religious affiliations to avoid sowing divisions among the colonists, the priest regularizes the marriages that have taken place and assists Crusoe in the reformation of the former mutineer Will Atkins, who thereafter becomes Crusoe's overseer among the English colonists and distributes the property in so just a manner that no grounds for complaint exist. No government is established, except for the rules the colonists wish to give themselves, and a general promise to Crusoe that they will "live in Love and good Neighborhood with one another" (3:59). The plain implication of Crusoe's failure to delegate any unitary authority over the several settlements on the island is that he does not think any is needed. He declares the island "a kind of Commonwealth" and prepares to abandon it, reserving to himself only the unoccupied land and a share of the rents after eleven years. Crusoe himself admits—retrospectively—that for him to have remained on the island as its governor would have been to act "like a Man of common sense," and he rebukes himself with having behaved "in a kind of haughty majestick Way, like an old Patriarchal Monarch" (3:80). but these reflections on his conduct are not endorsements of the idea of monarchy; they are reproaches directed at his failure to conquer the "impetuous Desire . . . to wander into the World" he had had from a youth (3:81). Had Crusoe remained on the island, the book might have become an investigation of "the subtle influences of culture, custom, precedents—the unconscious conditioners of political order" that Schonhorn has suggested did not interest Defoe.[28] An alternative explanation, however, is that it was monarchy that did not interest Defoe, and that having established religion and property rights on his island and guarded against the "Seeds of Division" (3:69) as much as possible, he reinvoked Crusoe's wandering compulsion in order to progress toward the book's real goal. For Defoe, the historical evolution of man and society did not end with the attainment of monarchy; there was still a further level of social and moral order for Crusoe to discover.

5. Crusoe as a Model for Mankind

The loss of Crusoe's "pilot," Friday, while on his last visit to his island colony, leaves Crusoe with no guide but himself through the moral wilderness of the world, but the scope of the world that Crusoe now has before him exceeds even Friday's knowledge, and so his services, though once highly valued, are not missed. With Friday's help, Crusoe has learned for himself how to judge when to venture and when not to venture, which is the real crux of his moral sensibility. How well he has learned to moderate his adventurism is suggested by his conduct during the massacre of the people of an Indian village by the crew of the vessel on which he is a passenger. An initial skirmish with these East Indians has resulted in the loss of one of the ship's crew, who disappeared in an attempt to molest one of the native women. Crusoe "could not satisfie my self . . . without venturing on Shore" to see if he can find the man; but when he is convinced that the man is lost and that a more than equal loss has been imposed on the natives, he proposes a return to the ship (3:88–89). The boatswain and his party, however, reject both Crusoe's proposal and his authority over them and make

their way to the Indian village. The discovery of the missing
seaman, who has been killed and hung by his arm, sets them
"on fire with Revenge, and made Devils of them all" (3:91).
Unable himself to restrain the men, Crusoe argues with the
ship's captain to stop them, on the grounds that the adventure
endangers the security of the ship and the interest of its owners
and merchants. The captain, however, as he later admits, "was
not Master of himself, neither could he govern his Passion,"
and neglects his duty as commander of the ship to join the
carnage himself (3:100). The incident clearly reveals the need
for the kind of authority that Schonhorn has called a "unitary
executive sovereignty," but not necessarily of the monarchical
sort. Political authority—in the form of the captain—is itself
overcome by passion and is unable to keep the situation in
hand. What is needed is moral authority in the form that
Crusoe suggests—that is, deference to the collective interests of
the voyage, represented in this case by the investments of the
shipowners and the merchants who laded her. Had the ship's
crew and captain respected the trading purposes of the voyage,
the massacre would not have happened, and the balance of the
voyage would have passed in ease and safety, instead of in the
several disasters and mutiny that follow.

It is tempting to conclude, on the basis of this incident, that
Defoe is suggesting that trade is itself a moral order with inher-
ently peaceful and humanitarian values, which if pursued
within the limits set by Providence and self-restraint will bring
us to a higher level of civilization that the pursuit of purely
personal or factional interests could possibly do. This impression is heightened by Crusoe's discovery of a new "pilot" in his
English merchant companion, whose "Wisdom" it was "to stick
to that as the best Thing for him, which he is like to get the most
Money by," and who was content to go "like a Carrier's Horse,
always to the same Inn, backward and forward, provided he
could, as he called it, *find his Account in it*" (3:111). The still-
imperfect state of Crusoe's knowledge prevents him from immediately accepting this wisdom as his own, and he joins this
merchant more for the adventure than the profit; yet, after a
few voyages he tells his new partner that "I begin to be a Convert to the Principles of Merchandizing," and warns him that he
will pursue it not like a draught horse, but eagerly and tire-
lessly, once he has conquered his "backwardness" (3:112). Were
this the conclusion of the novel, it might seem that Defoe's

ideological purpose was to reconcile the clash of interests between landed and moneyed men, merchants and manufacturers, or domestic and international traders by creating in Crusoe
a larger-than-life figure who absorbs all these interests in himself and subordinates them to the interest of the collective en-
terprise, just as Defoe had attempted to describe Shrewsbury
and Harley as emblems of the Country interest that reconciled
and moderated the clash of political factions. Given the fact
that the English merchant represents a specific interest, however—the emerging commercial interest, which threatens to
displace the established interests with which it competes—
Defoe cannot and does not allow Crusoe entirely to come under
the English merchant's sway. To do so would be to make the
novel no more than a disguised appeal for the ideological
hegemony of the commercial class, which was evidently not
Defoe's intention.

Readers who are familiar only with the first volume of
Robinson Crusoe frequently do not find any moral order proposed in the novel, or if they do, they find it in that very pro-
pensity to wander that Crusoe so ineffectively laments.
According to this reading, Crusoe's wandering compulsion is
the secret motor behind his accomplishments in the world, a
secret that his own precapitalist consciousness seems unable to
appreciate. But as Paul Alkon has recently reminded us,
Crusoe's narrative must be understood "from the perspective
of the end without forming any decisive judgment of character
until arriving at the last moment," which means, in effect, until
the completion of Crusoe's saga in the *Farther Adventures*.[29] It is
true that Crusoe's compulsion to wander has kept the novel
going and has forced Crusoe to recapitulate the stages of human and societal evolution, but his knowledge is not perfected
until he learns to subdue that compulsion. He conquers it
amidst the wastes of Siberia, where he is guided, now by his
"old Portuguese Pilot" (3:214), into the company of an exiled
minister of state from the Russian court. Crusoe lets the old
courtier know that, as sovereign of the island, he had enjoyed
greater authority than the czar, since he had "not one Person
disaffected to my Government, or to my Person, in all my
Dominions." The courtier surprises Crusoe by telling him that
"the true Greatness of Life was to be Master of our selves," that
"he found more Felicity in the Retirement he seemed to be
banished to there, than ever he found in the highest Authority

he enjoyed in the Court of his Master the Czar," and that he was happier in his exile than his enemies who possessed his former wealth and power, because "those things chiefly gratified the coarsest of our Affections, such as our Ambition, our particular Pride, our Avarice, our Vanity, and our Sensuality" (3:200–201). Not doubting the sincerity of the courtier's words, Crusoe admits that the old man is a greater sovereign than he, "for he that has got a Victory over his own exorbitant Desires, and has the absolute Dominion over himself, whose Reason entirely governs his Will, is certainly greater than he that conquers a City" (3:202). Yet, though Crusoe does not doubt the courtier's sincerity, he tests his conviction by offering to assist him in an escape from exile, much as he had once wanted Friday's assistance to help him escape from the island. Though greatly tempted, the old man rejects the offer on the grounds that, should he return to court, "all the Seeds of Pride, Ambition, Avarice and Luxury, which I know remain in Nature, may revive and take Root," while if he stays, he shall be "an honest Man still, though not a free Man" (3:208–9). The world-renouncing example of this old courtier, whose exile strongly resembles that of Harley and Shrewsbury and whose opinion of the honesty of courtiers resembles Defoe's in *Old Whig and Modern Whig Revived,* guides Crusoe to his knowledge of "the Value of Retirement, and the Blessing of ending our Days in Peace" (3:220), a perspective which, as Alkon has said, conditions the interpretation of the entire book.

Crusoe's compulsion to wander, his individualism, his temporary and illusory monarchy, even his success as a trader—none of these are the ultimate subject of the book. Defoe sought to develop in Crusoe a model of moral restraint that included in itself elements of all social classes, from the mechanic to the monarch, from the country gentleman to the merchant adventurer. It was his purpose to show that the passions awakened by new opportunities for wealth and advancement could be tolerated and encouraged, as long as ambition and adventurism were moderated by self-restraint and the dictates of experience. The restraint had to be self-imposed, or else it would merely be the domination of one interest by another and lead to more strife. If this self-restraint, this pursuit of ease and safety, came as early in life as it had come to the duke of Shrewsbury, then one could hope to live a moderately successful life without sacrificing one's honesty; if it had been adopted by the culture generally during Shrewsbury's lifetime, then the clashes of interest over the Treaty of Commerce, over the succession, over the division of power in the Whig party in 1717, or over the prosecution of Harley would not have happened, and the country would have been spared these political crises. Since, as Crusoe's life attests, it does not come so easily to everyone, then Defoe offers it as a perspective that comes to Crusoe at the end of his life, and colors his recollection of his own history. Like death, it reveals the vanity of life; but unlike death, it also suggests a way to live so as to avoid the worst effects of ambition, pride, and folly. To ministers of state, as well as ministers of the church, it suggests that moderation and toleration are the only honest forms of service. Under the historical circumstances, this advocacy of restraint and moderation might in practice have served the emerging commercial interests more than those that were struggling to retain their dominance. It was not, however, Defoe's purpose to advocate the ideological supremacy of any one component of his culture, but rather to provide them with a model of how their competing claims might be reconciled one with another, and of the benefits that would result from doing so.

Notes

1. Ian Watt, *The Rise of the Novel* (London: Chatto and Windus, 1957); Maximillian Novak, *Defoe and the Nature of Man* (London: Oxford University Press, 1963); G. A. Starr, *Defoe and Spiritual Autobiography* (Princeton, N. J.: Princeton University Press, 1965); J. Paul Hunter, *The Reluctant Pilgrim* (Baltimore, Md.: Johns Hopkins Press, 1966).

2. James Sutherland, *Defoe: A Biography* (Philadelphia: Lippincott, 1938), pp. 227–28; John Robert Moore, *Daniel Defoe, Citizen of the Modern World* (Chicago: University of Chicago Press, 1958), pp. 223–24.

3. Maximillian Novak, "Defoe's Theory of Fiction," *Studies in Philology* 61 (1964): 63, 67.

4. Isaac Kramnick, *Bolingbroke and his Circle* (Cambridge, Mass.: Harvard University Press, 1968), pp. 188–89.

5. Paul Alkon, *Defoe and Fictional Time* (Athens: University of Georgia Press, 1979), p. 43.

6. John Richetti, *Defoe's Narratives* (London: Oxford University Press, 1975), pp. 14–15.

7. Maximillian Novak, *Economics and the Fiction of Daniel Defoe* (New York: Russell and Russell, 1962), p. 32; Starr, *Defoe and Spiritual Autobiography*, p. 81.

8. Kramnick, *Bolingbroke*, p. 189.

9. J. H. Plumb, *Sir Robert Walpole* (Boston: Houghton Mifflin, 1956), 1:248–49.

10. The quarrel between father and son to which Defoe alludes may well be the one between George I and the Prince of Wales in 1717; he was to use it again as a paradigm of social disorder in *The Family Instructor* (1718) and, of course, in *Robinson Crusoe*.

11. J. A. Downie, *Robert Harley and the Press* (Cambridge: At the University Press, 1979), p. 189; Romney Sedgwick, *The House of Commons, 1715–1754* (London: History of Parliament Trust, 1970), 1:132; Ragnhild Hatton, *George I, Elector and King* (Cambridge, Mass.: Harvard University Press, 1978), pp. 204–5.

12. Defoe's account of Shrewsbury's life is in large measure supported by Dorothy H. Somerville, *The King of Hearts* (London: George Allen & Unwin, 1962). See also Dennis Rubini, *Court and Country 1688–1702* (London: Rupert Hart-Davis, 1967), pp. 21–22.

13. Hatton, *George I*, p. 179.

14. Geoffrey Holmes, *British Politics in the Age of Anne* (London: MacMillan, 1967), pp. 189–92. See also G. H. Healey, *The Letters of Daniel Defoe* (London: Oxford University Press, 1955), pp. 29–39.

15. Daniel Defoe, *Memoirs of Publick Transactions in the Life and Ministry of his Grace the Duke of Shrewsbury* (London; 1718), pp. i–ii.

16. For a fuller discussion of Defoe's use of memoirs, see Novak, "Defoe's Theory of Fiction," pp. 656–58.

17. Daniel Defoe, *The Secret History of the White Staff*, Parts I and II (1714); Part III (1715); *Some Account of the Life, and most remarkable Actions, of George Henry Baron de Goertz* (London, 1719).

18. For a definition of the novel as "false document" and a discussion of *Robinson Crusoe* as "this first of the great false documents in English," see E. L. Doctorow, "False Documents," in *American Review, No. 26*, ed. Theodore Solataroff (New York: Bantam Books, 1977), pp. 215–32. Doctorow perhaps relies too heavily on the Selkirk story as the source of *Robinson Crusoe*, but shows how, through false documents, "it was possible for fiction to give counsel."

19. Manuel Schonhorn, "Defoe: The Literature of Politics and the Politics of Some Fictions," in *English Literature in the Age of Disguise*, ed. Maximillian Novak (Berkeley: University of California Press, 1977), p. 22.

20. Ibid., pp. 17–18.

21. Ibid., p. 22.

22. Ibid., p. 35.

23. *The Life and Strange Surprizing Adventures of Robinson Crusoe of York, Mariner, and The Farther Adventures of Robinson Crusoe*. The Shakespeare Head Edition, 3 Vols. (Oxford, 1927), 1:82–85. Subsequent references in the text are to this edition.

24. Schonhorn, "Defoe," p. 32.

25. Michael Shugrue, *Journal of English and Germanic Philology* 62 (1963): 403–5, cited with approval by Hunter, *The Reluctant Pilgrim*, p. 6n.

26. Starr, *Defoe and Spiritual Autobiography*, pp. 12–21.

27. Schonhorn, "Defoe," p. 37.

28. Ibid., p. 48.

29. Alkon, *Defoe and Fictional Time*, p. 89.

Epilogue

Of all the many criticisms to which Defoe's writing is vulnerable, the one whch has probably done the most damage is the allegation that Defoe did not believe in what he himself wrote—that he was a propagandist with great powers of persuasion, but with little concern for the truth. In some critical accounts, this failing has been converted into the secret of his success as a maker of fictions: his excellence as a liar is supposed to have qualified him to found the tradition of the English novel. Such praise tends to eviscerate not only Defoe's reputation, but the validity of fiction itself, while it brings us no closer to understanding the kind of knowledge that Defoe believed fiction to be and the uses to which he tried to put it.

The problem is complicated by the fact that, to a certain extent, Defoe *was* a propagandist. Alan Downie, reviewing the roots of the Defoe-Harley relationship, has shown that in 1702 Harley specifically sought "some discreet writer of the government's side . . . to state facts right," and thus to counter the impositions upon the public of "ill-designing men."[1] This search led to the founding of Defoe's *Review*, which Downie describes as the first "full-time propaganda weapon" in the struggle for popular opinion. For the best part of the next twenty years, Defoe was to be engaged in propagating the viewpoint of one ministry or another. The fact that he was a propagandist, however, does not preclude his also being an ideologist, and it is this second vocation that is much more important to his development as a maker of fictions.

As Downie uses the term, *propaganda* in Harley's ministry was exclusively a form of action, not of knowledge. Harley "used propaganda positively to explain government policy to MPs and to the political nation. The aim was to achieve policy objectives," or to discredit the propaganda of the opposition; it was

172

never Harley's intention to create a system of belief or of knowledge for its own sake.[2] But Defoe's reason for serving Harley—as this study has attempted to point out—was not merely to preserve Harley against his enemies or to attain Harley's policy objectives, but to reconcile the clashes of interest among the various cultural and political formations that were struggling for dominance from the Revolution to the emergence of Walpole's ministry in 1722. The focus of Defoe's "propaganda" was not Harley himself or his ministry, but rather the idea of a peaceable kingdom free from internal divisions, and thus secure from external threats; Harley was nothing more than the best candidate to bring about such a reconciliation, and, after his fall, a suitable emblem of the idea for which he stood in Defoe's mind. While Harley may have had no loftier aspirations than to advance himself and his ministry through the use of propaganda, his propagandist Defoe seems to have believed that he had been chosen to develop a complete moral system that, by teaching through examples the value of reflection and self-restraint, would help to eliminate the factionalism and partisanship which marked the politics of his own times. The fact that this moral system reached fruition long after Harley's fall—notably in the *Memoirs of the Duke of Shrewsbury* and *Robinson Crusoe*—indicates strongly that Defoe was more interested in creating a way of knowing the world through his writing than in protecting the career of an individual politician.

Of course, many writers have created ways of knowing the world without becoming ideologists. Defoe's work, however, is ideological in the sense defined by Gramsci and Williams—that is, by describing a moral and political order that resolved contradictions in the dominant class, Defoe helped create the conditions for a hegemonic culture that was the basis for the long Whig and Hanoverian supremacy. The moral and political order that Defoe described did not yet exist, but was merely projected in his work; the reality that he described was neither historical nor fictional, but a potential reality that he sought to bring into existence. Defoe subordinated both fiction and history to this ideological intention, which he regarded as legitimating whatever liberties he had to take with historical or literary probability. The preeminence of a correct ideological intention and its capacity to legitimate a fiction are revealed by an incident that occurs in the first volume of *Robinson Crusoe*.

The English captain whose ship has been taken over by mutineers enlists the aid of Crusoe's party in the capture of Will Atkins and some of the mutinous sailors. Their repentance of their crime is perfected by a ruse employed by the captain: he informs the men that the "Governour" of the island, who has remained out of sight, has them in his absolute power and may choose to hang them on the spot or to send them back to England to be hung. "Though this was all a Fiction of his own," remarks Crusoe in his narrative, "yet it had its desired Effect" in that it restored the captain to his rightful supremacy and obtained the sincere penitence of the rebels (1:62). Crusoe's authority, both over the island and over the lives of the men, is fictitious, because it has never been ratified by any higher power; yet its effect is terrifying, largely because it is invisible. The captain's invocation of an unseen governor's power puts the men in mind of the natural or ideal order of things, which they themselves recognize to be just, though the governor's power itself is a fiction.

In such ways, *Robinson Crusoe* advances a theory of moral knowledge and behavior that makes it more than mere propaganda for Whiggism, or even for the dominant class as presently constituted. Though the book may in fact have been of greater assistance to the emergent elements of English culture than to the residual ones, it was based on ideas of personal conduct and social organization that Defoe considered to be valid in themselves, and that he intended should be applied universally. However much one might agree with Marx's criticism that no system of ideas could be universally valid apart from its historical and social context, it is nevertheless certain that Defoe had these ambitions for his work, that these ambitions raised his work above the level of mere propaganda, and that his desire to project a system of moral and political order in *Robinson Crusoe* explains his choice of fiction as the vehicle for this ideology, despite his misgivings about the acceptability of fiction as a form of knowledge.

If Defoe's claim for the validity of his fictions rests on their subordination to an ideological intention, which is itself valid, then the final proof of the worth of his work depends not on the validity of the idea of fiction itself, but on the validity of ideology as a form of knowledge. During the course of this study, two different claims for the validity of ideology as a form of knowledge have been advanced. One is Gramsci's "psycho-

logical" validity—that is, that certain ideas which are "historically organic" and "necessary to a given structure" will appear
to be valid, and a system of thought which arranges them into a
workable order is likely to become hegemonic. By thus removing ideology from the realm of universal and timeless truth to
the psychological dimension of what men believe is historically
necessary at a given time, Gramsci provides a way in which an
ideology can be valid at a specific historical time and place.
Within this limited context, ideologies can be used to attain
historically necessary ends, without thereby reducing them to
mere propaganda. Such a historically necessary end, it may be
argued, was the reconciliation of the clashes of interest among
the factions of the dominant class in England in the early eighteenth century.

The second claim for the validity of fiction as a form of
knowledge lies in Defoe's efforts to bring order out of chaotic
phenomena by the use of what Paul Alkon has called "the perspective of the end."[3] The "end" that Alkon refers to is not only
the teleological end of history, but also the end of fictional time.
Defoe chose to write his fictions from the end of time, looking
back at events whose meaning had been invisible or ambiguous
to his narrator, because this method gave him the opportunity
to review those moments as secret "hints" of a moral order or
Providence existing outside time. Crusoe's frequent reflections
on his own conduct ("whenever I found those secret Hints, or
pressings of my Mind, to doing, or not doing any Thing that
presented . . . I never failed to obey the secret Dictate . . .
besides many Occasions which it is very likely I might have
taken Notice of, if I had seen with the same Eyes then, that I
saw with now." 1:203) are the best-known instances of Defoe's
use of this method, but the embittered reflections of the Jacobite narrator of *A True Account of the Proceedings at Perth* or the
exposure of a conspiracy against Harley made by the historian
of the White Staff are no less important in their discovery of a
moral end in historical events. To the degree that *A True Account* helped sustain the climate of emergency, it encouraged
passage of the Septennial Act and thus might be considered
propaganda; but in a larger sense, by attributing cowardly and
anti-British actions to the Jacobite leaders, it undermined the
association between the Stuart cause and the ideas of heroism
and divine right that were its ideological basis. Similarly, the
defeat of the Pretender's forces at Preston was not merely the

176 DEFOE AND THE IDEA OF FICTION

victory of a large and well-fed army over a smaller and more
desperate band of men, but an emblem of the rightness of the
Hanoverian claim to the throne, an imperative encoded in history that would remain whether the Septennial Act passed or
not. The knowledge that history is governed by preordained
ends which man can discover, but not modify, discourages the
pursuit of personal ambition and reconciles clashes of interest.

The validity of Defoe's fiction for its own time, therefore, was
twofold: in expressing ideas that men believed to be true in
themselves and necessary to their condition, it achieved a psychological validity; and in reconciling the Old Whig and Country values with the urge to venture that belonged to the
emergent culture, it achieved a historical validity. To the extent
that the beliefs and cultural needs that gave rise to the fictions
still exist, the fictions retain their validity. It is true that to make
these contributions to the ideological hegemony of the emergent culture, Defoe had to take more than a few liberties with
historical and factual truth; yet it may be said of him, as he said
of the English captain, that though it was all a fiction of his own,
yet it had the desired effect.

Notes

1. J. A. Downie, *Robert Harley and the Press* (Cambridge: At the University Press,
1979), p. 58.

2. Ibid, p. 183.

3. Paul Alkon, *Defoe and Fictional Time* (Athens: University of Georgia Press, 1979),
p. 89.

Bibliography

DEFOE AND HIS CONTEMPORARIES

Books, Pamphlets, and Periodicals

(The place of publication is London unless otherwise noted. A question mark indicates that the attribution is probable, not certain.)

Atterbury, Francis, Bishop of Rochester. *English Advice to the Freeholders of Great Britain.* 1715.

Boyer, Abel. *An Impartial History of the Occasional Conformity and Schism Bills.* 1717.

Clement, Simon. *Faults on Both Sides. 1710.* Reprinted in *Somers Tracts,* edited by Walter Scott, vol. 12. 1809–15.

The Conduct of the Earl of Nottingham. Edited by W. A. Aitken. New Haven, Conn.: Yale University Press, 1941.

The Conduct of His Grace the Duke of Ormonde, in the Campaigne of 1712. 1715.

Dunkirk or Dover. 1713.

Defoe, Daniel. *An Account of the Conduct of Robert Earl of Oxford.* 1715.

———. *An Account of the Great and Generous Actions of James Butler.* 1715.

———. *Advice to the People of Great Britain.* 1714.

———. *An Answer to a Question that No Body Thinks of, Viz. But What if the Queen Should Die?* 1713.

———. *An Appeal to Honour and Justice.* 1715.

———. *An Argument Proving that the Design of Employing and Enobling Foreigners, is a Treasonable Conspiracy.* 1717.

———. *An Argument Shewing, That a Standing Army, with Consent of Parliament, is not Inconsistent with a Free Government.* 1698.

———. *And What if the Pretender Should Come?* 1713.

———. *Bold Advice: Or, Proposals for the entire Rooting out of Jacobitism in Great Britain.* 1715.

———. *The Case of the Protestant Dissenters in England.* 1716.

———. *The Conduct of Parties in England.* 1712.

———. *The Conduct of Robert Walpole, Esq.* 1717.

————. *Considerations upon the Eighth and Ninth Articles of the Treaty of Commerce and Navigation.* 1713.

————. *The Defection Farther Considered.* 1718.

————. *An Essay on the Treaty of Commerce with France.* 1713.

————. *An Essay Upon Publick Credit.* 1710.

————(?). *An Examination of a Book Intitled, The Conduct of the Duke of Ormond, Anno 1712.* 1715.

————. *An Expostulatory Letter to the B[ishop] of B[angor].* 1717.

————. *A General History of Trade, Part IV.* 1713.

————. *A General Pardon Considered.* 1717.

————. *A Farther Argument against Enobling Foreigners.* 1717.

————(?). *The Fears of the Pretender Turned into the Fears of Debauchery.* 1715.

————. *His Majesty's Obligations to the Whigs Plainly Proved.* 1715.

————. *History of the Reign of King George,* Vol. 2. 1718.

————. *An Impartial Enquiry into the Conduct of the Right Honourable Charles Lord Viscount T[ownshend].* 1717.

————. *A Journal of the Earl of Marr's Proceedings* (emended and introduced by Defoe). 1716.

————. *A Letter from a Member of the House of Commons.* 1713.

————. *A Letter to the Whigs.* 1714.

————. *The Life and Strange Surprizing Adventures of Robinson Crusoe of York, Mariner, and the Farther Adventures of Robinson Crusoe.* Oxford: The Shakespeare Head Edition. 3 Vols. 1927.

————. *Memoirs of Count Tariff &c.* 1713.

————. *Memoirs of Publick Transactions in the Life and Ministry of his Grace the D[uke] of Shrewsbury.* 1718.

————. *Mercator.* 26 May 1713 to 20 July 1714.

————. *Mercurius Politicus.* May 1716 to March 1720.

————. *Minutes of the Negotiations of Monsr. Mesnager.* 1717.

————. *Not[tingh]am Politicks Examin'd.* 1713.

————. *The Poor Man's Plea.* 1698.

————. *The Old Whig and Modern Whig Revived, in the Present Divisions at Court.* 1717.

————. *Reasons Against the Succession of the House of Hanover.* 1713.

————(?). *Reasons for Im[peaching] the L[or]d H[igh] T[reasure]r.* 1714.

————(?). *Remarks on the Speeches of William Paul Clerk, and John Hall.* 1716.

————(?). *The Repeal of the Act against Occasional Conformity, Considered.* 1717.

————. *A Reply to a Traiterous Libel.* 1715.

————. *Review*. Edited by A. W. Secord. New York: Columbia University Press, 1938. Vol. 1 (9).

————. *Rogues on Both sides*. 1711.

————. *A Seasonable Expostulation with, and Friendly Reproof unto James Butler*. 1715.

————. *The Secret History of the White Staff*. 1714.

————. *The Secret History of the White Staff, Part II*. 1714.

————. *The Secret History of the White Staff, Part III*. 1715.

————. *Some Account of the Life, and Most Remarkable Actions, of George Henry Baron de Goertz*. 1719.

————. *Some Considerations on a Law for Triennial Parliaments*. 1716.

————. *Some Thoughts upon the Subject of Commerce with France*. 1713.

————. *The Succession to the Crown of England, Considered*. 1701.

————. *A True Account of the Proceedings at Perth*. 1716.

————. *What if the Swedes should Come?* 1717.

————. *Whigs Turned Tories, and Hanoverian-Tories, From their Avowed Principles, proved Whigs: Or, Each Side in the Other Mistaken*. 1713.

Leigh, E. *The Plot Discovered; or, some Observations upon a late Jesuitical Pamphlet, written and published by the desperate Agents and Understrappers of Count Gyllenborg, intitled, Fair Payment No Spunge*. 1717.

Letters which Passed Between Count Gyllenborg, the Barons Goertz, Sparre, and Others. 1717.

No Punishment, No Government. 1712.

St. John, Henry, Viscount Bolingbroke. "The Idea of a Patriot King." In *The Works of Lord Bolingbroke*, Vol. 2. London: Bohn, 1844; reprinted 1967.

Rae, Peter. *The History of the Rebellion*. 1746. First published in 1718 as *The History of the Late Rebellion*.

A Report from the Committee of Secrecy. 1715.

Sewell, George. *The Resigners Vindicated*. 1718.

Tindal, Matthew(?). *An Account of a Manuscript, entitled Destruction the certain consequence of division*. 1718.

Toland, John. *Anglia Libera, or the Limitation to the Succession of the Crown of England*. 1701.

————. *The Second Part of the State Anatomy*. 1717.

————. *The State Anatomy of Great Britain*. 1717.

Ward, Patience, et al. *A Scheme of the Trade, as it is at Present Carried on between England and France . . .* 1674. In *Somers Tracts*, edited by Walter Scott, vol. 8. 1809–15.

Wotton, William(?). *Observations Upon the State of the Nation in January 1712/13*. 1713.

————(?). *A Vindication of the Earl of Nottingham from the Vile Imputations,* and *Malicious Slanders, which have been cast upon Him in some late Pamphlets.* 1714.

Manuscripts and Letters, Published and Unpublished

Healey, George H., ed. *The Letters of Daniel Defoe.* Oxford: Clarendon Press, 1955.

Historical Manuscripts Commission, 72 Laing II, 188–89.

Lockhart, George. *The Lockhart Papers.* Edited by F. Aufrere. 1817.

de Robethon, Jean. *Letterbook.* Letters to de Robethon from Baron von Bothmer, L. J. Schrader, Daniel Pulteney, [?] Martines, [?] Gatke, C. F. Kreienberg, John Churchill duke of Marlborough, William Cadogan, James Jefferyes, Arch. Hutcheson, George Ridpath, and Robert Goes. Huntington Museum, HM 44710.

SECONDARY SOURCES

Books

Alkon, Paul. *Defoe and Fictional Time.* Athens: University of Georgia Press, 1979.

Appleby, Joyce Oldham. *Economic Thought and Ideology in Seventeenth Century England.* Princeton; N.J.: Princeton University Press, 1978.

Baynes, John. *The Jacobite Rising of 1715.* London: Cassell, 1970.

Beattie, John M. *The English Court in the Reign of George I.* Cambridge: At the University Press, 1967.

Bennett, G. V. *The Tory Crisis in Church and State.* Oxford: Clarendon Press, 1975.

Béranger, Jean. *Les Hommes de Lettres et la Politique an Angleterre.* Bordeaux: Faculté des Lettres et Sciences humaines de l'Université de Bordeaux, 1968.

Biddle, Sheila. *Bolingbroke and Harley.* London: George Allen and Unwin, 1975.

Blewett, David. *Defoe's Art of Fiction.* Toronto: University of Toronto Press, 1979.

Booth, Wayne. *The Rhetoric of Fiction.* Chicago: University of Chicago Press, 1961.

Carabelli, Giancarlo. *Tolandiana.* Firenze: La Nuova Italia Editrice, 1975.

Clark, G. N. *Guide to English Commercial Statistics, 1696–1782.* London: Royal Historical Society, 1938.

———. *The Dutch Alliance and the War against the French Trade, 1688–1697.* New York: Russell and Russell, 1923, 1971.

Coates, Willson H.; White, Hayden V.; and Schapiro, J. Salwyn. *The Emergence of Liberal Humanism.* New York: McGraw-Hill Book Co., 1966.

Coxe, William. *Memoirs of the Life and Administration of Sir Robert Walpole.* London: Longman & Co., 1816.

Daiches, David. *The Last Stuart: The Life and Times of Bonnie Prince Charlie.* New York: G. P. Putnam's Sons, 1973.

Davis, Ralph. *The Rise of the Atlantic Economies.* Ithaca; N.Y.: Cornell University Press, 1973.

Dickinson, H. T. *Liberty and Property: Political Ideology in Eighteenth-Century Britain.* New York: Holmes and Meier, 1977.

————, ed. *Politics and Literature in the Eighteenth Century.* Totowa N.J.: Rowman and Littlefield, 1974.

Downie, J. A. *Robert Harley and the Press.* Cambridge: At the University Press, 1979.

Eagleton, Terry. *Criticism and Ideology.* London: Verso Editions, 1978.

Earle, Peter. *The World of Defoe.* New York: Atheneum, 1977.

Fisher, H. E. S. *The Portugal Trade: A Study of Anglo-Portuguese Commerce, 1700–1770.* London: Methuen, 1972.

Francis, A. D. *The First Peninsular War, 1702–1713.* New York: St. Martin's Press, 1975.

————. *The Methuens and Portugal, 1691–1708.* Cambridge: At the University Press, 1966.

————. *The Wine Trade.* New York: Barnes and Noble, 1972.

Fritz, Paul. *The English Ministers and Jacobitism.* Toronto: University of Toronto Press, 1975.

Gramsci, Antonio. *Selections from the Prison Notebooks.* New York: International Publishers, 1971.

Green, David. *Queen Anne.* New York: Scribner's, 1970.

Hanson, Laurence. *Government and the Press.* Oxford: Clarendon Press, 1936, 1967.

Hatton, Ragnhild. *George I, Elector and King.* Cambridge, Mass.: Harvard University Press, 1978.

Holmes, Geoffrey A. *British Politics in the Age of Anne.* New York: St. Martin's Press, 1967.

————, ed. *Britain after the Glorious Revolution, 1689–1714.* London: Macmillan & Co., 1969.

Hunter, J. Paul. *The Reluctant Pilgrim.* Baltimore, Md.: The Johns Hopkins Press, 1966.

Katouzian, Homa. *Ideology and Method in Economics.* New York: New York University Press, 1980.

Kenyon, J. P. *Revolution Principles: The Politics of Party, 1689–1720.* Cambridge: At the University Press, 1977.

————. *The Stuarts: A Study in English Kingship.* New York: Macmillan Co., 1959.

Kramnick, Isaac. *Bolingbroke and His Circle.* Cambridge, Mass.: Harvard University Press, 1968.

Larrain, Jorge. *The Concept of Ideology.* London: Hutchinson, 1979.

Leadam, I. S. *The History of England, From the Accession of Anne to the Death of George II.* London: Longmans, Green, 1909, 1969.

Lee, William. *Daniel Defoe: His Life and Recently Discovered Writings.* London, 1869: Reprinted by George Olms Verlagsbuchhandlung, 1968.

McInnes, Angus. *Robert Harley, Puritan Politician.* London: Victor Gollancz, 1970.

Marx, Karl, and Engels, Frederick. *The German Ideology.* New York: International Publishers, 1947.

Miliband, Ralph. *Marxism and Politics.* Oxford: At the University Press, 1977.

Moore, John Robert. *A Checklist of the Writings of Daniel Defoe.* Bloomington: Indiana University Press, 1960, 1971.

————. *Daniel Defoe, Citizen of the Modern World.* Chicago: University of Chicago Press, 1958.

Murray, John J. *George I, The Baltic, and the Whig Split of 1717.* London: Routledge and Kegan Paul, 1969

Novak, Maximillian. *Defoe and the Nature of Man.* London: Oxford University Press, 1963.

————. *Economics and the Fiction of Daniel Defoe.* New York: Russell and Russell, 1962, 1976.

————, ed. *Conjugal Lewdness: Or, Matrimonial Whoredom.* Gainesville, Fla.: Scholar's Facsimiles, 1967.

Petrie, Sir Charles. *Bolingbroke.* London: Collins, 1937.

Plumb, J. H. *The Origins of Political Stability.* Boston: Houghton Mifflin, 1967.

————. *Sir Robert Walpole.* Boston: Houghton Mifflin, 1956.

Pocock, J. G. A. *The Machiavellian Moment.* Princeton, N. J.: Princeton University Press, 1975.

Richetti, John. *Defoe's Narratives.* London: Oxford University Press, 1975.

Riley, P. W. J. *The Union of England and Scotland.* Manchester: Manchester University Press, 1978.

Rogers, Pat. *Robinson Crusoe.* London: Allen and Unwin, 1979.

Rubini, Dennis. *Court and Country 1688–1702.* London: Rupert Hart-Davis, 1967.

Sedgwick, Romney. *The House of Commons, 1715–1754.* London: History of Parliament Trust, 1970.

Sinclair-Stevenson, Christopher. *Inglorious Rebellion.* London: Hamish Hamilton, 1971.

Somerville, Dorothy. *The King of Hearts.* London: George Allen and Unwin, 1962.

Speck, W. A. *Stability and Strife.* Cambridge, Mass.: Harvard University Press, 1977.

———. *Tory and Whig: The Struggle in the Constituencies, 1701–1715.* London: Macmillan & Co., 1970.

———, and Holmes, Geoffrey, eds. *The Divided Society: Parties and Politics in England, 1694–1716.* New York: St. Martin's Press, 1968.

Starr, G. A. *Defoe and Spriritual Biography.* Princeton, N.J.: Princeton University Press, 1965.

Stevens, D. H. *Party Politics and English Journalism, 1702–42.* New York: Russell and Russell, 1916, 1967.

Sutherland, James. *Defoe, A Biography.* Philadelphia, Pa.: Lippincott, 1938.

Thompson, E. P. *The Poverty of Theory and other Essays.* New York: Monthly Review Press, 1978.

Watt, Ian. *The Rise of the Novel.* London: Chatto and Windus, 1957.

White, Hayden. *Tropics of Discourse: Essays in Cultural Criticism.* Baltimore, Md.: Johns Hopkins University Press, 1978.

Williams, Raymond. *Marxism and Literature.* Oxford: At the University Press, 1977

Wilson, Walter. *Memoirs of the Life and Times of Daniel Defoe.* London: Hurst, Chance & Co., 1830.

Articles

Chance, James F. "The Swedish Plot of 1716–17." *English Historical Review* 18 (1903): 81–106.

Clark, J. C. D. "The Decline of Party, 1740–1760." *English Historical Review* 93 (1978): 499–527.

Cruickshanks, Eveline G. "The Tories and the Succession to the Crown in the 1714 Parliament." *Bulletin of the Institute of Historical Research* 46 (1973): 176–85.

Curtis, T. C., and Speck, W. A. "The Societies for the Reformation of Manners: A Case Study in the Theory and Practice of Moral Reform." *Literature and History* 3 (1976): 45–64.

Davis, Ralph. "English Foreign Trade, 1660–1700." *Economic History Review* 7 (1955): 150–66.

———. "English Foreign Trade, 1700–1774." *Economic History Review* 15 (1962): 285–303.

———. "The Rise of Protection in England, 1689–1786." *Economic History Review* 19 (1966): 306–17.

Dickinson, H. T. "The October Club." *Huntington Library Quarterly* 33 (1970): 155–73.

Doctorow, E. L. "False Documents." *American Review* 26 (1977): 215–32.

Downie, J. A. "Anthony Hammond Miscellanea." *Notes and Queries* NS 24 (1977): 219–21.

———. "Arthur Maynwaring and the Authorship of the Advice to the Electors of Great Britain: Some Additional Evidence." *British Journal for Eighteenth-Century Studies* 2 (1979): 163–66.

———. "Political Literature as Literature." *British Journal for Eighteenth-Century Studies* 2 (1979): 70–73.

Gregg, Edward. "Was Queen Anne A Jacobite?" *History* 57 (1972): 358–75.

Harkness, D. A. E. "The Opposition to the 8th and 9th Articles of the Commercial Treaty of Utrecht." *Scottish Historical Review* 21 (1924): 219–26.

Hill, Christopher. "Robinson Crusoe." *History Workshop Journal* 10 (1980): 6–24.

Holmes, Geoffrey. "The Sacheverell Riots: The Crowd and the Church in Early Eighteenth-Century London." *Past and Present* 72 (1976): 55–85.

Ivanyi, B. G. "Defoe's Prelude to the Schism Bill." *Times Literary Supplement,* 7 April 1966, p. 312.

Lichtheim, George. "The Concept of Ideology." *History and Theory* 4 (1965). Reprinted in *The Concept of Ideology and Other Essays.* New York: Random House, 1967.

Moore, John Robert. "Defoe's Hand in *A Journal of the Earl of Marr's Proceedings* (1716)." *Huntington Library Quarterly* 18 (1954): 209–28.

Novak, Maximillian. "Crusoe the King and the Political Evolution of his Island." *Studies in English Literature* 2 (1962): 337–50.

———. "Defoe's Theory of Fiction." *Studies in Philology* 61 (1964): 650–68.

———. "Fiction and Society in the Early Eighteenth Century." In *England in the Restoration and Early Eighteenth Century,* edited by H. T. Swedenberg, Jr. Berkeley: University of California Press, 1972, pp. 51–70.

———. "History, Ideology, and the Method of Defoe's Historical Fiction." *Studies in the Eighteenth Century,* Vol. 4, edited by R. F. Brissenden and J. C. Eade. Toronto: University of Toronto Press, 1979, pp. 99–122.

O'Gorman, Frank. "Fifty Years after Namier: The Eighteenth Century in British Historical Writing." *The Eighteenth Century: Theory and Interpretation* 20 (1979): 99–120.

Pocock, J. G. A. "Machiavelli, Harrington, and English Political Ideology in the Eighteenth Century." *William and Mary Quarterly* 22 (1965): 549–83.

Priestly, Margaret. "Anglo-French Trade and the 'Unfavorable Balance' Controversy, 1660–1685." *Economic History Review* 4 (1951): 37–52.

Rogers, Nicholas. "Money, Land, and Lineage: The Big Bourgeoisie of Hanoverian London." *Social History* 4 (1979): 437–54.

————. "Popular Protest in Early Hanoverian London." *Past and Present* 79 (1978): 70–100.

Rogers, Pat. "Addenda and Corrigenda: Moore's *Checklist* of Defoe." *PBSA* 75 (1981): 60–64.

Schonhorn, Manuel. "Defoe: The Literature of Politics and the Politics of Some Fictions." In *English Literature in the Age of Disguise*, edited by Maximillian Novak. Berkeley: Univeristy of California Press, 1977, pp. 15–56.

Seidel, Michael. "Crusoe in Exile." *PMLA* 96 (1981): 363–74.

Shennan, J. H., and Shennan, Margaret. "The Protestant Succession in English Politics, April 1713–September 1715." In *William III and Louis XIV*, edited by Ragnhild Hatton and J. S. Bromley. Toronto: University of Toronto Press, 1968.

Snyder, Henry L. "Daniel Defoe, Arthur Maynwaring, Robert Walpole, and Abel Boyer: Some Considerations of Authorship." *Huntington Library Quarterly* 33 (1970): 133–53.

Williams, Gwyn A. "The Concept of 'Egemonia' in the Thought of Antonio Gramsci." *Journal of the History of Ideas* 21 (1960): 586–99.

Index

Abingdon, first earl of (James Bertie), 42–46
Alkon, Paul, 111–12, 148, 168–69, 175
Anglesey, fifth earl of (Arthur Annesley), 42–46, 67, 74, 97, 105, 117
Anne (queen of Great Britain), 20, 24, 29, 41, 48, 51, 56, 63,69, 85–87, 90, 96, 103, 141–44
Appleby, Joyce Oldham, 17–18, 33, 39
Argyll, second duke of (John Campbell), 87, 110, 113, 123, 127, 151
Atterbury, Francis (bishop of Rochester), 85, 87, 89–91, 92, 97, 100, 105, 108, 118, 130
Augustus II (king of Poland), 73

Baker, John, 115
Barbon, Nicholas, 18
Bennett, G. V., 87
Benson, William, 72, 77
Bernstorff, baron von, 108, 131
Bolingbroke, Henry St. John (viscount), 16, 29, 45, 85, 87, 91, 105, 139, 150
Booth, Wayne, 25
Bothmer, baron von, 108, 131
Boyer, Abel, 155
Bradbury, Thomas, 83
British Merchant, 33, 34
Bromley, William, 105
Burnet, Thomas, 72, 77

Charles VI (emperor of Austria), 114
Charles XII (king of Sweden), 56, 57, 114, 134, 155
Clement, Simon, 60–61

Davenant, Charles, 14, 33–34, 60, 61
Defoe, Daniel: and emblematic method, 47–48, 49, 53, 92, 118, 149; and fiction, 11, 24, 26, 30, 43–44, 46–47, 52–53, 88–93, 110–18, 126, 144, 163; and historical biography, 48, 53, 111, 153–54; and liberal humanism, 14–16, 126, 132, 140, 144, 158; and Robert Harley, 11, 23–25, 45, 56, 57, 61–62, 66, 72, 77, 81, 96–97, 102–3, 172–73; and satire, 47, 65, 75, 127–28; and spiritual autobiography, 111–12. Works: *Account of the Conduct of Robert Earl of Oxford, An*, 139, 140; *Advice to the People of Great Britain*, 85–86; *And What if the Pretender Should Come?*, 75; *Answer to a Question that No Body Thinks of, An*, 76–77; *Appeal to Honour and Justice, An*, 77, 96–97; *Argument Proving that the Design of Employing and Enobling Foreigners, An*, 131; *Bold Advice*, 105–7; *Compleat English Gentleman, The*, 148; *Consolidator, The*, 52; *Dyet of Poland, The*, 66; *Essay Upon Publick Credit, An*, 58; *Fair Payment No Spunge*, 136; *Family Instructor, The*, 96; *Farther Adventures of Robinson Crusoe, The*, 165–69; *Fears of the Pretender Turned into the Fears of Debauchery, The*, 99–102, 152; *General Pardon Considered, A*, 140; *Jure Divino*, 158; *Letter from a Member, A*, 45, 47; *Letter to the Dissenters, A*, 82; *Letter to the Whigs, A*, 82–83; *Life and Strange Surprizing Adventures of Robinson Crusoe, The*, 11, 16, 24, 26,

190   Defoe and the Idea of Fiction

Test Act, 131
Toland, John, 130–36
Toleration, Act of, 66–67, 71
Tory party, 18; Country Tories, 60,
    66, 123, 1255, 127, 132, 135, 141;
    Hanover Tories, 44, 47, 51, 71, 73,
    74, 77, 78, 96, 97, 99, 105; and
    High Church, 61, 85, 97, 99, 100,
    105; ideology, 14, 16, 33, 40, 63;
    votes in Parliament, 42
Townshend, Charles (viscount), 48,
    67, 98, 104, 105, 117, 121, 123,
    126–29, 137, 151–52
Treaty of Commerce with France,
    16–17, 18, 24, 25–26, 29–46, 58,
    69, 71, 78, 81, 85, 97, 118, 139, 141,
    144, 170

Union with Scotland, Treaty of, 11,
    32, 71, 150

Utrecht, Treaty of, 23, 32, 37, 56, 69,
    86, 122

Walcott, Robert, 13
Walpole, Robert, 19, 43, 48, 98, 105,
    106, 121, 126–28, 136–38, 142,
    149–52, 155–56
Watt, Ian, 148
Wharton, Thomas, 75–76
Whig party, 18, 122–23; and Defoe,
    56, 67, 72, 82–83, 97–98, 104, 149–
    52; ideology, 12, 14, 16, 38, 40, 74,
    75–76, 101, 108, 118, 135, 174; and
    Junto, 61, 85, 88, 130, 150; Old
    Whigs and Modern Whigs, 26, 60–
    61, 96, 108, 117, 121, 138, 139,
    150–52; votes in Parliament, 30, 85
William III (king of England), 48, 56,
    63, 101, 106, 154
Williams, Raymond, 20–22